UCLA Slavic Studies
Volume 5

THE ORIGINS OF RUSSIAN GRAMMAR

Notes on the state of Russian philology
before the advent of printed grammars

Dean S. Worth

Slavica Publishers, Inc.

Slavica publishes a wide variety of books and journals dealing with the peoples, languages, literatures, history, folklore, and culture of the peoples of Eastern Europe and the USSR. For a complete catalog with prices and ordering information, please write to:

>Slavica Publishers, Inc.
>P.O. Box 14388
>Columbus, Ohio 43214
>USA

ISBN: 0-89357-110-5.

Copyright © 1983 by the author. All rights reserved.

The cost of typesetting this book was partially supported by a grant from the National Endowment for the Humanities to Slavica Publishers, Inc.

Text set by Kathleen McDermott and Randy Bowlus at the East European Composition Center, supported by the Department of Slavic Languages and Literatures and the Center for Russian and East European Studies at UCLA with grants from the Joint Committee on Eastern Europe of the American Council of Learned Societies and Social Sciences Research Council and the Research and Development Committee of the American Association for the Advancement of Slavic Studies.

Printed in the United States of America.

For Emily

CONTENTS

0. Foreword 7
1. The Earliest Texts 11
2. The "Eight Parts of Speech" 14
3. Konstantin the Grammarian 22
4. Написаніє ѧзыкомъ словенскимъ о грамотѣ 35
5. О мнѫжествѣ і о єдінствѣ 51
6. Книга глаголемаѧ буквы 56
7. Maksim Grek 65
8. The Donatus translation 76
9. Concluding Remarks 166

Notes 167

0. Foreword

The late Roman Jakobson used to warn his students not to confuse the process of scientific investigation with the happenstance of their own biographies. This book, I fear, is the result of just such a confusion. Its structure betrays its partly accidental origins, and it seems only fair to warn the reader about these.

While doing the reading for a projected *Historiography of Literary Russian* (itself intended as a first step toward a history of the Russian literary language), I realized how very little I knew about Russian philology prior to the appearance of the first printed grammars in the late sixteenth century. Surveys by Bulič, Jagić, Karskij, Vinogradov, Levin and Grigor'eva, and Kuznecov were rich in many ways, but contained little specific detail about the origins and manuscript tradition of philological thought in Russia.[a] With very few exceptions,[b] the only real source of information about this tradition remains Jagić's monumental *Rassuždenija južnoslavjanskoj i russkoj stariny o cerkovno-slavjanskom jazyke.*[c] Jagić's labors in ferreting out and editing the manuscript material were enormous, and his commentaries on the mss. and their Greek and Latin models are invaluable; this small book could never have been written without them. Nonetheless, the texts themselves are so numerous, so complex in their filiation, and often simply so difficult to understand, that not even Jagić could fully systematize and analyse their content. Some further efforts in this direction seemed possible, and this book is the result.

If the book had a Russian title, it would begin with *Očerki po . . .* or *Issledovanija v oblasti . . . .* It does not pretend to give a systematic historical survey of Russian philological thought, and it does not claim to describe or analyse all the mss. material published by Jagić, much less to present the results of original archival research. A systematic account of the rise of Russian philology will not be possible until the manuscript tradition has been investigated more closely than by Jagić (who in some cases had to depend on handwritten copies provided by colleagues in Russia). And, to be frank, it is not clear that the intellectual and cultural-historical importance of the subject matter would really justify such close scrutiny of mss. which are all too often naive attempts to transplant Greek and Latin habits onto Russian soil. What this book does offer is a fresh reading of several of the Jagić mss., a reordering of their often confused material into a more systematic (often, a paradigmatic) format, and in a number of cases, an analytic description more detailed than that provided by Jagić (for example, in the phonological material of the Написаніє ѧзыком словенскым о грамоте on pp. 35-50). I have tried to present my own interpretations of the complex material wherever I felt capable of doing so, but have not hesitated to fall back on Jagić's views there where I had nothing new to offer. My interest throughout has been not to study the origins or filiation of the mss. (the chapter on Maksim Grek is a partial exception to this statement), but rather to try to find out what aspects of language interested the medieval scribes and how much they knew about the phonology and grammar of their own language or of Russian Church Slavonic. As it turned out, they were interested primarily in the graphic and diacritic externals of language, they knew precious little about either phonology or grammar, and they seem to have had no idea that Church Slavonic was anything other than "their" language.[d] But it would be unfair and ahistorical to expect the medieval grammarian to share our modern concept of the form-function relation, and in their own way, the scribes who authored or copied these mss. showed considerable ingenuity in arranging their material to illustrate their views (cf., for example, the analysis of the at first glance totally unorganized paradigms of the Книга глаголемаѧ буквыı, pp. 56-64 or the use of the vernacular iterative to render the Latin pluperfect in the Donatus translation, pp. 100-101).

Our choice of mss. has been selective, not exhaustive. A brief introductory section surveys the oldest texts, which contain some information about the origins of Slavonic writing, but have almost nothing to say about language itself. We then discuss in more detail the two principal South Slavic sources of Russian grammatical thought, the so-called "Eight parts of speech" (of which there were really only four, as the second half of the original translation seems to have gotten lost), and the prescriptive fulminations of the Bulgarian expatriot Konstantin Kostenčeskij (too flatteringly referred to as "the Grammarian").[e] Of the confusing variety of anonymous medieval treatises, we have chosen three which seemed most interesting and most representative of the best that this period could offer, the Написаниѥ ѧзыıком словенским о грамотѣ, О мнѡжествѣ ı о ѥдıнствѣ, and Книга глаголемаѧ буквыı. There follows a section examining the contribution (or, in my opinion, the non-contribution) of Maksim Grek to the development of Russian grammatical thought. The final section, which occupies half the book, is devoted to a detailed presentation of the grammatical material in the Donatus grammar translation of Dmitrij Gerasimov and his copyists.

In transcribing the Slavonic texts, I have tried to stay as close to the Jagić forms as possible, although this was not technically feasible in all cases. In the later mss., which are concerned with grammatical categories and forms more than orthography or diacritics, I have brought raised letters down onto the line without specifically marking them in any way. Real philological precision is in any case impossible without access to the mss. themselves, and is not really essential for our purposes here.

Most of the research and part of the writing of this book was accomplished while on leave from U.C.L.A. on a grant from the Kennan Institute of the Woodrow Wilson Center in Washington, D.C. I should like to record here my gratitude to James Billington, S. Frederick Starr, and the many staff members of the Center and the Institute, both for the generosity of their support and for the grace with which they dispensed it. I should also like to record my gratitude to those colleagues whose close reading of my original manuscript helped me to eliminate at least some of my mistakes: Professors James Ferrell, Robert Mathiesen, and Richard Pope, as well as Henrik Birnbaum, Thomas Eekman, and Alan Timberlake, of the Editorial Board of *UCLA Slavic Studies*. Without the financial assistance of the James Duke Fund, administered by Professor Bariša Krekić, Director of UCLA's Center for Russian and East European Studies, and that of the National Endowment for the Humanities, a book of this complexity could never have been prepared in camera-ready copy. Andrew Corin and Pamela Russell were the careful typists of the original text, while J. Randall Bowlus and, most particularly, Kathleen McDermott managed to keep smiling while preparing the camera-ready copy of what must be the most difficult text ever to pass through the IBM composer. I shall not forget their help.

1. The Earliest Texts

The first written records about writing among the Slavs go back to the 10th, and perhaps even to the 9th century. They deal with the Cyrillo-Methodian origins of the Slavic alphabet, the content of the early translations, and in a few cases with certain correspondences between Slavic lexical items or grammatical categories and those of Greek. However, we know next to nothing about when or how such materials reached the Eastern Slavs. It is reasonable to assume that at least a few elementary facts about the Moravian Mission, perhaps including some information on the first translations from Greek, were known in Kievan Rus' even before the official Christianization in 988, but the oldest actual manuscript containing any material of linguistic interest dates only from 1073. None of these early records contains any grammar in the strict sense, that is, they are in no way prescriptive and hence made no contribution toward standardization of the written language. Indeed, the very idea of "correct" and "incorrect" language was unknown to Kievan Rus' and would arise only centuries later in the post-Euthymian Balkans. Nonetheless, the earliest texts do present a certain interest, if only because they demonstrate the existence of an awareness of the cultural importance of the invention of Slavic writing.

The *Life of Constantine* recounts that Constantine/Cyrill, having agreed to undertake the mission, "сложи пи́смена и́ нача́ бесѣду писати є̄ѵглъскую· искони бѣ̀ сло́во и̇ слово бѣ ѵ̇ бга и̇ бгъ бѣ сло́во, и̇ про́чаꙗ".[1] The *Life of Methodius* adds a little more detail: "да тоу ꙗви бг̄ъ философоу словѣньскъі книгъі, и абиѥ оустроивъ писмена и бесѣдоу съставль ... (later) посажь два попъі скорописьца ѕѣло прѣложі въ бързѣ вьса книгъі испълнь, разве Макавѣи, отъ грьчьска ꙗзъіка въ словѣньскъ шестию̇ мс̄цъ".[2] The *Primary Chronicle* (*Povest' vremennyx let*), in a section probably set down in the second quarter of the 11th c., recognizes the original unity of the Slavic tribes and the Moravian origins of written Slavonic: "Бѣ единъ ꙗзъікъ словѣнескъ, словѣни же сѣдаху по Дунаєви, ижже приꙗша оугри, и марава, чеси и ляхове и поляне, ꙗже нъінѣ зьвомаꙗ Русь, симь бо первоє преложенъі книги маравѣ, ꙗже прєзва сꙗ грамота словѣньскаꙗ, ꙗже грамота єсть в Руси и в болгарѣх(ъ) дунаискъіхъ",[3] the last clause of this passage indicates an awareness that the Eastern and Southern Slavs shared a common written language.[4] The Chronicle continues with the story of the Moravian mission: "Сима же (i.e., Cyrill and Methodius) пришедъшема начаста съставливати писмена азъбуковьнаꙗ словѣньски, и преложиста апл̄ъ и єѵглиє. Ради бъіша словѣни, ꙗко слъішиша величьꙗ бж̄ьꙗ своимь ꙗзыкомь. По семь же приложиста (read: преложиста) псалтрь и ѡктаикъ и прочаꙗ книги."[5]

In addition to this general knowledge of the origins of Slavonic culture, those Kievan Russians who were literate could discover a few details about the relation of Church Slavonic to the Byzantine Greek from which it was translated. The 1073 *Izbornik Svjatoslava* contains a few lexical glosses змарагдъ, анфраксъ) and periphrastic explanations of the poetic terminology in George Xeroboskos' treatise on tropes and figures (*μεταφορά* > прѣводъ, *ἀλληγορία* > инословие, etc.).[6] The only other "lexicographic" work of the Kievan period is the so-called *Rěč' židovskago jazyka preložena na ruskuju* . . . in the Novgorod *Kormčaja* of 1282; it glosses 174 Biblical names, Hellenisms (хризма, олтарь), foreign Slavisms (ков = лесть, бритва = стригольникъ), etc.[7] In the preface to his translation of John Damascene's *Philosophy*, Ioan Exarch of Bulgaria notes the non-correspondence of gender between Greek and Slavonic: *βάτραχος* and *ποταμός* are masculine but жаба and рѣка feminine, whereas *ἡμέρα* and *ἀνατολή* are feminine but дьнь and въстокъ masculine (Ioan mistakenly gives море as masculine when comparing it to feminine *θάλασσα*). This is the beginning of a centuries-long tradition of comparison of Greek and Slavonic letters, words and grammatical categories. Contrary to what is often assumed, however, Ioan Exarch had absolutely nothing to say about the grammar of either Slavonic or Greek.[8]

The treatise О писменехъ by the pseudonymous Černorizec Xrabr goes back to the 10th c. but is preserved in mss. only from the 14th; whether it was known in Eastern Slavic territory before the 15th century cannot be ascertained. Xrabr's work opens with an intriguing reference, "Прѣжде оубо словѣне не имѣхѫ книгъ, нѫ чрътами и рѣзами чьтѣхѫ и гатаахѫ погани сѫще"; what these "marks and slashes" looked like is unknown.[9] After they had been baptized, the Slavs were burdened with the inappropriate Latin and Greek alphabets ("римьсками и гръчьскъıми писменъı нѫждаахѫ сѧ") until St. Cyrill invented the 38-letter Slavic alphabet. Xrabr provides some specifics as to why the Greek alphabet was inappropriate to Slavonic: "како можеть сѧ писати добрѣ гръчьскъıми писменъı: б҃ъ, или живѡтъ, или зѣлѡ, или ц҃рковь, или чаание, или широта, или ꙗдь, или ѫдоу, или юность, или ѫзъıкъ (read: ѧзъıкъ), и инаа по(до)биаа симь" (the underlined letters mark sounds missing from Byzantine Greek),[10] but most of his text is given over to proving the superiority of the Slavonic alphabet over the Greek, a fact of some importance in Byzantino-Bulgarian historical relations but of little relevance to the study of language. A somewhat later Russian copy of this popular treatise divides the Slavic alphabet into those letters which are similar to Greek (а, в, г, д, е, з, и [= η], і, к, л, м, н, о, п, р, с, т, оу, ф, х, ѡ, и [=υ], пѣ [=ψ], хлѣ [=ξ], тъ [= ѳ], а [= ja ?], г [= г'], н [= ?]) and those which are purely Slavonic (б ж ѕ л [= л'?] ц ч ш ъ шь [= щ]¹¹ мь [= ?] ъ [= ь] ѣ ѧ ю ѫ); this division into Greek vs. Slavonic letters would be repeated in later grammatical works (cf. p. 23 below).¹² Xrabr is also the first Slavonic text to utilize a variant of the question-and-answer format taken over from the Byzantine "erotēmata", e.g. "аще ли въпросиши словѣнʼскъіѧ боукарѧ гла҃· кто въі писмена створилъ е́сть, или книгъі прѣложилъ; то вьси вѣдѧть, и̇ ѿвѣщавше рекѫтъ· ст҃ъіи Кѡнстантинъ философъ нарицаемъіи Кирилъ. тъ̏ намь писмена створи и̇ книгъі прѣложи."¹³

The scattered works discussed so far were concerned primarily with the origins and Byzantine heritage of Slavic literacy. They show no interest in the systematic exposition of grammar or with the concept of "correct" and "incorrect" language, i.e. with linguistic normalization, standardization. Such concerns arose only in the last century of the atrophying Byzantine Empire, in the Turnovo circles around Patriarch Euthymios and somewhat later at the Serbian court of Despot Stefan Lazarević, and, most notably of all, in the Greek and Slavic monasteries of Mount Athos. Here, in the deepening shadow of the Turkish Empire, there appears first a concern for, then a preoccupation with *form*, an interest not only in the meaning of grammatical categories but in the religious significance of the pettiest spelling details, a tendency, one might say, to equate orthography with orthodoxy. Interest in form soon became mere formalism, and incipient scholarship deteriorated into a stultifying scholasticism which, transplanted to the receptive soil of the Muscovite Empire, would soon choke off whatever Slavonic originality had been growing there.¹⁴

2. The "Eight parts of speech"

The first attested Slavic grammatical treatise is entitled *On the eight parts of speech*.[15] Originally considered a translation by Ioan Exarch of an in fact nonexistent grammar by John Damascene,[16] it is actually an early 14th c. Serbian compilation from two or more late Byzantine sources, a compilation which found its way via Bulgaria and Moldavia to Russia. Aside from the later Slavonic translation of Donatus' Latin grammar, the "Eight parts of speech" were the only significant attempt to systematize Slavonic morphology until the appearance of printed grammars in the very late 16th and early- to mid-17th centuries. For this reason, the text deserves fairly detailed examination.[17] We shall refer here to Jagić's edition of the Russian recension, with references to the 15th c. Serbian original where appropriate.

Of the eight parts of speech this treatise announces it will describe (и́мѧ substantive, рѣчь verb, причѧ́стіе participle, разли́чіе article [in the Slavic text = anaphoric and relative pronouns], мѣ́сто и́мени pronoun, предло́гъ preposition, наречіе adverb, сою́зъ conjunction), only the first four are discussed at all, and the bulk of the text deals with the substantive and the verb.

The substantive has three genders (му́жеско masculine, же́ньско feminine, сре́днее neuter), three numbers (еди́но singular, дво́йно dual, мнѡ́жно plural), and five cases including the vocative (пра́ва nominative, ро́дна genitive, вино́вна accusative, да́тельна dative, зва́тельна vocative; n.b. the unusual order, not however maintained in all Russian mss.). The most striking feature of the substantive paradigm is the substitution of a nominative-case possessive adjective form for the expected genitive case ending in all three genders of the singular, in the feminine dual (with the exception of one Russian mss., Syn², which has the classical – оу), and (but only in the Serbian ms.) in the neuter plural. Noteworthy, too, is the neuter singular accusative ending -а, apparently patterned on the animate masculine, in all Russian mss. (though the Serbian ms. has -о). There are some minor distributional differences between the Serbian and Russian mss. Serbian uses only the digraph -оу throughout the singular and the dual, while Russian fluctuates: dative masc. -ѹ but neut. -оу and acc. fem. -оу, gen. masc. and neut. dual -ѹ. Serbian uses ѡ only for the interjection ѡ and for the masc. plur. -ѡмь while Russian uses it for the neut. plur. as well.[18]

We can arrange the nominal paradigm into tabular form as follows:

"EIGHT PARTS OF SPEECH"

Nom.	ч͞лкъ	жена̀	е͡стѐтво
Gen.	ч͞лковъ	женина̀	е͡стѐтвово
Acc.	ч͞лка	женоу̑	е͡стѐтва[a,b]
Dat.	ч͞лкѵ	женѣ̀	е͡стѐтвоу[a]
Voc.	ѿ ч͞лче	ѿ жено	ѿ е͡тво[c]
Nom.	ч͞лка	женѣ̀	е͡ствѣ[c]
Gen.	ч͞лкѵ	женинѣ[d]	е͡стѐтвѵ[a]
Acc.	= nom.	= nom.	= nom.
Dat.	ч͞лкома	женама	е͡ствома
Voc.	ѿ ч͞лка	ѿ женѣ	ѿ е͡ствѣ[c]
Nom.	ч͞лци	жены̀	е͡ства[c]
Gen.	ч͞лкъ[e]	же́нъ[e]	е͡стествъ[e]
Acc.	ч͞лкы	= nom.	= nom.
Dat.	ч͞лкѡмъ	женамъ	е͡ствѡмъ
Voc.	ѿ ч͞лци	ѿ жены	ѿ е͡ства[c]

[a] sic spiritus asper
[b] S ѥстьство
[c] sic different abbreviation (in nom. and voc. only)
[d] Syn.² женоу
[e] S ч͞лов ѣкьъ, женьь, ѥстьствовьь with –ьь a harbinger of new -ā; **n.b.** possessive −ов− in neut.

The "Eight parts of speech" divides substantives into ѡбщиѥ (κοινά) and собнꙑѥ (κύρια), which to the Slavic compiler meant generic vs. specific or personal nouns: ч͞лкъ vs. Петръ, Па́вель, жена̀ vs. Сарра, Анна, and соуществѡ vs. н͞бо, дрѐво (ms. дрѐвъ), желѣзо. There are also some words whose gender cannot be predicted from their endings and which would require the presence of an article (разлиуиѥ) in order to mark them as masculine, feminine, or neuter. These are (1) feminines ending not in −а but in jer (кровь, соль, трость, персть), which for the original

15th c. Serbian compiler, with his single ь from both ь and ъ, of course looked like masculines; (2) feminines ending not in -а but in -и (мати, дш͞и, свекри, the last of which is included here because the Russian copyist blindly imitated his Serbian or Bulgarian prototype, which had collapsed и and ъı into и and thus no longer distinguished the old ū-stems from those in -[er]i); (3) neuters ending not in -о but in -е (сл͞нце, ороужие, копие), which could have seemed anomalous only to a scribe who was uncritically following a Greek model and who confused the Greek neuter ending -ον with the Slavonic name for the letter о, онъ ("соуть же и в сре́днемъ и́мени несконча́вающеся о́номъ, но е́стемъ"); (4) masculines ending not in jer but in -и (ками, гво́зди, черви, again confusing formerly separate declension types).

A good deal of the "Eight parts of speech" is given over to discussion of the grammatical categories (послѣдоующа or послѣдствоующа, παρεπόμενα[19]) of the substantive. In addition to those of the paradigm adduced above (ро́ди γένη, чи́сла ἀριθμοί, паденіе [or more rarely and later падеж] πτώσεις), Slavonic nouns are said to manifest "aspects" (види εἴδη) and "schemes" (начертанія σχήματα). The "aspects" of the noun are in effect derivational types: primary nouns (первобы́тно и́ма πρωτότυπον) are underived (e.g., у͞лкъ), while the derived, превод́ное παραγωγόν (the terms are adduced by Jagić 62 but do not appear in the mss. themselves) are the deverbatives (действено ἐνεργητικόν?) which include the obvious, like кова́чъ, древодѣла but also "ѿ ро́да же (i.e., родода́тню γενετικόν), я́ко се͞ · Маніакъ, Шоумакъ" (other mss. Шоума), and the "imputational" (повѣстно ἀποφαντικόν?), which appear to generalize some quality: "ѿ по́вѣсти же, я́ко се͞ · обѣшенникъ. обѣшенникъ бо пода́стъ всемоу ро́доу обѣшенія и́ма", an explanation of less than crystalline clarity.

The nominal "schemes" refer to depths of morphological embedding (compounding and derivation). A word's "scheme" can be simple (проста́ ἀπλοῦν), e.g. Петръ, Па́велъ, Фома́, Мило́шь, Драго́шь (the Russian scribe didn't take the trouble to substitute Russian names for these Serbianisms), compound (сло́жна σύνετον) like Доброславъ, Радославъ, Добромиръ (which, as he somewhat ponderously explains, "ѿ двою части ю ... слага́ются. Ино бо добро́ и ино же сла́ва ..."), or surcompound (пресло́жно παρασύνετον), "е́же ѿ тре[х] часте́й сло́ва слежи́тся (sic; read сложи́тся), a vague and not entirely appropriate description, as the examples show (бл͞гоповѣстникъ, бл͞гопроизво́ле[н], бѣдношёмлемъ, злопрія́тенъ).[20]

The discussion of the verb begins with an overview of tense and voice. Only the three major tenses are identified here (but see below). For the active voice (действенъı́и зало́гъ ἐνεργητικὴ διάθεσις), these are: past (мимошедшее, later referred to as предбы́вшее παρεληλυθώς), illustrated by the

3rd person sing. contracted imperfects оу̓ча́ше, посъіла́ше, бл͡гове́ст-
вова́ше; present (настоа́щее ἐνεστώς), e.g. оу̓чи́тъ, посъіла́етъ,
бл͡говѣ́ствȣетъ; and future (бȣдȣщее μέλλων), for which the scribe
can find only the illustration ти́ вамъ соу̓да́тъ (the Serbian text also
gives ти вамь бȣдȣть соу̓дїе). Full parallel paradigms are provided
for the passive voice (страда́льнаıа з. παθητικὴ δ.): past х͡ртосъ
распа́тса, сл͡нце поме́рче, ка́менıе распаде́са (here, the aorist
rather than the imperfect), and similarly распина́етъса, померца́етъ,
распада́етса and ра́спнетса, поме́ркнетъ, распаде́тса. Slavonic
is also said to have a mediopassive (за́логъ е́же г͡летса посреди́
дѣ́нства й стра́сти μέση διάθεσις), illustration of which is promised for
later ("по разделе́нıи време́ннемъ ска́жемъ").

The verb manifests eight grammatical categories, most of which are merely
listed, not described: moods (и́зложе́нıа ἐγκλίσεις), voices (cf. above),
"aspects" (ви́дъı εἴδη), "schemes" (начерта́нıа σχήματα), numbers (ἀριθμοί), "persons" (о́бразъı or ли́ца πρόσωπα), tenses (времена̀ χρόνοι),
and conjugation (сȣпроу́жьства συζυγίαι). The moods are divided into
imperative (повеле́нное ἔγκλισις προστακτική), optative (моли́твенное
ё. εὐκτική), interrogative (вопро́сное ё. ἐρωτηματική), hortative (зва-
тельное κλιτικός λόγου?), declarative (повѣ́стное ἀποφαντικόν), and a
separately treated infinitive (необа́вное ἀπαρέμφατος ё.), e.g. е́же честѝ
поле́зно, е́же е́сти потре́бно, е́же и́гра́ти оу̓ко́рно, пове-
лѣва́ю ти бъ́іти.

Verbal "aspect" has nothing to do with the modern use of this term, but
as with the substantive refers to derivational status. Aspect is either primary
(первоо́бра́зное πρωτότυπον εἶδος), e.g. хощȣ̀, прїи́мȣ or transferred
(преводное παράγωγον εἰ.), for example восхощȣ̀, воспрїи́мȣ̀, or
воспрїа́тıе from прїа́тıе. In the same way, the verbal "schemes" parallel
those of the noun; they are simple (просто ἁπλοῦν), e.g. да́мъ, compound
(сложно σύνετον), like возда́мъ, or surcompound (пресло́жно παρασύντετον), for an illustration of which our grammarian had to dip into his syntactic repertoire: возда́мъ ёмоу̓.

The three numbers are illustrated by both transitive and reflexive paradigms,
the most interesting feature of which is the utterly artificial Middle Bulgarian 1st
person sing. ending -а (in all Russian mss.; the Serbian ms. has творȣ):
n.b. also the secondary dual -ва for older -вѣ, and the Bulg. (-Ukrainian?)
1st person plur. in -мо (Serbian -мь; the Russian mss. have the usual -м
before the reflexive particle:

творѧ́		творѝва		творѝмо
творѝши	}	творѝта	{	твори́те
творѝтъ				творѧ́тъ

бїа́сѧ	бїе́васѧ	бїе́мсѧ
бїе́шнсѧ	} бїетасѧ {	бїе́тесѧ
бнетсѧ		бї ю́тсѧ

There are three persons, illustrated by г͞лю а́зъ, г͞лєшн т͞ы, г͞лєтъ о́нъзн (a Serbianism misunderstood by some Russian copyists, who changed it to онъ сн or simply онъ).

Tense is given a fuller treatment here than in the overview above. Past tense is now called прєдвъıвшєє, and has four subdivisions, durative (= imperfect) (протѧженое παρατακτικόν), unlimited (= aorist) (непредѣльное ἀόριστον), and two which are not illustrated because they are "unpleasant to the tongue" (ѩзъıкѹ непрїѧ́тнѣ), an "overcompleted" or "pluperfect"? (надпредѣлѧемое ὑπερσυντελικόν) and a "resultative" or "perfect"? (предлежнмое παρακείμενον). The present tense remains undivided, no distinction being made between imperfective and perfective forms of the present (although the perfective present-future was used to illustrate the passive future in the initial overview, cf. above; this is in fact the only recognition of aspectual distinctions in the entire "Eight parts of speech", and only an implicit recognition at that). However, the future tense is split into two, a distinction unknown to canonical Old Church Slavonic, a proximate future (помалѣ бъıва́ю - щеє) with the auxiliary хощю etc. and a simple future (бѹ́дѹщеє) with нмамъ (correspondingly, the Serbian text has a series in кю = ću and one in нмамь). The narrative illustrations to this scheme can be reorganized into the verbal paradigm below, which bears little relation to either the classical Old Church Slavonic or the evolving Russian conjugation pattern. Nor was our grammarian troubled by the petty bugbear of consistency: in the initial overview, −сѧ forms were given as passive, but here they appear as mediopassives, while the passive column is occupied by ordinary active (transitive) forms, which can be considered passive only from the point of view of the addressor, that is as a kind of deixis projected from the speech situation back into the underlying grammar. One also notes other evidence of verbal confusion: the Russian scribe has the incorrect aorist 3rd person plur. бѧ́хѹ мѧ̂ for бѧ̀ша мѧ̂ (the Serbian original was correct, бнше ме), as well as the Middle Bulgarian 1st person sing. present tense ending -ѧ, supported perhaps by analogy with the imperfect 1st sing. бїахъ (again, the Serbian prototype was correct, бню). The paradigm:

	active	passive	mediopassive
Imperfect	бїахъ	бїа́хѹ мѧ̂	бїа́хсѧ
Aorist	бнхъ	бн́хѹ^a мѧ̂	бн́хсѧ

Present	Бıа*ᵇ*	Бıютъ ма̂	Бıа́са*ᵇ*
Proximate future	Бити хощю*ᶜ*	Бити ма̂ хотѧтъ*ᶜ*	Битисѧ хощоу̂*ᶜ*
Future	Бити имамъ	Бити ма̂ имѫтъ	Бити сѧ имамъ

*ᵃ*Serbian бише ме
*ᵇ*Serbian бию, бию се
*ᶜ*Serbian бити кю, бити ме те (sic) бити се кю

It is clear from such paradigms that the original Serbian attempt to bend Slavonic to a Greek mold, together with the Russian copyist's deteriorating knowledge of Slavonic verbal morphology, resulted in a verb system that bore little resemblance to any Slavonic recension in any country. Fortunately, the Slavic grammarians were content merely to note that Greek had had thirteen separate conjugations ("со́проуж҄ьства же рѣчи око́нчеваѥмъıми словесъı съ си́лами (= diacritics) ꙗвлѧ́ема соу́ть. Дѣлѧт же сѧ въ три́ на́ десѧть ѿ е̋ллинъ"), but did not feel obliged to illustrate them with Slavonic material.

The third part of speech discussed in our treatise is the participle, correctly identified as expressing both verbal and nominal categories ("имѣѧи нѣкаѧ послѣдствꙋюща рѣчи и нѣкаѧ послѣдствꙋюща имению"). Only the present participles are adduced as illustrations, and these only in the nominative singular; for no apparent reason, all masculine participles are in the long form, all neuters in the short form, while the feminines are short in the active but long in the passive voice:

Active	masc.	пишаи̂	гл҃аи̂	бıаи̂
	fem.	пи́шущи	гл҃ющи	бıющи
	neut.	е̋же пишуще	е̋же гл҃юще	е̋же бıюще
Passive	masc.	пишемъıи	гл҃емъıи	бıемъıи
	fem.	пишемаѧ	гл҃емаѧ	бıемаѧ
	neut.	пишемо	гл҃е̂мо	бıе̂мо

It is not clear how much credence, if any, one should place in the final stress marks of the masc. active (пишаи̂ etc.) or in the circumflexed neut. passive бıе̂мо.

The grammatical categories of the participle are listed but not illustrated: nominal gender, "aspect", "scheme", number, case (both падежи and падения) and verbal voice, tense, and conjugation, with the same labels as above. Only case declension is illustrated, and ineptly at that: глава́ Па́влова and живо́тно Петро́во are genitive (n.b. that, as described above, genitive case appears only in the guise of a possessive adjective), although it is hard to discern anything participial in such constructions. The dative is illustrated by да́мь Петру́ хлѣ́бъ ("сіе́ оу́бо Петру́ да́тельно е́сть") and the accusative by ѹ́лка ра́ди сни́де бг҃ъ на́ землю́ ("сіе́ оу́бо ѹ́лка вино́вна е́сть"). Overlooking the confusion of genitive and accusative in ѹ́лка (which could only be accusative for our scribe, since the genitive of ѹ́лкъ was ѹ́лковъ), we can see that what is meant by "case" is not declension but syntactic valence; here, as in the substitution of the possessive adjective ѹ́лковъ for the genitive case form ѹ́лка, syntactic categories are substituted for morphological.

The final paragraph of the "Eight parts of speech" concerns the article (разли́чіе πτωτικὸν?). Articles can be preordinate (предчинны́е προτασσόμενα), of which there are none in Slavic, or subordinate (подчинны́е ὑποτασσόμενα), by which is meant the relative pronoun иже ꙗже еже. The paradigm is incomplete (there are no nominative forms in the singular), and the forms themselves are a curious mixture: most of them could pass for Russian Church Slavonic, but the acc. sing. fem. ꙗже betrays a Bulgarian confusion of ѫ and ѧ, as was the case with the 1st person sing. present passive бїа́сѧ (cf. p. 18 above); the Serbian ms. shows the correct ю́же, and also has gen. sing. fem. ѥѥ for the Russian е́ѧ (= еѧ). The nom. and acc. plur. feminine, on the other hand, are Serbian: е́же. The paradigm:

		masc.	fem.	neut.
Singular	Nom.	[и́же]	[ꙗ́же]	[е́же]
	Gen.	его́ же	еꙗ́	его́ же
	Dat.	емоу́же	е́й	емоу́же
	Acc.	——	ꙗ́же	——
Plural	Nom.	и́же	е́же	ꙗ́же
	Gen.	и́хже	и́хже	и́хже
	Dat.	и́мже	и́мже	и́мже
	Acc.	ꙗ́же	е́же	(ꙗ́же)[a]

*a*The ms. reads "ро́дно же и̇ вино́вно я̈коже и̇ въ мꙋ́жьскомъ и̇ же́н'скомъ", where "вино́вно" is clearly an error for "да́тельно".

The grammatical categories of the "article" are listed as gender, "aspect" and number, but as Jagić 66 points out, "aspect" is an oversight for "case"

As a normative description of Church Slavonic, and especially of Russian Church Slavonic, the "Eight parts of speech" is far from ideal. The adjective is not even listed among the parts of speech, and of those that are listed, nothing is said about the pronoun (as such; the relative pronoun however does appear as an "article"), preposition, adverb or conjunction. Within the noun, the major categories are correctly identified (gender, number, case), although the case system is restricted to the four cases of Greek [nom., gen., dat., acc.], plus the vocative), and the gen. appears consistently not as a true case form, but syntactically disguised as a possessive adjective. Animation appears only implicitly, the acc. sing. masc. у҃ка, but is otherwise ignored. Among the verbal categories, aspect is notable by its absence, although perfective present-future forms are used to illustrate the passive future (х҃с ра́спнетсѧ, etc.). The three major tenses are identified (past, present, future), the past being subdivided into four individual tenses, two having imperfect and aorist forms respectively but the other two being "offensive to the tongue" (perhaps the perfect and pluperfect?). There are two compound futures, a proximate future with хощю̀ etc., and a generalized future with и҆мамъ. There are three voices (active, passive, mediopassive), but the verbal types illustrating them vary from one part of the treatise to another. Moods are listed but not illustrated. Only the present participles are mentioned, in a strange selection of long and short forms. Both nouns and verbs are said to manifest "aspects" and "schemes", which amount to various kinds of derivational and syntagmatic patterns. The Greek article appears in the form of the Slavonic relative pronoun. The forms themselves are mostly adequate for Russian Church Slavonic, but betray some confusion (of aorist and imperfect), and occasional intrusion of Serbian and Middle Bulgarian (ѧ ≅ Russian у, ю). The fact that this treatise was modeled on Greek is evident throughout. Still and all, it cannot be dismissed as entirely incompetent; in particular, its discussion of grammar in terms of parts of speech and the grammatical categories they express is modern in spirit if not in detail, and is far closer to the heart of grammar than the dry dissection of diacritics of which so much medieval Russian "grammar" consisted.

3. Konstantin the Grammarian

It was not so much grammar itself as its graphic expression and diacritic decoration that occupied the attention of the second major Balkan grammarian, *Konstantin Kostenčeski* ("*Filosof*" or "Grammarian").[21] Konstantin had been educated in Trnovo by Andronik, a disciple of Patriarch Euthymios, and had found his way to the Belgrade court of the Serbian Despot Stefan Lazarević. Stefan had apparently sent Konstantin to Constantinople, Jerusalem, and the Mount Athos monasteries, in return for which his eager protege offered to reform Serbian letters, the хоула и разврашенїе of which he attacks repeatedly. Konstantin saw himself as a guardian not only of proper orthography but also of the faith itself, even going so far as to suggest that badly spelled books be consigned to the fires together with their authors.[21a] Konstantin's dream was to be the reformer of Serbian letters, in the image of Euthymios or the grammarian Manuil Mosxopoulos of Constantinople, but he was hindered in this ambition by two perhaps related factors: on the one hand, he did not receive as much assistance from his royal patron as he had hoped for, and on the other, he was incapable of writing a simple declarative sentence.[22] What has come down to us is not a grammar, but an "обличенїе" of the sorry state of Serbian letters, mixed together with pedagogical suggestions, Church history, and symbolic exegeses of a few religious texts.

Konstantin's "обличенїе", the title of which begins Сказанїе изьѧвлѥнно ѡ писменех, is the first consciously normative work of Slavic grammar. It is concerned almost exclusively with orthography and diacritics; grammar itself is important only to the extent that grammatical distinctions can be lost if orthography is faulty (e.g. nominative апостоли vs. acc. апостоль1). In fact, orthographic and diacritic distinctions are assigned grammatical roles far beyond those envisaged by the founders of Slavic literacy. The о ~ ѡ distinction, for example, is used to mark number (о̃блакь, водаа̀ sing. vs. ѡ̃блаци, во̃ды1 plur.) and also gender (ѡ̃нъ masc. vs. о̀наа̀ fem.), a function also (but less consistently) assigned to the diacritic "силы1" ' and '. The spelling едѝнаа is nom. sing. fem., while едѝнаѧ is nom. dual masc. (J. 128). These and similar artificialities recur throughout medieval Russian manuscripts.

Konstantin's "Сказанїе . . ." begins with a table of 43 letters and 23 diacritic marks (many of which appear to have been copied from Greek and are not commented on by K.), a brief preface, and a table of contents, unique among medieval grammatical treatises and perhaps reflecting Konstantin's acquaintance with similar tables in Mount Athos manuscripts.[23] One may speculate, too, that Konstantin had become acquainted with specifically Russian Church Slavonic mss., and with Russian monks, in the Panteleimon Monastery on Athos; otherwise it would be hard to account for his assertion that the original (= Old) Church Slavonic mss. had been written neither in Bulgarian nor in Serbian, but primarily in Russian:

тѣмⸯ же проразсоуди҆вше до́брі҆и ѡ҆ни и ди҆вні҆и
моу́жі҆е, и҆ и҆зⸯбра́вше тⸯнⸯчаиши҆и и҆ краснѣиши҆и
роу́шⸯкыи ѥ҆зы́кь, кь н҆ѥмуже по́мощь вда́ссе
бл҃га́рⸯскы҆и и҆ срⸯбⸯскыи и҆ бо́снⸯскыи и҆
словѣнⸯскы҆и и҆ чешⸯкаго чес и хрⸯва́тⸯскы҆и
ѥ҆зы́кь. въ ѥ҆же въмѣсти́ти бж҃твнаа҆ писа́ні҆а
(10ᵃ)

an assertion which would doubtless have pleased the later Russian grammarians, had it not been left out as Konstantin's treatise made its way, via Bulgarian and Moldavian excerpts, to Russia.[24] Konstantin adduces lexical evidence of the Russian origins of Slavonic holy writ, e.g. the verb ла́яти 'reproach' and the noun моу́ка 'food', and even provides the first written instance of awareness of the *trat*~*torot* correspondence, quoting Matthew V, 40, " а҆ще кто пои҆метⸯ те за ри́зу твою҆, си҆ рѣу свитоу, да́ждь ѥ҆моу҆ и҆ срачи́цоу," and commenting, " и҆ н҃нѣ ру́си кошу́лю соро́укоу гл҃ють " (10ᵇ). Citing some rather whimsically selected lexical items which Slavonic took from other Slavic languages (Bulg. н҃нѣ и҆ прс҃но, Serb. моу́жь, мъуь, Bosnian ты҆, мы҆ Croatian рѣх, дѣлⷬ҇а), Konstantin concludes that the original Slavonic had indeed been an international Slavic language, in which Russian had however been the primus inter pares:

того ра́ди и҆ книже́вні҆и сни ни бл҃га́рⸯскоу
ни срⸯбⸯскоу сі҆ю (sc. рѣуь, DW) нари́чють, нь
словѣнⸯскоу, ѥ҆же ѥ҆с въсѣхь си҆хь пле́мень, нь
ѡ҆ба́че ру́сь вещⸯше (11ᵇ).

Konstantin's 43-letter alphabet has no front ь (although he himself uses both ъ and ь, non-etymologically, e.g. кь 'towards' въса 'all things', etc.) and no nasals, but adds several vowels to those found in Xrabr's much older list: both υ and ΰ, not only o and ѡ but also ѳ ⊙ ⊚ and digraph ѿ ; ы , ѥ. In addition, the diacritic ⸯ (паерок), which replaced ь and (more rarely) ъ on morpheme boundaries (трⸯно́вⸯскы҆ихⸯ, си҆мⸯ, посила́етⸯме, възⸯ- гара́есе) and evolved into an all-purpose interconsonantal syllable – boundary marker (ва́рⸯва́рⸯства, анⸯдро́никⸯ) or a pure decoration (сⸯтрань), is in one case opposed as ь to ъ : въньже оу҆пова́хь 'in whom I trusted' vs. вънъже 'outside, outdoors'.[25] Konstantin describes the origin of the letters (the opposition of Greek vs. Slavic going back to Xrabr) and gives their names; noteworthy is the fact that except for и҆́же, о́нъ (ὄ μάλο ὄ μικρόν) and ѿ вели́ко (ὄ μέγα), the vowel letters have no names (ӓ, ё instead of а́зъ, е́сть etc.), a fact which Jagić 215 interprets to mean that Konstantin taught his pupils to read by pronouncing syllables, not the names of letters.

Konstantin's accusations against the degenerate state of Serbian letters can be summarized as follows: three letters had dropped out of use and should be restored (ы ѣ ѫ), an additional twelve were being used incorrectly (є ѕ з и і ꙃ о ѡ ю ѥ ѱ ь), and Serbian texts betrayed ignorance of various prosodic and punctuational conventions. Konstantin elaborates on this state of literary deterioration in a series of statements scattered thoughout his treatise and couched in language which is often hard to understand; we will adduce only the essentials here.

The distinction ы : и, ї is important as a marker of differing grammatical categories, "ꙗко да не прѣтвориши виновноую рѣч на дательноую или мѣстноу"; the actual grammatical oppositions adduced are, however, nom. vs. acc. plur. (про҃рци : про҃ркы) and nom. sing. vs. nom. plur. adjectives, confusion of which could even result in the Nestorian heresy, for example were one to mix up єдинородѣныи сы̃ снь with plur. єдинородніи сн̃ (13ᵇ). Konstantin does not insist on correct pronunciation of ѣ, but requires that it be used properly in writing, in order to preserve such lexical distinctions as свѣть 'light' : свѣть 'holy' (< *svęt-); the same distinction is artificially introduced to create a pair of opposed gerunds, смѣавь 'having dared' < смѣти : смеавь (се) 'having laughed' < смеатисе (68ᵇ). ѣ : є is also essential to the dat. : acc. contrast in the pronouns, e.g. тебѣ даше : тебе́ више. The grammarian has little to say about the third "lost" letter, ѫ, contenting himself with listing a few words where ѫ should be written (ѫеос, матѫеи) and warning against such hypercorrect spellings as ѫимоѫеи for тимоѫеи.

Similar remarks appear à propos of letters other than the three lost ones. ѥ is to be used after palatal [ń], e.g. гн̃ѥ, ѡ нѥ, конѥ, and also for the distinction, apparently invented by Konstantin, between ѥзы́кь 'language' and єзы́кь 'tribe' (for a different interpretation of ѥ : є cf. p. 27 below). Equally artificial is Konstantin's proposal to use ю : оу to distinguish not only the old *i*-stem dat. sing. поутю 'road' from the *o*-stem поутоу 'cord', but also ю́же 'already' : оу́же 'cord', a distinction which could in Konstantin's opinion be rendered equally efficiently by diacritics, оу̂же 'already' : оу̂же 'cord'; here, as so often in medieval Slavic grammatical treatises, we see an attempt to devise new graphic oppositions in order to prevent the homophony and homography resulting from the collapse of older phonological distinctions.

On the ѡ : о marker of plural : singular and masculine : feminine, see above (later copies of this treatise indicate that ѻ was probably used in anlaut in the singular, о internally); ⊙ and ⊚ are used only in ⊙ко, ⊚у̏и, paralleling the number-marking о : ѡ already discussed. і is used in borrowings (ісаа́кь, іа̃кѡ́вь), and with the dieresis (авѣ̀ зрьн҄ци) before final vowels, e.g.

разⸯвращенїа. Upsilon appears in borrowings (сѵрїа), and is made to contrast with и in the pair мȣрʹно 'sweetly' : миρʹно 'calmly'.

All in all, the functional load of vowels (whether inherited or invented) is greater than that of consonants, although the latter are termed господствȣющїа and the former покорителʹныı а. In fact, the consonants are really the males of the graphic family: vowels, when they occur internally, are subordinated to preceding consonants, and do not require breathing marks ("силы", i.e. ʼ ˘), just as a woman at home with her husband does not need to wear a hat. However, when a woman goes out in public, she must cover her head, and so must vowels, out in anlaut, cover themselves with apostrophe or dasija (29[b]); cf. p. 31 below.

Chapters 13-17 of Konstantin's work deal with diacritics and punctuation. He lists words written under the titlo (primarily *nomina sacra*), permitting some variation in the extent of abbreviation (б͞гоу or б͞оу, у͞лвкь or у͞лкь), and mentions superscript $\widehat{\text{д}}$ but not $\widehat{\text{с}}$, which he himself uses frequently. Quite irrelevantly for Slavonic, Konstantin shows off his knowledge of Greek stenography (καὶ = $\in$ and some convoluted scribbles which — I can only associate myself with Jagić 138 n. — " я даже совсем не понимаю").

Konstantin lists five principal "силы": ´ о̓зїа, ˋ варїа, and three emotive markers, ῀ периспомени (used with heartfelt words, which "и̓зʹ срдца въсе͞ю кре́пости͞ю възʹдви́жутсе"), a sign of disapproval с\ (ѿıавленїе г͞лоу поругáнїе), and a kind of all-purpose exclamation point, ⸗\ (по́хвалʹно въ оу́дивленıи, и́ пакы́ поно́сно тáкоже). The apostrophe ʼ is associated with masculines and the dasija ˘ with feminines, although Konstantin does not say how, and the printed text shows almost no instances of the latter mark. The apostrophe is also used to mark reliable quotations, e.g. from Scripture, while the double » is reserved for heretical or apocryphal citations. The semicolon ; functions as a question mark (тебѣ̀ подбáеть ц͞ртвı́е; = ты̀ ли есѝ досо͞инь ц͞ртвı́ю), ∼ is a hyphen employed when a word must be divided at line-end, \\ signals the end of short words (сѐ тебѣ̀ г͞лю, въ и́мѣе три́ сн͞ы; it also distinguishes the demonstrative pronoun сѐ from the reflexive particle се (stressed сѐ), and apparently functions as a dual marker as well (ѐ же и въ мнѡ́гыих͞ или нѣкое две́ ве́щи гависти сѐ на потрѣ́боу снце·«роу́кь» или «нѡ́гъ», или и́но тáково). The comma (междостроуı́е) and period (строка) are used in the usual way, while † divides a text into verses. No mention is made of the superscript period functioning as a colon (снце· in the just-adduced quotations), but Konstantin felt it necessary to comment on ⸖, used to mark the place in a line where some originally omitted but marginally supplied form belongs, and even on the Greek stenographic J (=´´). Stress must be of course be correctly placed: гависѐ and оучи́сти are aorists but гави́се, оучистѝ imperatives, and to say "повѣсисе г͞и на др[в]ѣ" (instead of повѣ̀сисе) is to invite Christ to be crucified a second time. Here and throughout, Konstantin is concerned with grammatical categories and grammatical distinctions only to the extent to which they illustrate the graphic distinctions with which he was preoccupied. Konstantin is also concerned with correct verbal endings, but not always for the right reasons: he complains that видѣста ѻчи мои is a разъвращеніе because -ста is dual masculine and the neuter ѻчи should have видѣстѣ; this intrusion of gender marking into the conjugational paradigm was presumably triggered by similar marking in the *l*-participle.

In chapter 37, Konstantin gives a brief sample of a типикь, i.e. the erotēmata-type grammar he would like to write if only the Despot asked. However, one suspects that Stefan Lazarević may have been a ruler with some philological acumen of his own, since as Jagić 227-228 points out, Konstantin's knowledge of Greek was so weak that, " Судя по этому отрывку, едва ли нужно жалеть, что более обширный труд в этом роде не состоялся" (228). This poor knowledge of the very Greek grammars he wished to emulate, plus his shaky command of Serbian itself (confusion of cases, e.g. въ добрьінх писаніи 33^a; spelling hesitations, e.g. великьінх моужен and сицевьінх моужии in the same sentence, 9^b; the same spelling confusion he railed against, e.g. both рыбоу and рывію in the same line, 22^b, etc. etc.) force one to conclude that, for all his enthusiasm, Konstantin Kostenčeski was ill-suited for the profession of grammarian, and was perhaps unduly harsh on his Serbian colleagues (" не во зде въ тънъчаншінх мьісль полагають, по емуже ѡбразу съкръвеннаа моудрости ѡбрѣсти, нь моудрѣншаа безумие [sic] мнѣть, 18^a). Was it only the hapless Serbian scribe, who was, in Konstantin's own words, " невѣжа сьі, не мѡгьіи преда собою ѡсла познати " (18^b)? Be this as it may, Konstantin's treatise, at least in abbreviated form, found its way eastward into Russia.

There is no evidence that Konstantin's Сказаніе изь ѣавлѣнно ѡ писменех ever came to Russia in its full form, but it was widespread in an abbreviated Russian version containing additional material from the "Eight parts of speech" and from two other medieval Russian treatises known as the Сила существу книжного слова and the Начало буквам по орѳографии.

The original abbreviated version of Konstantin's word arose in Serbia in the late 15th or early 16th century and bears the title Словеса въ крацѣ избранна ѡ книгьі Константіна. This is a semi-competent compilation of some of Konstantin's rules, adduced in an order even less logical than that of the original, and in which the illustrative material frequently bears no relation to the orthographic or diacritic convention being discussed (for example, the copyist – a "бестолковый же эпитоматор", in Jagić's phrase – adduces the imperative : indicative [aorist] pairs ѡпоусти: ѡпоусти, прости : прости 2^a, but instead of placing them in a discussion of stress as

Konstantin had done, includes them totally inappropriately in his discussion of the ы : и contrast). The compiler gives new illustrative material for certain orthographical contrasts: въ себѣ пришедь:въ себѣ бывь 5ᵃ, раѹи́таса masc.: раѹи́тѣса fem. 8ᵇ, and repeats in a condensed and inaccurate way Konstantin's assertion that OCS had been primarily Russian: " рѹшкъı же... «соуршукоу» кошоульо глать, мъı же «сраѹнца», или «аира» мъı же «разрано» 3b. The back jer is "великъı", the paerok "малъı иже еръпь", but the illustrative мѫжь, петрь make it clear that the "large" jer could be either ъ or ь and that the scribe did not distinguish etymological ъ from ь (cf. въсѣхъ, dat. plur. симь, etc.). Furthermore, Konstantin's clear distinction between вънъ 'outside' and вънˢ 'to him' (cf. p. 23 above) is completely lost in the condensation, " и аще въпишеши великъı съ ъ вмѣсто малаго сего ˢ, то растлѣваеши глъ и не глеши на ба ѵпоβати, нѫ́ вънѣ, изврьженїе изˢ двора" 4ᵃ. The same scribe, interestingly, himself follows fairly strict rules for the distribution of ъ and ь, although these rules are never mentioned in the text: ъ is absolutely consistent in prepositions (въ къ съ) and almost so in prefixes (exceptions: безьсънѣдъı 2ᵃ, изъоѹчивь 10ᵇ), and is by far the more frequent in other inlaut positions, e.g. зе́млънаа, въсѣ, босънскъıи́ (exceptions: тънькота 3ᵇ, вънѹтрь ю̈доу 6ᵃ, разньствоѵеть 7ᵃ, Бельградь 8ᵃ, шньсица 8ᵇ, проѵьствіа 9ᵃ, изъоѹчивь 10ᵇ, богатьство 10ᵇ, ӓггльми 12ᵃ, дѣвьствѵа and дѣвьствоѵ 12ᵇ, ѵьтение 12ᵇ, поѹтьшествїе 12ᵇ, ѵьсть 12ᵇ, and some dozen and a half cases between root palatals and the adjectival suffix -ск-, e.g. грѣѵьскаго 3ᵇ, мѫжьска 8ᵇ, еретиѵьскъıа 9ᵃ); ь, on the other hand, occurs regularly in auslaut, e.g. хощеть, азъıкь, вънь 'outside'(cf. p. 23 and above), съıрь (exceptions: добръ 2ᵇ, тъ 7ᵃ, въводѧть 8ᵇ, книгахъ 9ᵃ, нарекль 12ᵇ, книгъ 12ᵇ, вѣкшмъ 12ᵇ and ten instances with words under the titlo like бъ 4ᵃ, апль 7ᵃ, глъ 9ᵇ).[26] In other words, the "бестолковый эпитоматор" was both incapable of understanding the system he was trying to transmit and unaware of the quite different system by which he himself was governed. In a few cases, however, he did manifest a certain originality. For example, where Konstantin had attempted to exploit the е : ѥ distinction lexically (езъıкь 'tribe' : ѥзъıкь 'language' 16ᵇ), his epigon proposes it as a number marker (" сё ѥ ѥзъıкь единь навлѣеть, се же е езъıкъı мншгъıи" 5ᵇ). He also gives a new name for the comma (коука alongside the older междоѹсроѵїе 9ᵇ), and lists some additional Greek diacritic names (макра, врахїа́, ѱили, ӱфень, ѵподїастоли), without however explaining to his Slavic audience how these signs were used or even what they looked like. He copies Konstantin's remark that the nasal vowel letters caused some problems for Serbian scribes ("сїа́ же писмена двѣ, Ӓ. Ѫ̈. ꙗкож нѣкое врѣмѧ сръблемь ю̃авнٓшӕ̃" 6ᵇ), and unlike Konstantin uses the юсы quite liberally — if not always etymologically correctly — himself, e.g. "ты же, ѡ҆писа́телю, а́ще въ писа́нїи ѡ҆ сила́ˣ не въни́маеши и̇ разнˢствїи глш̃м, нѫ та́уїѫ красотѣ рукы̇ı въни́маеши, то̑ тво́риши кнı́гѫ своѫ̇ красотоѫ̇ по́бнѫ̇ ц҃рци, е̑ство́м, же ста́нїа рѫкы̇ı твоеѫ̇ го́рши е̑ блѫ́ница 6ᵇ. The use of ѫ and especially of ѧ (e.g. in глѧ̃ть) shows that this short version of Konstantin's treatise had moved East from Serbia through Bulgaria — or at least via a Bulgarian copyist to Wallachia and Moldavia, from which area it would then spread out to Russia (Jagić 229-230, 266), where in various combinations with other South Slavic and Russian works, it was to become the major source of Russian preoccupation with orthographic and diacritic detail.

The condensed version of Konstantin's work was incorporated into 16th and 17th c. mss. which arose on East Slavic territory,[27] and which showed a certain degree of initiative in rearranging the material from the condensed version of Konstantin's work and in combining it with other sources, including the "Eight parts of speech".

The Russian recension begins with an expanded version of its source's comments on diacritics. Most of the diacritics and their names remain the same, although ⁀ периспоме́ни has been converted to перелиспоме́нı̇, ˘ дасı́а̇ is also called уашˢка, the question mark ; is labelled поˆстолїа̇ instead of the earlier съпроти́вная , and the паерок is now called not only е̇рˢти́ца but also р̇еунı̇къ, while the comma , , formerly междоу-с(т)роуı̇е or коу́ка, is now the slightly misspelled but otherwise modern запатаа ; similarly, the modern though non-diminutive term кавы̇ıкы̇ı is used for 〉〉 . The single and unnamed short-word auslaut marker \\ (се̏, тъ̏ etc.) has been split into \\ пı̇а́сма and \\ кенˢди́ма , the functions of which are not explained. ѵ̇ и̇жница appears, mysteriously, in the same place as the earlier и̇ѱи̑ (Konstantin, full version), while ⁀ ѱи́ли is listed at the very end, as was the case in the condensed Konstantin text. Four diacritics are newly introduced: ⸍ и̇сѡ (unless this corresponds to ᷉ and ⸍ of the full and condensed sources, which seems unlikely, since the latter of these is repeated in the Russian mss.), ʺ сквады̇ı , ⌒ камура (which "и̇нде гл̃етсѧ периспомени̑ ," sic), and a real exclamation point ! called прибы̇ıлица, the difference between which and ⸜ (поноси́телна) and ⌒ (похва́лна) is left to the reader's imagination. Overall, one has the impression that the Russian scribe was assiduously compiling a list of diacritic terms without knowing much about their functions or the Greek from which they derived (cf. the twice misspelled периспоме́ни and the miscopied макра̀, врахїа̇ , which are rendered as ма́рˢко and влахı̇а̇ respectively).

The second part of the Russian recension consists of an incomplete orthographical compendium, derived mainly from the condensed version of Konstantin but also drawing on the "Eight parts of speech" and on two other

Russian treatises known as the Сила существу книжного слова and the Начало буквам по ор∂ографии. Jagić 269-70 concludes that this compilation, titled ѿ вүкваⷯ. сирѣ̈ ѿ слѡваⷯ аꙁⷭбуцѣ , was made on Russian soil, both because of the just-mentioned borrowings from other Russian texts and because Greek συλλαβή is translated скла́дъ; to this we might add the translation, "аще погрѣшиши, сиреү̈ аще о́пишешсѧ " (Jagić 278), which indicates that the Russian scribe was aware of the different meanings of грѣхъ in Church Slavonic ('sin') and East Slavic ('error'); cf. also the typical Russian Church Slavonic spelling of *tert groups (посрⷣественоⷨ 277, времⷩана 277, пре́вы́вⷭшее́ 277, etc.) and the etymologically (usually) correct rendering of *tьrt etc. troups (серьⷠвки sic 276, вѐрхⷡ 277, съвершително 277, etc.). Surprising in this clearly Russian recension, however, is the absence of any mention of the primarily роуⷭкыıн origins of Old Church Slavonic.

The compilation ѿ вүкваⷯ repeats much of the prescriptive data from the condensed Konstantin, not always in easily comprehensible form. For example, where the Moldavian text explained that the spelling -аа was (nom.) singular feminine but -а ѩ (nom.) dual masculine ("прѣ̈ста́а, еди́наа. ӓще ли въпи́шеши едина ѩ, два̀ мүжа г҃лешн"), the Russian recension apparently wants to prescribe -аѧ as the fem. sing. and -аа or -а ѩ as the masc. dual, but this is far from clear in the text, " прⷮта́ѧ еди́наѧ. ӓще ли напи́шеⷲ еди́наа два̀жⷣы , и́ли боⷧшое́ ѩ, мүжа г҃лешн " On the other hand, the Russian scribe is stricter than his South Slavic predecessors in his treatment of the titlo: while permitting either бг҃ть or бт҃ь in the previous section (ѿ тон си́лѣ кни́жном, Jagić 275), he now insists that the root-final consonant be preserved in бг҃ъ, бж҃е etc. (not б҃ъ, б҃е); furthermore, he introduces a new distinction between Holy Family names and their homographs: pagan gods are to be spelled out, with no titlo ("бѡ̈ꙁи иже не сътвориша нб҃се и ꙁемлѧ̀ да погибнү̈ " 277) and all Marys other than the Virgin Herself are to be spelled out (" всѣⷯ ма́рен беꙁ въꙁмѐта пиши сⷭкла́доⷨ, ӓще и ст҃ы сүть. еди́нү бц҃ү пиши поⷣ въꙁметоⷨ мр҃ı̈а, мр҃ı̈е́ " 278), and similarly молитва 'prayer' is to be written under the titlo, мл҃тва, but мо́ле́нı̈е, молⷭба [28] моли̂, мо́лисѧ, " то̂ всѐ сⷭкла́доⷨ пишı̂, не покры́ван" 278.

Remarks on individual letters of the alphabet call for little comment, with the exception of є and н, where the scribe seems to be concerned more with variant accusative forms than with the distribution of the letters themselves: 'н̂ се е̋ е̂ ꙁвателⷭное́ ("objective"? DW), пишеⷮ сѧ ꙁа е́го и ꙁа ѐѧ̂ и ꙁа нⷯ, ѩ̂кожⷤ бы̀ ре́ши̂. иꙁⷭ́бавиⷯ е̂ и сп҃еть е̂, оу҆ѹѧ́ще е̂, въꙁми е̂, твое́, мое́, мнӥмое́, даёмое́, и про́ѹаѧ̂ 278. This е̂ seems to be a kind of all-purpose accusative, representing the neut. acc. sing. as well as a combination of the Serbian *ę reflex є and its East Slavic equivalent ѣ . Similarly, after giving examples of н in anlaut (нача́льствүеⷮ , e.g. и҆зьı́де, и҆ да́сть) and auslaut (покоряе́тсѧ or повїнова́телнож, e.g. твои́, сн҃ъ), ʒвателнож again appears to mean 'objective', or perhaps 'enclitic': " и҆ʒмү и҆, прославлю҄ и҆, приведеши́ и, в҃мѣсто его̀ і и҆хъ", after which the scribe generalizes, "мнѿгьı г҃льı и҆сполнае҃, си́це оу҆бо і̇, е҆и а пишю҄ сѧ въ приѧуѧающихъсѧ мѣстех҄ и ʒа ег҃, и ʒа их҄, и ю҄ ʒа еа҃" 278). From all of this it would appear that the Russian scribe was trying to cope with animate and inanimate accusatives (и̇ vs. его̀, ӗ [and а̃?] vs. ихъ, etc.), and perhaps with Serbian e<*ę (<*ę₃) vs. Russian ѣ and Russian Church Slavonic ѧ; however, the passages are not entirely clear. The scribe seems also not to have understood his source's correlation of ш : ф with masc. : fem.: the condensed Konstantin says explicitly: " ѡ҃н, ѡ҃ньсѝца ѡ̇ мѫ҃жи. ф҆на, ф҆н҅сица ф҆жена҆х҄ " 8ᵇ, out of which the Russian recension saves only the incoherent, " ѡ̈ о҃нъсѝце, ò мүжи· она̀, о҄нсица, ò женѣ " (Jagić 279).

The most unexpected feature of ѡ̈ бүква҆хъ is the appearance, in the discussion of the orthography of Б, of the "passive" paradigm (страда́лнаг҃ оу҄бо ʒало́га времѧна) of бити, actually a combination of what in the "Eight parts of speech" were "passive" (бıа҆хү мѧ҆ etc.) and mediopassive (бıа҆хсѧ) forms. The мѧ҆ "passives" are illustrated by the third plural forms of the same five tenses as in the "Eight parts of speech", but in slightly different order:

пре́бьıв҅шее҆ ("past", sc. aorist) :	бихү мѧ҆
протѧжен҅ное҆ непредѣленое҆ (imperfect) :	бı́ѧ̆хү мѧ҆
настоѧ҃щее҆ (present) :	бью҄ мѧ҆
по малѣ бьıва́ющее҆ (proximate future) :	бити мѧ҆ хотѧ҃
бүдѫщее҆ (future) :	бити мѧ҆ и҆мү҃

This is followed by another "passive" (страдалнаж сүть та́ко), this time reflexive, but with the first and second persons plural in the wrong order, perhaps because the copyist first took бı̈ётесѧ to be a third person dual: (... бı̈етасѧ, бı̈етесѧ, бье́мсѧ̃...). Put into the usual order, the paradigm is as follows:

бı́ѧсѧ̃		бье́мсѧ̃
бı̈е̂шисѧ̃	} бı̈ётасѧ {	бı̈е́тесѧ
бı̈ётесѧ̃		бью҄тсѧ

Aside from the mysteriously erratic diacritics, which we shall not even attempt to explain, attention should be called to the combination of South Slavic and East Slavic tense jer reflexes in the root, and to the "Bulgarian" first person singular spelling -а (< ѧ < ѫ).²⁹

As is the case with all works connected with the name of Konstantin, this Russian recension is concerned above all with orthographic and diacritic details, and in particular with the positions within the word in which a given letter or mark can or must occur. As we saw in the treatment of jers in the condensed Konstantin text (see p. 27 above), medieval grammarians were hardly aware of the systematicity — or lack thereof — with which they themselves were writing. The same is true of the Russian recension, which for example says not a word about the use of ъ, ь and ѕ паерок (е҄рѕтица, рѣунікъ), although it cannot have escaped this scribe's attention that his own use of ъ and ь differed radically from that of his South Slavic model. Nor did this Russian scribe, such a stickler for accuracy — not to say pettiness — in other ways (бз҃ бa҃ тыж пиши сz҃ глаголем, бг҃а бг҃ъ 277) even make an effort to follow his source as far as the jers are concerned: of the app. 390 etymological jers in his text, 165 (42%) are used correctly, another 201 (52%) are replaced by ѕ, omitted, or vocalized (all normal, if not exactly fastidious East Slavic developments, and a mere 23 (less than 6%) show confusion of ъ and ь (съоѵзь 275, дръжи҃ 275, подобънаа 276, глаголь 277; six of these 23 cases are third-person verb forms in -ь, which could reflect East Slavic phonology as well as the Serbian distribution). In other words, the Russian scribe simply used the jers his own way, being affected by his supposedly authoritative source in hardly one case out of twenty. The same is true of other letters as well, for example in the case of оѵ and ѵ: where the condensed version of Konstantin used only the digraph оѵ, the Russian scribe employs the two letters in complementary distribution, with оѵ occuring in anlaut (оу҄сты 275, оу҄чаше 277 etc.), after ъ in the word съоѵзь 275, 278), and after і in borrowings (і оу҄даѷдь 275, іоу҄да 277 etc.), while ѵ is used in all post-consonantal positions (and ю post-vocalically). Nor is our scribe much concerned with consistency, for example in his use of ѣ and е : (вѣлѣгь 276 but белѣгыі 278, греѵесѕких and греческїе 276, възмѣта and възметом in adjacent lines 278), or in the distribution of ы and и after velars (12 occurrences of кыі, гыі to 15 or ки, ги, e.g. па́кы 275 but па́ки 276, муж҄скых and женьских 275, мнѡ́гыі 278 but мнѡ́гим 280).

It is in the use of diacritics that the Russian recension differs most noticeably from its South Slavic forebears. If the older texts treated their vowels in Moslem metaphorics (vowels inside the word, like women inside the house, do not need to wear diacritics or head-coverings, respectively, whereas vowels exposed in anlaut, like women in public, must be covered; cf. p. 25 above), the Russian recension is more like a Victorian girls' dormitory where one hardly ever undresses at all: diacritic marks are obligatory on all vowels in anlaut or post-vocalic position, all stressed vowels, and a good many others whose need for diacritic decorum is unclear, at least in our own less restrictive age. The result is a profligate scattering of purely decorative diacritics, e.g. о҄зїа́ 275, о҄пира́ющї е҄ѧ 275, прїйде 276, о҄зїе҄ю 276, оу҄лїанїи 275, бїа́са̑ and бїе҄тса̑ 276, etc. etc., in the confusion of which it is hard to discern much that is systematic. Nor is this difficult to understand: the Russian scribe (or perhaps a

Ukrainian; cf. the ы~ъ confusion mentioned above, and also the occasional use of the паерок over the s of the adjectival suffix -ск-, e.g. еретичесκӹ е 276, грѣчески͞х 276, всл̈чес̈клА 277; however, there are no clear cases of confusion of ѣ and и) was working from a Bulgaro-Moldavian version of a Serbian original written by a Bulgarian emigrant trying to imitate Greek. Nonetheless, certain regularities can be observed in the use of diacritics.[30]

The distribution of ″ and ′ on initial vowels depends both on stress and on the front~back distinction in the vowels themselves. Initial и (i) and є take ″ when stressed (и̋сш, и̋стин͞ную, и̋збра͞ному, и̋же, и̋мА, etc.; ѐсть, ѐже, ѐгдà(?), but ′ when unstressed (илѝ, ѝ, ı̀, идѐж, ıн̀де, ı̀нако, ѝсх̣одити, ıоу̀ад̈ь, ıоу̀лита, ѝз′гони͞, ѝподıа́столи, ѝкш͞н; ѐА, ѐю, ѐдıно, ѐретичесκые, у̀фѐнь), but there are some exceptions (и̋жица, и̋сповѣдую͞, ѐдıносу̀ш′на). Back vowels take ″ regardless of stress (о̋стра, о̋брѣтаѐтсА, о̋при, о̋зıа̀, о̋пира̀ющı̈, о̋пише͞сА, о̋ца, о̋дѣжи͐, о̋но̀, ш̋но̀; а̋пострѡфь, а̋ще, а̋зь, а̋гглъ, а̋плъ, а̋минь, а̋з′вуцѣ, г̋̈ако̀ж, г̋̈азы́ıку [га was considered simply a vowel letter, not /ja/] оу̀сты̀ı, оу̀бо̂, оу̀пишеши [sic⸪], but again there are a few exceptions: о̀зıа̀ and а̀п͡сла alongside о̋зıа̀, а̋плъ, and ѝкаа̀н′не . Whereas the preposition ѡ (used with feminine or plural nouns) takes ″ or ′ (ш̋ мни̋сѣх̣, ш̋ о̋нъсице, ш̋ женах̣), the exclamation ѡ takes ⸰ when apposed to substantives in what the scribe calls "зва́телно" usage (i.e. approbatory exclamations, cf. " Сѐж па́ки ѡ̀великоѐ зва́телно нарица́етсА, зва́телноеж высоуа̋йши͞м гла̀сш͞м гл̀етсА, пишетсА сице· ш̋ глубѝна̀ бога́тества̀, ш̋ бл̀гти твоѐа̀, ги, ш̋ дивное чюдо..." 279; note the mixture of Slavic nominatives and Greek genitives after ш̋) but with ⸰ in the hortative (" м̋олтивноѐ жѐ· ѡ̀ г͡сни спасѝж, ш̋ г͡си поспѣшиж " 279), and simply ′ in derogatory exclamations ("поноси́телнож· ш̋ невѣрı̀а̀ ва́ше͞г, без′закон′нı̋ıı ю̀дѣѝ, ш̋ле неразумı̀а̀ ва́ше͞г" 279). The scribe seems not to notice that his usage conflicts with the rules he had been copying only a few pages earlier (" сѐ а̋пострѡфь вели́кı̋ıı· ⸰ сı̀а̀ похва́лна, ⸰ сı̀а̀ поноси́телна " [and no mention of the expressive function of ′] 275).

The single apostrophe ′ is used for unstressed vowels in postvocalic position, either internally or finally (о̋брѣта́етсА, о̋пира́ющı̈, оу̀лıа́нı̋ıı, погрѣша́еши, прı̀ıдѐ, любодѣ̀ı̀чища, сı̀а̀, варı̀а̀, запата̀А, про́речествı̀а̀, поклоненı̀ѐ, бладословı̀а̀). The same function is filled by ″ in C__V position (вели́кı̋ıı, нѣкı̋ıı, чтущı̋ıı, прı̀ıдѐ, посла́нı̀а̀, беззакон̈ı̀ѐ), in competition with the dieresis ¨ (даси̋а̀, мѣренı̋ıı, развращенı̀а̀, бı̋ı̀ах̣у, слı̀анı̋ıѐ) the latter otherwise occurring, for reasons which escape me (perhaps to save space at line-end?), in interconsonantal position in a few words (ѐдıн—

regularly, кнїжном, повїновательнїх, глѵвїна); the demonstrative *sьje takes a variety of diacritics (сї̆а, сї̆е, сей, сїа̂, сїе̂, but only ¨ before final barytone, сїа̑, сїе̑, сїа̑).

῾ frequently substitutes for ᾿ over final unstressed vowels (срᴬѵньїй, велнкїй, проѵаа̑, нѣкїй, вывающеѐ, etc), although its more usual role is to mark stressed vowels in auslaut (ö̂стра̀, ддсїа̀, рещѝ, ѵто̀, прїйдѐ, йлѝ, пра̀, зрѝ, ѵрьна̀, мы̀, вы̀, пнсмена̀, своѓ, задѐ, пнсмо̀, твоѐ, моѐ, пншѝ, земла̀, женѣ̀, двѣ̀, два̀, etc.); in this function, ῾ is in complementary distribution with ´, which marks stressed vowels internally (вѡ́нъ, ö́пнра́юшї, сѝце, лѓввѐ, про́ѵаа, поẋва́лна, па́кы, про́пасть, глаго́лю̋, ню́зьїкѵ, степе́нї, сѣ́сти, да́ти, ма́лъ, велн́къ, etc.); exceptions being rare (сѐ, сѵдѝ, скваดы̀, слѡва̑ẋ, двд҃ы̀, гла́-голем sic, въззрѝте but во́зрите). Stressed internal vowels can also be marked by ¨ postvocalically, though such instances are few (а̑вр̋аӓмъ, бї̋нӓẋѵ, бї̋ёваса, бї̋ётаса, вь̋ёмса̀; cf. ѡ̏ка̀а́н˒не, ѝпо-дї̑а́столи, настоа̑ще̏е̏, бїе̏шнса̀, бїе̋тса̀, вь̋ютса, оѵ̑-стрѡе̋нїе̏; clitics and intonation appear to play no role in these variations). In general, ¨ is the most ubiquitous of all diacritics; in addition to the functions already noted, it can also mark both unstressed and stressed vowels in postconsonantal and interconsonantal position (ре́ѵнїкъ, запїна́ютса, кнї̋-гаẋ, възйма́ю̋, ѿ҃навлае̋, едїнӓг̏, в҃горшднѵї̋но, в˒нїтѝ), like ¨ (see p. 28 above).

One diacritic mark is used on consonants as well as on vowels: the circumflex (периспоме́ни and assorted misspellings thereof). With vowels, it is frequent in unstressed or weakly stressed auslaut position, especially with conjunctions, pronouns, and clitics (й̑, лй̑, йлй̑, но̑, во̑, оѵво̑, се̂, се́же̂, сй̂, сй̑це̂, сй̑це, то̂, ѡ̑но̂, ö̑но̂, еда̂, ма̂, са̂, е̂сй̑), but also and without apparent motivation in ѡ̑ѵй̑, в˒нити̑; ѵ̂лколю́вѵе̂ is best grouped with three cases of interconsonantal ⁀ in which the diacritic marks the preceding consonant cluster (ѱ̑или, ѡ̑вла̑цы, исẋож̑е̏нїе), merely being displaced to the right. The use of ⁀ in consonant clusters, curiously enough, appears to depend on phonological criteria. The general rule is that clusters ending in sonorants and /v/ never take ⁀, while those ending in obstruents generally do so, but with quite some variation. The prohibition against ⁀ is absolute for clusters in /l/ and /v/ (поклоненїе̏, гла́голъ, еладо́сло-вїа̑, ти́тлѣ, посла́нїе, слѡва̑ẋ, разли́ѵно, влахїа̀, гор-лом, земла̀; скваดы̀, вѵква̑ẋ, е́стество, лѣствицї [n.b. ц̑ = [t͡s]] сътвориша, надвор, два, свѣдете́⁀ство, поẋвална) and for /stop + r/ (въкра̑⁀цѣ̀, кромѣ̀, греѵе⁀ски, погрѣша́ешн, ö̑при, привєдешн, пра̀, православнн҃ы̑ẋ, врьзопи́сцеẋ, до́бром, изо-вра̑⁀номѵ, ö̂стра̀, внѵтръ, страдалнаг̏, дръжи), whereas /cont. + r/ clusters show more or less free variation (с̑рока, зрѝ, а̑враӓмъ, on

the one hand, but more frequently, conforming to the general rule, по-
средственож, зри, возрите, въззрйте, врьстѣ, развращенїа,
времана on the other). The /affricate + r/ cluster /čr/ takes ⌢ in both of
its appearances: у̑ревѣ, у̑рьпа. Clusters ending in nasals also tend not to be
marked by ⌢ (кнїгах, погибну, перисномені sic, косне⌢, зна́-
мені, назнаменáхом, похвална, внутръ; пи́смена, писмо́,
сматря́и on the one hand, but rarely, with dental continuants, назна-
менáти, писме, есмь, on the other). Obstruent clusters show a much more
even distribution: /st⁽ʲ⁾/ and /sk/ never take the diacritic (оу́сты, е́сть,
в'мѣсто, и́стинную, стихw͡в, естеством, степéнї, сѣсти, про́-
пасть, мужскы͡х, греческїе), while the other voiceless clusters vary,
regardless of the order of stop and continuant (го́с͡пwдем с͡пасиж, but
перелиспоме́нї sic, списáтелїе, и́сповѣдую⌢; г͡летса, обрѣтáетса, w͡вращáютса, et. al., but г͡летса, обрѣтáетса, запїнá-
ютса, et. al.; за̑ѣ, позде, инде, онде, нѣкогда on the one hand but
за́ѣ, инде, е́гда on the other). The remaining obstruent clusters do not take
⌢, but there are too few of them to permit any conclusions (верху, исхо-
дити, съвершително, болгарским). Overall, the use of the circumflex
seems to depend primarily on consonantal distinctive features, perhaps influenced by — and of course in some cases coincident with — syllabic and/or
morpheme boundaries, which themselves coincide with dropped jers, of which
our scribe may have been dimly aware, although he makes only a most inconsistent effort to mark such jers with a паерок (cf. p. 31 above) and not at all with
the circumflex. Be this all as it may, in the use of diacritics, as in the distribution
of jers, the Russian recension of the condensed Konstantin treatise is governed —
albeit inconsistently — by distributional principles of which the scribe himself
was seemingly unaware. Overall, this strange and derivative mixture of fact and
fancy, with its preoccupation with the pettiest of linguistic entities and its
almost total neglect of genuine grammar, was hardly an auspicious beginning for
the Russian grammatical tradition.

4. Написаніє ꙗзыком словенским о грамотѣ

The closest thing to a phonological description of Slavonic is found in a rather long (and, in some passages, rather obscure) treatise entitled Написа́нїе ꙗзы́ко{м} словенски{м} о гра́мотѣ і҆ о є҆ѧ̀ строє́нїй, в нє́йже о҆ бу́квѣ и҆ о є҆ѧ̀ писмєнє{х}, вопроша́нїа о҆у҆чи́тєл{ь}скаꙗ, ꙗ҆́ко в{ъ} лицѐ о҆у҆ченичєско, и҆ ѿвѣща́нїа о҆у҆ченичєска, ꙗ҆́ко в лицѐ о҆у҆чи́тєл{ь}ско.[31] Needless to say, the author's principal interest was not phonology but graphology; he is interested above all in the grouping (classification) and especially in the combinatorics of the vowel and consonant letters, not of sounds. His phonetic descriptions are couched in obscure metaphors: vowels are "notable" (ꙁнамєни́т), "adequate" (дово́лєнъ), "firm" (крѣ́пок), and so forth. Nonetheless, a certain amount of phonological insight, largely accidental, can be glimpsed through the graphic screen.

The treatise begins by drawing a clear parallel between the spoken and written forms of language: " Гра́мота є́сть сѐ. о҆у҆мѣ́нїе ү҆лүєскоє словєсємъ вса́кого вѣща́нїа гласова́нїємъ и҆ꙁъа҆влєно̀ въ слы́шанїє і҆ в раꙁу҆мѣ́нїє, а҆ писа́нїємъ и҆ꙁложєно̀ в видѣ́нїє и҆ прєдложє́нїе" (360). It is worth noting in passing that the spoken as well as the written form of language is Slavonic; there is no trace of awareness in our medieval texts that Church Slavonic differed from the vernacular, and no attempt to equate the former with written and the latter with spoken language.

The alphabet (бу́ква) is said to contain forty-five letters, arranged in what is basically the modern order:

а б в г д є ж ꙁ н і к л м н о п р с т у ф х
ѿ ц ч ш щ ъ ы ь ѣ ю ꙗ ѧ є ѡ ꙃ ѱ ѵ ѹ а ꙽ й.

The digraph о҆у҆ is missing from this list, although this letter is included in the vowel classification (see p. 37 below).

The most important thing to know about the letters of the alphabet seems to have been how they can be combined into clusters (usually, syllables). Here the terminology is not always clear. Слоги́на appears to be "combinatorics" in general, and consists of two parts: слогъ is the act of combining one letter with another, or perhaps the syllable as such, abstracted from its concrete manifestations, while сложє́нїє is the resulting cluster ("Слоги́на є́сть сѐ· прави́тєлница вѣща́нїа, вса́кого ра́ꙁу҆ма прєда́ннаго ѿ бга о҆у҆му́ у҆лү́ескому҆, и҆мѣ́єтъ в{ь} сєбѣ̀ вєсь слогъ і҆ вса́ко сложе́нїе стѧ҆жи̃"; "Слогъ є́сть сѐ· писмана к писмано{м} присовоку҆пла́а во є҆ди́нў ү҆ет҆у вѣща́нїа, прибира́ѧ по є҆ди́номў писмани ма́ло и҆ мно́го вса́ко сложе́нїе и҆сполна́а і҆ вса{к} гл̃{ъ}"; "а сложе́нїе є́сть сѐ· в{ъ}ку҆пѣ сложєно̀ рєщѝ два́ писмани или́ три і҆ли чєты́рє и҆ли пѧ́ть"365).

Clusters of two to five (in one ms., up to nine) letters are labeled and illustrated: двѡнкьı (ба, ва, га, ...), трѡнкьı (бра, вра, гра, ...), четверицьı (стра, стре, стри), патерицьı (сквра). The слогъ thus contains, or produces, four different сложенїа: "первое двойное, второе тройное, третїе четверичное, четвертое патеричное" (with one ms. continuing on to "ѡсмое девятеричное"). Сложенїе, in spite of the examples just adduced, is considered not only a permissable but also a meaningful combination of letters: separate, uncombined letters are "dead" ("а еже не слагаются кюн писманá, по разници пристоятъ к' реченїемъ, то именуются мертвеныя" 366), and the syllable itself (слогъ), apart from such meaningful clusters, is compared to a body without a soul or a soul without a body, only "сложенїе уподобляе оживленїе" (366).

After this general introduction, the treatise proceeds to a classification and "description" first of the vowels (звателныя), then of the consonants (полузвателныя [32]), and then continues with a complex description of the various combinations of vowels and consonants.

There are twenty-one vowels, divided into six classes (статїя), five built around the cardinal vowels /a e i o u/ and the sixth containing ъ ь й '. The phonetic descriptions are fancifully but, at first glance, not very usefully metaphoric:

статїя первая
    а   "a notable and simple sound" (азъ гласъ знаменїı̂ і простъ ѡбдержит')
    а̀   "significant" (назнáменателен)
    ѧ   "impressive" (внятеленъ)

статїя вторая
    е   "a thin sound" (скуденъ глас' ѡбдержит')
    ѣ   "flexible" (гибокъ)
    ԑ   "adequate" (доволенъ)

статїя третїая
    и   "a narrow sound" (узокъ глас' ѡбдержит')
    ы   "broad" (широкъ)
    ї   "flat" (плоскъ)

статїя четвертая
    о   "a sharp sound" (остръ глас' ѡбдержи)
    ѡ   "smooth and long-low" (гладокъ і логоватъ)
    ѡ̈   "smooth and slow"? (затянучвъ) [33]

статїа пѧтаѧ
- ѵ "expansive" (пространенъ)
- оѵ "adequate" (доволенъ)
- ю "constrained" (тѣсенъ);
  in some ms., "firm" (крѣпокъ)
- ѫ "nasal and (?) arbitrary" (гугнивъ і произволенъ)
- ѷ "indeterminate" (неуставенъ)

статїа шестаѧ
- ъ "broad and short" (толстъ глáсъ óбдéржѫтъ крáтокъ)
- ь "narrow and short" (тóнокъ і крáтокъ)
- й "shortened and (?) inverted" (сокращéнъ і опровéрженъ)
- ѕ "same as ъ" (нáкоже еръ) [34]

A certain degree of parallelism is evident in these vowel – letter sets. Each of the first five begins with the basic (positionally least restricted) vowel, which is followed by its positional variants. The positional determinants vary from set to set: in the а and ѵ sets, the first members (а, ѵ) occur alone or after unsharpened consonants, and the third members (ѧ, ю) after jot and sharped consonants (with various sequential restrictions), but н and і are distributed according to whether the following segment is a vowel or not. In all sets but н, the back-allophone letter comes first, but this is reversed for н/ь і.[35] The spatial and other metaphors which are supposed to describe the pronunciation of all these graphs are awkward and in some cases difficult to interpret (e.g. є and оѵ are both "adequate" [доволенъ], although in fact their principal characteristic is that they occur in anlaut). The only more or less consistent metaphor is that back vowel variants tend to be described as "large and heavy", while their front counterparts are "thin" or "narrow" (a metaphor with obvious physical characteristics: the tongue is raised and advanced for the second group):

ьі =	широкъ	н =	оузокъ
ѵ =	пространенъ	ю =	тѣсенъ
ъ =	толстъ	ь =	тонокъ
є =	доволенъ	е =	скуденъ

Incidentally, one may note in passing that our medieval grammarians were as fond of proliferating terms as they were of superfluous letters and meaningless diacritics. Indeed, if we had to describe the difference between medieval and modern grammatical viewpoints in a single (and of course vastly oversimplified) phrase, we might say that the seventeenth-century grammarian revelled in surface variety and was not much concerned with underlying and unifying regularities, while from the mid-eighteenth century on we have been concerned just with such regularities and have attempted to eliminate (or at least to dismiss as marginal) such surface facts as do not conform to the unifying principles we believe to have discovered.

The phonological classification of vowels is followed by a section on vowel distribution and diacritics. Unfortunately, without photographs of the actual mss., it is not easy to make sense of some of the distributional distinctions the author (or one of his predecessors) was striving to elucidate. For example, ten vowel letters are said to be "effective" (дѣлныхъ) and "cognomers" (вкѵпо иманныхъ); five of these occur in initial position (а́ е́ и ѡ́ оу̇[36]), while the other five are "coordinated with" them (? ; тѣм способны) (а̇ е и о ѵ̇), but the printed text does not allow us to distinguish between а and a, е and ε as easily as may have been the case in the ms.[37] Eight other letters, ѡ̈ ы ѣ ю ѧ ъ ь й, are apparently independent, i.e. unpaired by anlaut and non-anlaut positions (самооѡсобны ; не помогаю́ ни требую́ согласіа), while ѫ and ѵ̈ are free variants (пишутсѧ во иныхъ мѣсто писманъ). All vowels are the same length (имѣютъ слогъ ра́венъ), except ъ and ь, which are short (имуть слогъ кратокъ) and й, which is "shortened" (имать слогъ сокращенъ; all 367).

The classification of consonants into groups, just as was the case with that of vowels, shows both a certain phonological acumen and some inexplicable contradictions, and once again the phonetic descriptions are couched in not always comprehensible metaphoric terms. For the most part, the consonants are presented in voiced/voiceless pairs (the former are "clean" [у́исты1а] and presumably thus more basic than their voiceless counterparts, which are "dim" [ту́склы1а]) :

Б	П	"coarse" (гру́бы1)
В	ф, Ѳ	"rough" ? (свиблявы1)
Г	Х	"heavy, taut, nasal" (тя́жкы1, нату́жны1, гугни́вы1[38])
Д	Т	"simple, light, resonant" (про́сты1, легкы1, гро́мны1)
Ж	Ш	"delicate" (шепетли́вы1) ("whispering"?)
ѕ, З	с, З, ѱ	"sibilant" (сипа́вы1)
ц	ч, щ	"clear" (ясны1)

ѕ and з are said to be identical, as are ф and Ѳ. Most curious in this list is the appearance of ц in the column of voiced consonants, the explanation of which must be sought in some earlier, Serbian text in which ц indeed represented a voiced affricate.[39]

The last five consonants are not paired by voicing:

к, р   "gutteral" (кортавы)
л, м, н   "deaf" (нѣмы)

The only generalization which can be extracted from the descriptive metaphorics of these sets is that the grave (peripheral) phonemes were perceived synaesthetically as unpleasantly heavy and coarse (б п = грѵбы, в ф ѳ = свиблйвы, г х = тѧжкы, натѵжны), whereas the acute (central) consonants were lighter and more pleasant (д т = про́сты, легкы́ but also гро́мны; ж ш = шепетлйвы, ц ү щ = ѧсны). If we compare this situation with that obtaining among the vowel descriptions, an unexpected and striking parallelism emerges: the back vowels, like the peripheral consonants, are perceived as heavy (and large). In other words, one glimpses, even through the cumbersome metaphorical terminology at his disposal, that this medieval grammarian recognized in an inarticulate, subliminal way that the back vowels were allied with both the backmost (velar) and the frontmost (labial) consonants — a realization that was to be formulated only three hundred years later by Roman Jakobson and his associates and subsumed under the distinctive feature labels "grave" (b p v f, g k x; u o) and "acute" (d t z s, c č ž š; i e).[40]

A substantial part of the Написа́нїе ѩзы́ком словенским о̀ гра́мотѣ ı о єѩ̀ строєнїи is devoted to the combinatory properties of vowels and consonants. As expected, this section abounds in unusual and often apparently inappropriate terminology, and by no means all the classificatory principles are clear. Jagić 517 made a first step toward interpreting this material when he reordered the terms used for the various combinatory types into a branching diagram, but unfortunately stopped short of explaining either the terms themselves or the classificatory principles of which they were a manifestation. In what follows, we shall attempt to go a step further into this terminological thicket by reproducing Jagić's branching diagram, to which we have added a numerical key facilitating reference from the diagram to the following explanatory material.

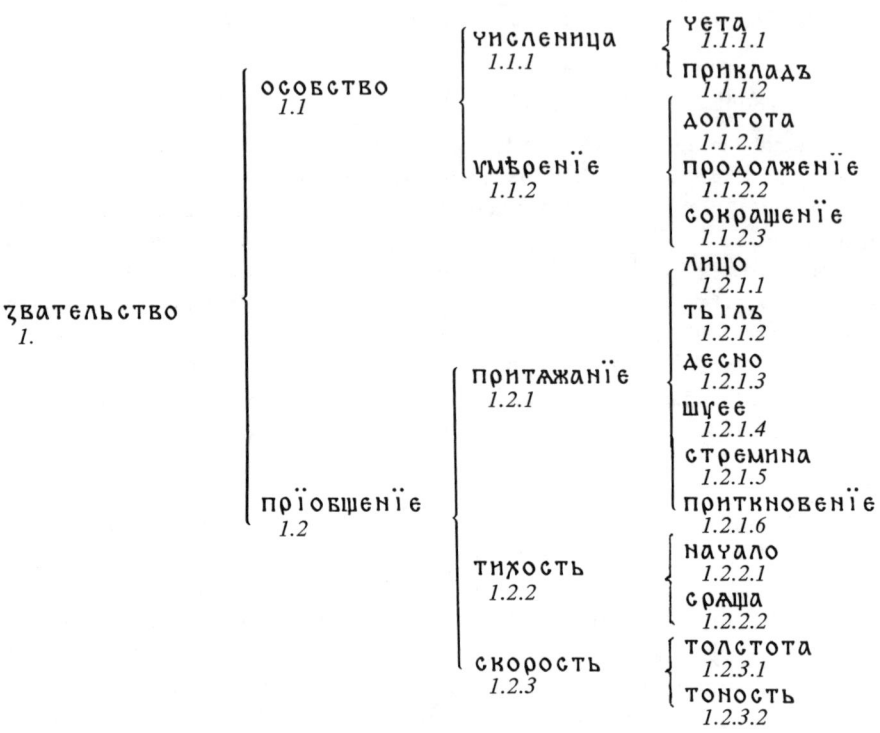

1./2. = ҅ꙁвателъство / полуꙁвателъство = *vocalism/consonantism*. Both vocalism and consonantism are defined in the same general terms, the sense of which appears to be that the vowel-consonant distinction reflects a dichotomy of intelligence basic to communication: " ꙁвателъство̀ е҆́сть се҄ гласова́нїе мнѡгоуа́стно раꙁдвоѐнїе ра́ꙁума, ѿ него́же похо́ди̅ всѧ́ко вѣща́нїе" (371); "Полуꙁва́телъство е҆́сть се҄ гласова́нїе мнѡгоуа́с̾тно раꙁ̾двоѐнїе ра́ꙁума ѻ҆бьа҆влѧ́етъ, ѿ него́же похо́ди̅ всѧ́ко вѣща́нїе" (377). The vowels are "free" and "full", whereas the consonants are "unfree", "poor", and "impotent"; the consonants are subordinated to the vowels, but both vowels and consonants "agree" with each other (how, we do not learn):

vowels	*consonants*
свобѡ́дныѧ пѡ́лныѧ гла́сы самодѐржны і҆мѣю̄ востагнове́нїе, по себѣ̀ притѧга́ю друг̾ыѧ гла́сы ску́дныі і҆ согласу́ю с ни́ми (371)	невѡ́лныѧ ску́дныѧ гла́сы мнѡголи́уныі і҆ не́мощныі раꙁвѣ при пѡ́лны̄х гла́сѣ̄х ꙗ҆влѧ́ю свою̀ ску́дость и҆ по нӣх вратѧ́тсѧ, коему́ждо гла́су свобо́дному повину́ютсѧ і҆ согласу́ю (377-378)

One notes that the superiority of vowels over consonants is expressed in approximately the same metaphoric terms as we saw above in the acute/grave opposition, although the metaphors here have only a syllabic, not a phonological interpretation.

The vowel and the consonant letters follow according to their sound value and their organizational structure (о́уста́въ):

| та́кож и҆ в писмѣ̀ писма́на̀ ꙁва́телнаѧ ѿ букв̾ы ѡ҆бдержа̄ и҆послѣ́дую по гласово́ᴹ свое́му ӣх о́у-ста́ву (371) | та́кож і҆ писма́на̀ бу́квенаѧ полуꙁва́телныѧ послѣ́дую сему о́уста́ву полуꙁва́телному (378) |

It is a curious fact that in an age where graphic entities were of paramount importance, this particular treatise seems to subordinate graphics to phonetics.

1.1/1.2 = о́со́бьство/прїо́бще́нїе = *independence/associativeness*. "Independence" refers to anlaut (= non-post-consonantal) position, whereas in "associativeness" the vowels attract consonants and join with them to form syllables:

осо́бʹство е́сть се́· про́сто
гласа́тсѧ свобѡ́днь́іѧ гла́-
сь́і междѹ невѡ́лнь́іˣ, не
прїѡбща́ющесѧ невѡлнь́іˣ
та́кожʹ и писмана̅ ꙁва́телʹ-
нь́іѧ про́сто ка́ко оу҄ча̅
та́ко і г͞лю, не слага́ѧ
с полуꙁва́тельнь́іми пис-
ма́ньі в҄ ре́чеˣ, ꙗ҄ко се́·
а ї є ю а ѿ ш у· сі́и
о́смь писмань та́ко об-
держа́ о́со́бʹство
(371-372)

Прїѡбще́нїе е́сть се́· сво-
бѡ́днь́іѧ гла́сь́і невѡ́лнь́іˣ
ѡбраща́ѧ і притага́ѧ по
свое́и си́лѣ, с невѡ́льнь́іми
совокѹпла́асѧ⁴¹ и́ гласа̅
в ре́чехъ о́бще· та́кожʹ и
писмана̅ ꙁва́тельнь́іѧ сла-
га́ѧ с полуꙁва́тельнь́іми
по́ два, по́ три, по четь́іре
і по пѧте́ру⁴² ѿвшиˣ, и́ гла-
са̅ в ре́чеˣ о́бще, ꙗ҄ко
се́· ба, бра, стра, сквра.
та́кожʹ і про́чаѧ.⁴³(374)

It is unclear why the vowel letters illustrating "independence" are partially just those which are positionally dependent (on preceding jot — which the scribe may not have recognized — or preceding consonant), namely ї ю ѧ.

1.1.1/1.1.2 = <u>чи́сленица</u> / <u>ѹ҄мѣре́нїе</u> = *enumeration/modification*. This is one of the most vaguely defined distinctions in the entire treatise, primarily because no illustrations are given of either of the two kinds of "enumeration". The definitions of "enumeration" and "modification" themselves don't help much:

чи́сленица е́сть се́· сво-
бѡ́днь́іѧ гла́сь́і в число́
ѹ҄страа́є в҄ речéнїаˣ
(372)

ѹ҄мѣре́нїе е́сть се́· пѡ́лʹ-
нь́іѧ гла́сь́і и́спо́лнено
воѡбража́ю в реúеˣ.
(372)

Examination of the subcategories (see below) leads to the conclusion that "enumeration" consists of one or two vowels in sequence, within a word, accompanied by other vowels and/or consonants, but not forming syllables; this is, however, at best a tentative and hesitant definition. "Modification" is much clearer, and refers to two vowels in sequence, considered from the point of view of whether they are identical or different (see 1.1.2.1 – 1.1.2.3 below).

1.1.1.1/1.1.1.2 = <u>чета̀</u>/<u>прикла́дъ</u> = *pairing/application*. Since no illustrations are given for either of these categories, it is no easy matter to puzzle out their meaning. Before trying to decipher them, let us give the full definitions from the treatise:

чета̀ е́сть се́· по́ два гла́-
са свобѡ́днь́іˣ по́ рѧдѹ
кроʹмѣ невѡ́льнь́іˣ гласѡ́вʹ

прикла́дъ е́сть се́· по еди́-
номѹ гла́сѹ свобо́дномѹ
междѹ вѡ́льнь́іˣ и междѹ не-

ѻбще́нїа ѻ є҆ди́ны іх҄ рече-
нїа х҄ та́коже и҆ писмана̀
ꙁва́телны ꙗ по два кромѣ̀
полуꙁва́телны іх҄ слогу̀.
(372)

во́лны іх҄, а҆ кромѣ̀ прїѻбще́нїа.
та́кож и҆ в писмане х҄ бу́квены х҄
по є҆ди́ному писмани ꙁва́тел-
ны х҄ между̀ ꙁва́телными і҆ по-
луꙁва́телными кромѣ̀ слогу̀.
(372)

The closest we can come to an interpretation of "pairing" is that it refers to two adjacent vowels, each of which forms a syllable with its own adjacent consonant (type паук); it is not clear just how чета̀ differs from долгота̀ , with the definition of which it has much in common (see below). "Application" is easier to understand, referring to a single vowel in position between a vowel and a consonant (между̀ вѡ́лны іх҄ и҆ между̀ нево́лны іх҄), not forming a separate syllable (а҆ кромѣ̀ прїѻбще́нїа; прїѻбще́нїа are various syllable-forming combinations of vowels and consonants).

1.1.2.1/1.1.2.2/1.1.2.3 = долгота̀ / продолже́нїе / сокра-ще́нїе = *length/continuation/shortening*. This set of terms is easily deciphered, thanks more to the abundant illustrations than to the definitions.

1.1.2.1 долгота̀ "length" refers to the combination of two unlike vowels. It is unclear in what way "length" differs from "pairing", since the two definitions are nearly the same: compare that for чета̀ above with that for "length": долгота̀ е҆́сть се́· свобѡ́дныꙗ гла́сы гласа̀ с свобѡ́дными же, е҆ди́нъ со другы́ м по два, и҆́н же кромѣ̀ невѡ́лны х҄ ѻ҆бще́нїа· та́кож и҆ в писманѹ х҄ ꙁва́телны х҄ кромѣ̀ полу-ꙁва́телны х҄ слогу̀ (372). One suspects that this or an earlier copyist may have confused two different definitions, substituting some part of that for чета̀ for an equivalent section of that for долгота̀. Examples of "length" are adduced for anlaut, inlaut, and auslaut:

Anlaut

є҆а̀	:	є҆а́же ли
і҆а̀	:	і҆а́ковъ
є҆ю̀	:	є҆ю́же ли
аи	:	анце
і ѿ	:	і҆ ѿ него̀
оу҆і҆	:	оу҆ і҆ны́хъ
і҆оу҆	:	і҆ оу҆ и҆но́го

Inlaut

і҆є̀	:	на і҆є҆рл҃мѣ̀
є҆а̀	:	на є҆а́ же ли

ιӑ	:	на ιӓковѣ
ѥго	:	не сѥго же ли
ѧн	:	даа́н же

Auslaut

ѥӑ	:	моѥӑ
ιӑ	:	аллилуιӑ
ѥго	:	сѥго
ѧн	:	даа́н

The persistent use of pro- and enclitics, which do not seem required by the definition of "length" itself, makes it clear that "length" obtains only when two consecutive vowels are sandwiched in between other vowels, consonants, and word-boundaries. We assume that initial *e,ѧ* etc. were felt simply as vowels, with no reference to jotation. The types which occur are:

Anlaut |v v C: ѥӑже ли etc.
           |v v V: і оу́ нного (one ex. only)

Inlaut   V v v C: на іерл̂мѣ etc.

Auslaut V v v |: моѥӑ etc.

Independent words such as ѥӑ are noticeably missing; our author is clearly concerned with them only in relation to their environments (ѥӑже ли, на ѥӑ же ли, моѥӑ). The second anlaut and the auslaut structures are mirror images of each other: |v v V, V v v|. The structures which would mirror the first anlaut and the inlaut structures are missing from the description, although illustrations would not be difficult to find: C v v| того, сιӑ, etc.; C v v V| сѥго, даа́н etc.

The three positions are referred to as "пред слогом і в'слозѣ і по слозѣ" (373), but these terms do not refer to *stressed* syllables, as e.g. іӓковъ makes clear. Rather, пред слогом means 'not preceded by but followed by a syllable', в слозѣ = 'both preceded and followed by a syllable', and по слозѣ = 'preceded by but not followed by a syllable'. That is to say, the classificatory scheme is conceived primarily in terms not of surrounding vowels, consonants and boundaries (see above), but of syllables (=S):

Anlaut: _S (S)
Inlaut: (S) S_S (S) } for examples, see above.
Auslaut: (S) S _

The vowel letters which are used in долгота́ are called, appropriately enough, дѡлгьιѧ. They are а́ і ѿ у ю ѧ є́ ѡ.[44] Cf. "continuation" below.

1.1.2.2 Продолженїе "continuation" refers to a sequence of two identical vowels (Продолженїе есть се҃· глашенїе гласѡвъ по̀ два є́диныӥ гласѡв взра҄, та́кож и писмана̀ ꙁва́телныѧ по̀ два 373). Examples are first adduced only for an- and inlaut positions (but see below):

Anlaut

а̄а̀	:	а̀ а́ще ли
і̄и̇	:	і̇ и́стина
ѡ̄ѡ̄	:	ѡ̄ ѡ̄цъ̑
ѡ̇ѡ̇	:	ѡ̇ ѡ̇нѣ҄
о҄у о҄у	:	о҄у о҄умнаго

Inlaut

а̇а̇	:	а̇враа́мъ
єє	:	сꙋщєє ли
і̇и̇	:	прї и́стинѣ
ѡ̄ѡ̄	:	і̇ ѡ̄ ѡ̄цъ̑
ѧѧ	:	дрєвнѧѧ жє ли
ѡ̇ѡ̇	:	і̇ ѡ̇ ѡ̇нѣ҄

The same three syllabic positions are then adduced as for "length" (пред слого́м, в сло́ꙃѣ, по сло́ꙃѣ). The vowel letters used in these continuation positions are termed продолˢжнаѧ 'continuants'; they are nearly the same as the "long" (долгы́ѧ) letters used in "length", but the order differs slightly: а і оу (not ѵ) ѡ̄ ѧ ю ѡ..

1.1.2.3 Сокращенїе "*shortening*" refers to any single vowel followed by jot (и̇, which was considered a vowel, albeit a "shortened and inverted" one (сокращєн̀ і̇ опровє́ржєн ; cf. the sixth "статїѧ", p. 37 above). Not that one would immediately deduce this from the definition in the text: "Сокращенїе есть се҃· єди́н гласˢ свобо́дєн, всѣ́м гласовы́м свобѡ́дны́ᴹ же, запина́ѧ вредᴬ гласи́ти, ꙗко возмѣтаѧ вы́гнꙋтїєм та́ко и̇ в пи́сманѣ҄ ꙁва́тєлныӥ є̇ді́но писма і̇ всѣ ꙁва́тєлныѧ писмана̀ сокращае҃" (374). Glancing over the examples below, we see that the є̇ди́н гласˢ свобо́дєн and the є̇ді́но писма̀ refer to и̇, which prevents all the other free vowels from continuing (всѣ́ᴹ гласовы́ᴹ свобѡ́дны́ᴹ жє запина́[єт] гласи́ти), i.e. from being followed by another like or unlike vowel, as in продолжєнїє and долгота̀ respectively; that is to say, и̇ raises a barrier (?) before these other vowels (ꙗко возмѣтаѧ вы́гнꙋтїєм). The examples adduced in illustration of "shortening" are:

а́и̇	:	да́и̇	о́и̇ : то́и̇	ю́и̇	:	оу́трєнюи̇
є́и̇	:	сє́и̇	ѣ́и̇ : андрє́и̇	єи̇[45]	:	твоєи̇

оу҆й : и҆манѵ҆й ьıй : мьıй ай[46]: а҆йнниненани
ıй : вıй шй : мой (sic)

Twelve letters appear in shortened position: а є и [о][47] оу ѣ ьı ѡ ю є ѧ ѩ ; they are called "shortened" (сокращéнньıѧ).

The section on о҆со́бство closes with a comparison of the three kinds of vowels which occur in "length", "lengthening", and "shortening": long vowels which command (others to appear after them, DW; до́лгьıѧ ꙗ҆ко повелѣва́ю҆тъ), lengthened vowels which insist (on their own presence? ; продо́лжньıѧ ꙗ҆ко понѹжда́ю҆тъ), shortened vowels which forbid (other vowels to follow them; сокращéнньıѧ же ꙗ҆ко запреща́ю҆⁓, all 374). The treatise then turns to the various ways in which vowels can be combined with consonants, i.e. to 1.2 прïо҆бщéнïе "associativeness".

1.2.1/1.2.2/1.2.3 = притажа́нïе / ти́хость /ско́рость = *assimilation / silence / brevity*. "Assimilation" refers to combinations of different vowels with any given consonant, "silence" deals with various consonants combining with a given vowel, and "brevity" describes consonant-plus-jer clusters. In "assimilation" the "free" vowels attract consonants and assimilate them each to its own "force": "Притажа́нïе е҆сть се҇· своб́ѡ҆дньı҃ˣ гла-сѡ́въ два̀ на́ десѧть, а кïйждо глас҃ˢ и҆ и҆ме҇е҇ си́лу таково ѵ҇· всѧ́кьıи глас҃ˢ нево́льньıи притага́е҇ на свое҇ подо́бïе" (374-375). Of the twelve vowels, ten sound the same, presumably as far as length is concerned, while two (ъ, ь) are short: "ı҆ десѧтѣ҃ˣ гласѡ́въ ра́вньı притага́ѧ прилага́ю҆ и҆ гласа҃⁓ о́бще " (375), forming minimal pairs based on the vocalic oppositions defined in the six vowel groups (статïа̀) discussed on p. 36 ff. above: ба̀ /бѧ, бе / бѣ, би/бьı, бо/бѡ, бу҆ / бю and бъ/бь, ва /вѧ etc. These vowels are the first and second (е/ ѣ, и/ьı, о/ѡ, ъ/ь) or first and third (а/ѧ, у҆/ ю) members of the vowel groups, and in four of the six groups (perhaps five, if we assume with some scholars that ѣ caused greater sharping than е[48]) the opposition is clearly one of fronting / backing, a feature the medieval scribe attributed primarily to the vowels, with the consonants assimilating themselves to the vowels in this respect.

1.2.1.1/1.2.1.2/1.2.1.3/1.2.1.4/1.2.1.5/1.2.1.6 = лицѐ/ты́лъ /де́сно / шу́ее / стреми́на / притꙁнове́нïе = *front / back / right / left / forward / adhesion*. These strange terms have nothing to do with the phonology of the vowels and consonants involved, but are simply a counting device borrowed from the acrostic alphabets intended to be learned by reading from right to left, left to right, top to bottom, bottom to top, etc., and by counting letters off on the front or back side (ꙁатьıлъ) of the fingers of the right or left hand. Even the syllables formed by these CV clusters are described in directional terms: а/ѧ "ѡ҆держа̄" сло́гъ, ꙗ҆ко с҃переди и҆ли в҃знаѹь", и/ы " ѡ҆держа̄ слогъ, ꙗ҆ко созади и҆ли ниць ", е/ѣ "со страны̀ пра́вы҄ѧ", о/ѡ "со страны лѣвы҄ѧ", ѵ/ю "к тѣмени" (375-376). It seems likely that these directional terms referred to the relative positions of the pair of vowel letters in the various acrostics, but we have no proof of this. Here, the six groups refer to the six vowel groups on p. 36 ff. In each group, a pair of vowels is adduced, bearing their metaphorical labels, and combined with each of the first two consonants, e.g.:

1.2.1.1 лицѐ "front": "Лице́ е҆сть се҃· е҆ди̑н̄ е҆сть глас҃ свобо́денъ зна́мени҄, а҆ вторы́и вня́теленъ, свобо́дны҄и же, ꙗ҆кож и҆ писмена̀ зва́телни́и (sic), а҆зъ да ѧ҆̄. ѡ҆держа̄ сло́гъ, ꙗ҆ко с҃переди. и҆ли в҃знаѹь та́ко· ба бѧ, ва, вѧ. тако́ж і҆ про́чаѧ (375). Similarly:
1.2.1.2 ты҄лъ "back": оу҆зо́къ / широ́къ, би бы, ви вы
1.2.1.3 де́сно "right": скѹ́денъ / дово́ленъ, бе бѣ, ве вѣ
1.2.1.4 шѹ́ее "left": о́стръ / гла́докъ і҆ логова́тъ, бо бѡ, во вѡ
1.2.1.5 стремни́на "forward": (i.e. in usual alphabetical order, as opposed to въ сра́щѹ, in reverse order): простра́нен̄ / тѣ́сенъ, бѵ бю, вѵ вю
1.2.1.6 притковеніе "adhesion": свобѡ́дны҄ѧ гла́сы два̀· е҆ди́нъ то́лстъ, а҆ дрѹ́гіи то́нокъ, а҆ ѡ҄ба ско́ры ("short"; cf. ско́рость below), ꙗ҆кож и҆ писмена̀ зва́тел҃ны҄ѧ, е҆ръ да е҆рь, ѡ҆держа̄ сло́гъ мимотекѹ́щь, неме́дленъ (in another ms., неме́длив̾). и҆збы́рив̾, недоста́тк҄ы и҆сполняѧ҄ си́це· бъ бь, въ вь, гъ гь. та́кож и҆ про́чаѧ (376). By this time we will not be surprised to find such a "minimal pair" as гъ гь ; cf. the exx. in the treatise О҃ мно́жествѣ і҆ о҆ е҆ди́нствѣ, p. 52 below.

1.2.2 Ти́хость "stability" refers to the constant length of the syllable formed by combining a vowel with any consonant in either VC or CV order: "Ти́хость е҆сть се҃· ра́венъ сло́гъ творѧ҄ въ рече́нїах҄ свобѡ́дны҄ѧ гла́сы с невѡ́льны҄ми гла́сы҄ма не протага́ѧ ни сокраща́ѧ, ꙗ҆ко се҃ и҆ писмена̀ зва́телны҄а слагаѧ҄ с полѹзва́тельны҄ми пис-

меньі, и полѹзва́телны͂͡х пи́сманъ по є҆ди́ному и҆ли̂ по̂ два и҆ли̂ по̂ три и҆ли̂ по ѹеты́і ре,⁴⁹ а ꙁва́телны і͂͡х к тому̂ по є҆ди́ному писмани а глас͞а ѻ҆́бще на своа҂ подоби҆а" (376).

1.2.2.1/1.2.2.2 = наѹа́ло / сра́ща = *forward / backward* are the two subgroupings of "stability", corresponding to the order VC and CV respectively, e.g. а б   а в   а г and б а   в а   г а . The two can be combined into three-letter clusters, which are, however, not dignified by a separate label, e.g. а б а   а в а   а г а   а д а, "тако͡ж і̂ про́ѹаа" (377).

1.2.3 Ско́рость *"brevity"* refers to combinations of consonant plus front or back jer. The obvious problem of describing such clusters in syllabic terms results in a considerable amount of verbal thrashing-around: "Ско́рость прі҆о҆́бщеніа є҆́сть се̂· кра́тк҇ыа гла́сы своб҆ѡ́дныа, кра́токъ і̂ со͡гоꙁъ и҆мѣа с невѡ́лнымн гла́сы, не протѧгаа, въ͡ско́рѣ миноу́а, пресѣца́а, и҆сполна́а и҆ꙁбироиво скѹдны͡м гласово́͡м сло́гъ дро́бныі воꙁражаа і̂ помета́а в ма́лѣ, ꙗко сі҆ѐ и҆ в пи́сманѣ͂͡х· тьма, търава̂. тако͡ж і̂ про́ѹаа. и҆ наконѹева́а тако͡ж· є҆фра́нтъ, ѹе́рвь. та́ко͡ж и̂ писмана̂ бѹк-
вена́а, ꙗако се̂· бъ бь, въ вь, гъ гь, та́ко͡ж и̂ про́ѹаа и̂ в конце́͡х и̂ въ средина͡х" (377).

1.2.3.1/1.2.3.2 толстота̂ / то́ность *thickness / thinness* refers to consonant + jer clusters containing a "thick" back or a "thin" front jer respectively, both of course being кра́ткыі : бъ въ гъ   and (omitted in the text) бь вь гь.

This completes the section on vocalism; we have learned that, "та́ко вса̂ гла́сы пѡ́лныа и҆сполна́ю͂ вса́кѹ рѣ́ѹь, а҆ по ни͡х писмана̂ своа̂ и҆ꙁра́ства" (377).

2. полѹꙁва́тельство *"consonantism"* describes consonant-vowel combinations from the point of view of the types and number of consonants forming clusters and of the kinds of vowels which can combine with a given consonant. The description is simpler than that of vowel combinatorics, having only three levels to the latter's four (cf. Jagić's diagram, reproduced on p. 40 above), and several of the consonantal categories are identical with those of the vowels, e.g. ба / бѧ appears among the vowels as 1.2.1.1 лице and among the consonants as 2.2.1 прилѹѵі҆е , that is, one and the same CV combination is described, Rashomon fashion, from the point of view of both of its participants.

2.1/2.2 = повинове́ні҆е / и҆ꙁвра́тъ = *subordination / modification*. These two categories describe consonant-vowel clusters from the quantitative and qualitative points of view respectively. Повиновенїе deals with the number and type of consonants that can join vowels to form syllables: "Повиновенїе есть се· с котѡрыⁿ гласоⁿ свобо́дныⁿˢ станетсѧ скѹдныи гласъ (= consonant; cf. p. 41 above), томѹ і согласѹетъ своего̀ силою всѧкомѹ свобо́дномѹ гласѹ" 378), a description which I suspect found its way by error into the section on "subordination", since it sounds more like a description of "modification", and is belied by its own subcategories (see below). Ѝзвра́тъ, for its part, is described in quantitative terms more appropriate to "subordination" than to "modification": "Ѝзвра̄ есть се· ска́занїе писманъ вˢ слѡ́зѣ до колика кѡ̈иⁿ с кѡ̈ими слѹчаетсѧ. скѹ́дныѧ гласы имѣю̀ силѹ таковѹ̀· всѧ́кⁿ гласˢ скѹденъ еди́нъ а̀ ѡбраща́етсѧ по всѣⁿ гласѡвшѡⁿ пѡ́лныіхъ і ӻавлѧю своюꙷ скѹдость патьма̀ положенїамъ· ѡбраща́ю̀тсѧ, приклоня́ю̀тсѧ, і прилагаю̀тсѧ. а̀ ко иныімъ ѡбраща́ю̀тсѧ, приклоня́ю̀тсѧ і притьі̂чѹ̀ю̀тсѧ, согласѹ́ю " (379), a repetitive and confused description the verbs of which refer to the assimilative "actions" of the consonants in position before vowels of each of the six vowel groups we have referred to more than once already; (cf. притьі̂чѹю̀тсѧ = 1.2.1.6 приткновенїе and 2.2.6 притоучїе).⁵⁰ What is intended is, however, made clear by the examples which follow: ба́ бѧ, бє бѣ, би бы, бо бш, бѹ бю . Combinations with ъ ь are singled out by a special description: " такоⱉ и всѝ шестомѹ положенїю в ма́лѣ ѹдарѧю̀тсѧ на своѧ̀ подѡбїѧ. тако́ⱉ и писмена̀, ӻ̀ко сѐ притьі̂чѹю̀тсѧ· бъ бь въ вь гъ гь такоⱉ і про́чаѧ "(379).

2.1.1/2.1.2/2.1.3/2.1.4 = ра́венство / тезоиманїе / сѹгѹ́бїе / приложенїе = *equality / homonymy / replication / accumulation*. "Equality" obtains when a single consonant combines with a single vowel, the former being subordinated in some unspecified way to the latter. Such clusters appear only in the order CV, e.g. ба ва га . If two identical (stop) consonants precede a vowel, — which is impossible within a syllable, although nothing is said about this in the text — the result is "homonymy", e.g. бба вва гга . If on the other hand the two consonants differ, one has consonantal "replication" and the clusters (those few which are adduced, at any rate) do form syllables: бра вра гра . Finally, "accumulation" refers to CCCV and CCCCV clusters like стра стре стри .⁵¹

2.2.1/2.2.2/2.2.3/2.2.4/2.2.5/2.2.6 = прилѹчїе / притьі̂лъ / придесно / пришѹее / пристремина / притоучїе = *frontward / backward / rightward / leftward / forward / adhered*. These labels simply repeat the six varieties of vocalic притѧжа́нїє dealt with on p. 46 ff. above. The subordinate position of the consonants is underscored ("зва́тельство притѧжа́е͞, а̀ полу̑зва́тельство повину́́́ется" 379). No examples are given, nor are any necessary, since they were all adduced together with the definition of the superordinate category и҆зврáтъ "modification": ба ба, бє бѣ, би бы, бо бш, бу бю, бъ бь.

With this the section on vowel and consonant combinatorics ends. There follows, more or less as a curiosity, a note to the effect that up to four or even five vowels can precede a single consonant within a (phonetic) word: і о̀ і҆а̑ковѣ, і о̀ і҆ӧнѣ, і о̀ і҆оі҆лѣ про̑цѣ (380).[52]

The Написа́нїє ꙗзы́комъ слове́нскимъ... continues on to discuss graphics and diacritics. There are three kinds of writing (писа́нїє): бу́квено = writing regular alphabet letters; разстоӓ́телно = punctuation marks of ten different kinds; вы́молвно = diacritics such as " ⁀ etc. (also ten in number). There are pauses of six kinds, from that on a word boundary to that at the end of an entire work. Letters come in four separate sizes, and can be used with various diacritics and other decorations to render numbers. But there is nothing of phonological or grammatical interest in all of this.

5. О мн҃жествѣ і о едиствѣ

The most consistent, even if not very successful, attempt to mark the singular/plural opposition graphically is found in a treatise entitled ô мн҃жествѣ î ô едінствѣ.[53] The anonymous author implores his reader to distinguish singular, dual, and plural ("едіньственыӏа рѣуь с҃ двойственою не смѣшай, й мн҃жественую рѣуь ѿ едíньственыӏа й двойственыӏа во всемъ ѿдѣлай. Село бо сїй межи себе разньствуютъ і ѿнюд ни вмалѣ не сходатса" 432), but as illustration of the dual he adduces a helpless mixture of grammatical and lexical duality and plurality: ѡ двѵ, ѡ двоихъ, двоих҃ ради винъ, etc. The situation is hardly improved in the verbal illustrations, into which ѣ seems to have found its way as a universal marker of the dual: мы́і есвѣ and also мы́і есмѣ, вы́і естѣ, писастѣ, глаго́ластѣ, прїидо́стѣ, сотвори́стѣ.

Ten vowel letters are divided into two groups: singular endings are to be spelled with о ь и а ѵ and plurals with ѡ ъ ы ѧ оу (є and ѣ are omitted, for reasons which escape me; so is й [treated throughout medieval mss. as a vowel], although the contrast -ей sing./-ей plur. appears among the exx. below). It is curious to note that the vowels in the latter, plural set are each more complex graphically than their singular counterparts, thus establishing a perhaps deliberate iconicity between the grammatical categories and their graphic expression. One can find some historical justification for the graphic distinction between singular and plural forms (дамь, ємь etc. vs. дамъ, ємъ, nom. sing. десѧть vs. gen. plur. десѧтъ participial gen. sing. masc. -ща vs. acc. plur. -щѧ, and even adjectival masc. nom. sing. -ый vs. plur. -ии, this last distinction of course being "backwards"), but it is doubtful if our 17th c. scribe had any idea of such matters; more probably, he was simply following the usual medieval practise of trying to hang grammatical functions onto whatever graphic pegs he had handy.

The differences between singular and plural spellings are illustrated by a fortuitous and etymologically absurd set of substantive, adjective, and present active participle forms identified only as singular and plural but not by case. In the list below we have rearranged these forms into contrasting sing./plur. pairs; the two bracketed forms have no plur. counterparts. With two exceptions, all words begin with а- or в-, which may indicate that the scribe originally intended to adduce a much longer list of illustrations in alphabetical order but lost interest in this task before he reached в, for which one can hardly blame him. We include all the illustrations of the ms. and group them into morphological and stem-consonant types (all consonants adduced together with the endings are so listed in the mss.).

	Singular		Plural
-аа	а҃гг҃льскаа	-аѧ	а҃гг҃льскаѧ
-їа	а҃гг҃льскїа	-ыѧ	а҃гг҃лскыѧ
-імъ[a]	а҃гг҃льскімь[b]	-ымъ	а҃гг҃льскымъ
-ньіѧ	б҃лвеньіѧ[c]	-ньіѧ	б҃лгвеньіѧ
-щїа	бл҃жащїа[d]	-щыѧ	бл҃жащьіѧ[d]
-щи	бл҃гващи[d]	-ще	бл҃гословаще[d]
-омь	а҃гг҃ломь	-шмъ	а҃гг҃лшмъ
⎧ -ымь	а҃гг҃ловыімь ⎫		
⎩ -овь	а҃гг҃ловь ⎭		
-ки	а҃збуки[e]	-кы	а҃збукы
-кь	а҃збууникь	-къ	азбууникъ
	ц҃рковникь[f]		ц҃рковникъ
-ца	а҃гнїца[h]	-цѧ	а҃гнїца[g,h]
-ць	а҃гнець[g]	-цъ	а҃гнецъ[g]
-ци	му҃нци	-цьі	му҃нцьі
-ей	а҃рхїерей	-ей	а҃рхїерѐй[i]

[a] sic ъ; sc. ь [b] preconsonantal ї is rare; it contradicts almost universal scribal practise [c] sic ыѧ, sc. їа [d] -а-/-ѧ- in the stems of the first pair may be an attempt to extend the sing./plur. spelling rule into the stem, but as the second pair shows, this was not done consistently [e] it is hard to imagine what case this spelling is supposed to represent [f] ms. "кь, ѩко ц҃рковникь"; Jagić's f.n. thereto, "Лучше въ [ms.] 318: къ ѩко црковникъ" is inappropriate, because the scribe was trying precisely to illustrate the singular in -ь; the fact that imported Serbian spellings like -кь were phonologically and graphically nonsensical bothered Jagić but not — typically — the medieval scribe [g] note the і, и for weak, but the є for strong jer [h] sic а; sc. ѧ [i] here as elsewhere the scribe is inconsistent with his diacritics; we would expect -ей̀; n.b. too that the й/и distinction is not included in the five-vowel sets mentioned above.

One of the two mss. of о҃ мнѡ́жествѣ і о҃ є҆дѝнствѣ adduces additional sing./plur. sets with pres. act. participles. Sing. -а contrasts with plural -ѧ in gen.-acc. sing. masc. а҆лу́чша о҆ного / acc. plur. а҆лу́чшѧ ѡ҆ны̀ and similarly вс҃лваща / вс҃лващѧ, глагóлюща / глагѡ́люща and nom. sing. fem. а҃лучша ӧна҄ / plur. а҃лучша ѡнь҄і and similarly зра҄ша / зра҄шѧ, вѣша́юща / вѣша́ющѧ, слава́ша / слава́шѧ. Nom. sing./nom. plur. masc. pairs illustrate the number contrast, but with other than the paired letter endings discussed so far: sing. а҃лующи о҄нъ і҆ли о҄на / а҃лующе ѡ҄ни and similarly бл҃ваши / бл҃ваше, глаго́лющи / гл҃юще. Finally, neut. sing. forms in -що are adduced with no contrasting members (а҃лущо бж҃тво су҄щества і҆пра́вды, у҆лу́ьское є҆сество а҃лущо су҄що сп҃нїа себѣ, бл҃ващо... і҆ гл҃ющо й слы҄шащо і҆ твора҄що... [note the alphabetical order of the exx.]), as is a single acc. sing. fem. а҃лующю ону҆ illustrating the correct -ю as opposed to -у (оу҆ же́н҆скаго і҆мени в҆ прилуче́нїихъ [= 'as a direct object', dsw] поставлѧй ю а не й҄къ, сице а҃лующю ону҆"). Note that in a few cases the sing./plur. vowels appear in the verb stems as well as in the ending глаго́люща / глагѡ́лющѧ, вѣша҄юща / вѣша҄ющѧ, whereas ү҆у / ү҆ю are used indiscriminately in а҃лующи, а҃лующе, а҃лущѧ, а҃луща, а҃лующю and both а҃луща ӧна҄ and а҃лующа ӧна҄.

What is most noticeable about these paradigm fragments is the extent to which they differ from the Old Russian recension of Church Slavonic: -щи forms used for nom. sing. masc. as well as the expected feminine, -ща forms for the nom. sing. fem., -що neuters, completely unknown at the older stage, etc., not to mention such anachronistically contrasting pairs as -ки / -кь҄і, -кь / -къ, -щї / -щь҄і etc. discussed above. In some cases (nom. sing. masc. participles in -щи, feminines in -ща) this text may codify actual practise in Middle (Ukrainian and/or) Russian Church Slavonic, but we cannot be sure of this until the history of this Russ. Ch. Sl. has been written. In other cases, however (sing. а҃збучникь / plur. а҃збучникъ, бл҃жащїа / бл҃жащьіа, etc.), we can be confident that the recommended contrasts never got beyond the chambers of the assiduous but rather naive copyist. At times, one has the impression that he must have felt nearly overwhelmed by the bewildering variety of forms he had to deal with (no wonder, considering what a hodgepodge of OCS, Bulgarian, Serbian, Ukrainian and Russian Church Slavonic he was faced with!) and sought to bring some order into this confusion by assigning grammatical function to every formal distinction he noticed (and to some he, or a predecessor, had simply invented).[54] In doing so, he occasionally displayed a certain originality, even if the result was a distorted description of his subject matter. Participles, for example, are distinguished from other adjectives by the presence/absence of the category of tense — a rather astute observation for that time and place — but the tense appears to be something like a perfect ("Вѣждꙋ й се҄, ꙗ҄ко єже рещи ста҄ добродѣтел҆на труда҄ жа́дна а҃луна, сї҄и рѣчь настоѧ҄ща суща, а є҆же рещи а҃лующа ӧна҄ і҆ли бл҃ваща і҆ли зра҄ща і҆ли вѣша҄юща і҆ли слава҄ща, сїа҄ рѣчь прѣбы҄вша суща, сп҃речꙋ҄ и҆здавна҄ зра҄ща й бл҃ваща й вѣша҄юща й слава҄ща" 435).

It comes as no surprise that a monk whose thoughts were frequently on the Trinity tended to think in terms of threes, even if it caused him to stray from his subject at times. Having reiterated the importance of distinguishing singular, dual and plural (" Вид́иши ли, господи́не, ꙗ́ко ѕело̑ мно́го ра́зньствуютъ еди́ньство ѿ двойственаго. мно́жайшо же па́че мнѡжьственое ѿ еди́ньственаго и̑ двойстве́наго во всемъ" 433), he then turns to a less grammatical trinity, namely that of high, middle, and low style vocabulary (стость, посре́дне and ѿпа́дшо). High style words are lawful, venerable, holy, honorable, spiritual; they must be spoken with veneration and should be written using the titlo or superscript letters (" гл҃ати сїю ст҃ости́ю, а́ не про́сто, и̑ писа́ти с ра́зумомъ і̑ почита́ти взме́томъ или покры́тїемь ꙗ́ко вен҄цо́мь сл҃вы во о́бразъ бу҃дущаго возда́анїа ст҃ымъ" 433); note the iconic " почита́ти взме́томъ … во о́бразъ бу҃дущаго возда́анїа ", reinforced by the distant alliteration вз-… воз-). Neutral middle-style words are for everyday material objects like чи́стъ сосу́дъ, чиста́ ри́за, чи́сто тѣ́ло (Посре́дне же е́сть е́же чи́стъ о́нъ сосу́дъ или и̑́но что веще́ствено, … се́ е́сть посре́дне, зе́м҄но и душе́вно человѣ́ческо су́що" 433); they are to be spoken in moderate tone (посре́дне) and written without the titlo or vzmet. Finally, low-style words are for false gods and lying words and unclean passions, etc. (Ѿпа́дшое́ же е́сть се̂, е́же а́н҄гелъ сопроти́вника и̑ бѡ́гы і̑до́льскыꙗ і̑ глаго́лы лѡ́жны і̑ су́етны … и̑ ду́хы лука́вьствиꙗ и̑ стра́сти нечи́стыꙗ, и̑ цари́ нечести́выꙗ и̑ мучи́тели злы̑ꙗ, і̑ человѣ́ка лука́ва и̑ кнѧ́зи ꙗ̑зы́ческыꙗ і̑ влады́кы еду́м҄скыꙗ … 433-434). How these "fallen" words are to be spoken is not specified, but they are not to be written under the titlo.[55] In general, our author is much enamored of triads. No sooner has he finished setting down the rules for the high/middle/low words than he compares them to the three numbers (" во все́мь т҄щи́сѧ стость ѿ посре́днего і̑ ѿ ѿпа́дшаго всѧ́ко ѿдѣлѧ́ти … та́коже і̑ еди́ньство и̑ двойственое и̑ мнѡ́жественое во все́мъ раздѣлѧ́и" 434), and even goes on to promise his reader a treble reward for observing the orthographic conventions ("да тро́е бл҃го полу́чиши"): first, he will commune with the angels ("пе́рвое со а́гг҃лы бесѣ́дованїе и̑мати"); second, he will profit from the respect of his audience ("второ́е са́мъ ползю̑ воспрїи́меши и̑ почита́ющихъ и̑ тѣ́хъ послу́ша ющи́хъ и̑ма́ши ползова́ти"); thirdly, he can earn a living doing this ("тре́тїее ѿ своего́ труда́ хлѣ́бъ свой стѧ́жеши і̑ [not to seem too materialistic about it,] ни́щему ѿ того́ подаси́ " all 434).[56]

Inconsistent and artificial as many parts of the о̂ мнѡ́жествѣ і̑ о̑ еди́нствѣ are, its author was at least primarily concerned with keeping grammatical functions distinct from each other. Unfortunately, he had only a vague notion of some of the categories he was discussing (e.g. the dual number, cf. p. 51 above), and he was so indiscriminately fanciful in inventing forms to illustrate his graphic oppositions (-къ / къ etc.) that he simply could not have been well-read in the very Church Slavonic texts whose graphic form he so assiduously tried to regulate.

6. Кни́га глаго́лемаѧ бѹквы

The fullest array of real grammatical material of any of the medieval treatises, and in a sense the culmination of the "grammatical tradition" (such as it was) which began in 14th-century Serbia with the "Eight parts of speech", appears in a compilation known as the Кни́га глаго́лемаѧ бѹквы.[57] This text opens and closes with sections on punctuation and diacritics which are no fuller and no less derivative than those of many other 16th-17th c. treatises, and need not be discussed here. The grammatical material itself is of two sorts. The first consists of minimal pairs illustrating such oppositions as singular/plural (слова̀ ихъ [м.] / слова моег̀ [е.]⁵⁸), masculine/feminine (бѣла̀ [мѹж.]/ бѣла̀ [женск.]), and indicative/imperative (говори́те / говори́тѐ); these will be discussed below. The second sort of grammatical material consists of actual paradigms, both inflectional and derivational.[59] We shall examine these first.

Most of the nominal (substantive and adjective) paradigms are found in a section of the Кни́га subtitled Нача́ло бѹкˢвъ по ѿртографі́и. This section lists twenty-four letters of the alphabet (а б в г д е ж ѕ і и к л м н п р с т оѹ/ѵ ф х ѿ ц ч),[60] each of which is illustrated by from two to seventeen inflectional paradigms, many of which are grouped into word-nests, e.g. тро́ица / тро́ице / тро́ицѹ / тро́ицы // тро́ическъ / тро́ическа / тро́ически / тро́ическо / тро́ическѹ // тро́иченъ / тро́ична / тро́ичне / тро́ично / тро́ичнѹ / тро́ичны.[61] The selection of case-number forms in the inflectional paradigms, and the order in which they appear, are quite inconsistent and more than a bit confusing; it is not always easy, or even possible, to identify the forms which appear, — all the more so because some of them are nonexistent, for example пророко or премѹдросте̄ . The paradigms contain from two to eight forms each. Those with only two members form identifiable singular/ plural pairs of the type mentioned above (e.g. го́ры ихъ [м.] / го́ры̀ моеѧ̀ [е.]) and will be included in the discussion of this type below (p. 59 ff.).[62] The variety, and the inconsistency, of the three- to eight-member paradigms can best be illustrated by adducing a sampling of them:

небо	ѹ́ченица	престо́ли	єсте́ственъ
неба	ѹ́ченице	престо́лѹ	єсте́ствена
небѹ	ѹ́ченицѹ	на престо́лѣ	єсте́ствены
дѹхъ	дѹшъ	крести́тель	премѹ́дрость
дѹха	дѹша	крести́телѧ	премѹ́дросте
дѹхи	дѹше	крести́тели	премѹ́дрости
дѹхо	дѹши	крести́телю	премѹ́дростѧмъ

КНИГА ГЛАГОЛЕМАЯ БУКВЫ

ѿтецъ	пророкъ	небесъ	церковь
ѿтца	пророка	небеса	церквамъ
ѿтцемъ	пророки	небесе	церкве
ѿтцу	пророко	небеси	церкви
ѿтцыı	пророку	небесѣ	церквѣ
мѹдрецъ	дѣвицъ	мѹдръ	троиченъ
мѹдреца	дѣвица	мѹдра	троична
мѹдрецемъ	дѣвице	мѹдре	троичне
мѹдрецыı	дѣвицѹ	мѹдри	троично
мѹдрецѹ	дѣвицыı	мѹдро	троичнѹ
мѹдрецѣ	дѣвицѣ	мѹдрѹ	троичныı
честенъ	свѧтъ		любомѹдръственъ
честна	свѧта		любомѹдръствена
честне	свѧте		любомѹдръствене
честни	свѧтїи		любомѹдръствени
честнѹ	свѧто		любомѹдръствено
честныı	свѧтѹ		любомѹдръственѹ
честнѣ	свѧтыıи		любомѹдръстvenѣ
крестъ	милосердъ		церковенъ
креста̀	милосерда		церковна
крестѐ	милосерде		церковне
крести	милосерди		церковнїи[63]
кресто	милосердо		церковно
крестѹ	милосердѹ		церковнѹ
крестыı	милосердыı		церковныı
крестѣ	милосердѣ		церковнѣ

The sequences of case-number forms are indeed inconsistent, but only from our modern point of view, which sees paradigms in the framework of grammatical meaning; for us, nominative, genitive and dative are sequenced as ineluctably as dawn, day and dusk, regardless of the actual endings which express these meanings (φ/a/u, a/i/e, φ/i/i etc.). Not so for our medieval grammarian, whose preoccupation with graphic detail led him quite naturally to order paradigms according to form, — specifically, according to the alphabetical order of the endings. His principles are simple: the paradigm begins with a form in -ъ or -ь if such exists (probably because this is the nom. sing. masc. ending, this being the scribe's only concession to function as an organizing principle), and other endings then follow in the usual alphabetical order: а е и о ѹ ыı ѣ. Which particular ending is used is not important, as long as it begins with the right letter (cf. the dative plural forms in the paradigms of ѿтецъ, церковь, and мѹдрецъ, the long nom. plurals свѧтїи and церковнїн etc.). Preoccupied — not to say obsessed — as he was with alphabetical order, our grammarian insouciantly added totally nonexistent forms to his paradigms, in order that the right letter appear in the right place: доухо, пророко, кресто, премоудросте. The only mystery is why he did not use existing endings like -омъ, -ехъ instead of the bare vowels -о, -е; this is perhaps a result of his predilection for single-vowel endings (cf. however the dat. plur. forms just adduced).

Departures from the order ъ/ь а е н о оу ы ѣ are infrequent. ѧ and ю substitute for а and оу in a few soft stems, e.g. 'ін҃ль /-ѧ/-е/-н/-ю/-ѣ, кре́ститель/-ѧ/-н/-ю, although ѧ comes in its usual place at the end of the alphabet in цесарь /-емъ/-н/-ю/-ѧ. Occasional departures from the usual order were caused by phonetic developments, e.g. the -ы for -н in моудрецъ /-а/-емъ/-ы/-оу/-ѣ. Morphological pressure (= the subconscious urge to place the nominative at the head of the paradigm) may be responsible for небо /-а/-оу and наша /-ъ/-е/-н. In several cases, however, no more rational cause suggests itself than scribal absent-mindedness, as with the misplaced loc. ѣ of мо҃ученицъ /-а/-ѣ/-е/-оу/-ы or the initial voc. -е of преподобне /-ъ/-а/-н/-о /-оу/-ын. At times, the scribe seems to have been too weary to cope with alphabetical order, the results of phonetic and morphological change, and archaic stem mutations all at once, which led him to produce such a paradigm as:

оученикъ
оученика
оученице   (correct vocative sing.)
оученичн   (ч for correct ц; nom. pl.)
оученичоу   (forgetting to replace stem-final -к-)
оученика   (for -о? and out of order)
оученикн   (for older -кы; acc. pl.)
оученикоу   (for -цѣ, Belorussian influence?)

Paradigms such as those just discussed, in which alphabetical order departs from the usual ъ/ь а е н о оу ы ѣ, can be called "incorrect", to distinguish them from those which are merely defective, i.e. missing one or more endings present in their fuller counterparts (for example, in the three-member paradigms above, небо is incorrect, while оученица, престоли and естественъ are defective, each in a different way). Both terms, "incorrect" and "defective", are to be understood in the same restricted graphic sense. The medieval "grammarian" was in fact quite unconcerned with grammar, and made no attempt to give full morphological paradigms for his sample words. He was concerned only with providing a more or less representative sample of the different vowel endings which could be attached to each of these words. If forms in -ѣ are omitted especially frequently in the defective paradigms, as happens to be the case, it is not the locative singular case which was neglected (there is, in fact, absolutely no evidence that any medieval grammarian even recognized the locative as a distinct grammatical meaning), but merely the graph ѣ which was awkward in a number of ways. It called for already unnatural velar mutations, it did not occur in endings after underlying -ц in an older period when the latter was still soft, the sound it had represented had undergone various mutations in areas from which the Russian grammatical tradition had sprung (Serbia, the Ukraine), etc.

As a result of the various pressures exerted by phonetic and morphophonemic change upon the graphic system, one observes what might be called mini-regularities in the defective paradigms. For example, in paradigms of less than six members, stems in -ц never take endings in -н, -o, or -ѣ (among five-member sets, мѣсѧцъ /-а/-е/-у/-ы and identically сердецъ, ѿецъ; four-member sets additionally omit either -ы, e.g. мертвецъ /-а/-е/-у or -ъ, e.g. троица /-е/-у/-ы and three-member sets both of these, as in ѹченница /-е/-у, солнца /-е/-у). It must be reemphasized, however, that grammar itself (the correlation of phonetic or graphic form with grammatical meaning, or the oppositional bundles of grammatical meanings themselves) plays no discernable role in any of this.

The closest our scribe comes to showing interest in actual grammatical facts is when he adduces binary pairs of case-number forms in order to illustrate the difference between singular and plural or, more rarely, other grammatical oppositions. In a few cases, more extensive paradigms are given.

Singular-plural pairs appear in alphabetical order, but are scattered throughout three different sections of the treatise: pairs with initial letters а-н are under the corresponding sections of the Начало буквъ по ѿрографїи, those beginning in м, н, and ѡ follow the subtitle двогласно во єдиныхъ лежаще, and п-ѧ appear in the following section, троегласно во єдиныхъ; к and л are missing altogether. At some point in the history of this compilation, a scribe must have been copying from two sources and combining them into a single work. He began by adding singular-plural pairs to the case-number paradigms described above, doing this consistently throughout the first ten letters of the Начало буквъ по ѿрографїи, but then forgot to add the singular-plural pairs until he had finished copying the Начало буквъ and was into the stress-opposed pairs of the дво- and троегласное sections, at which point he again began adding singular-plural pairs from his second source, forgetting however pairs in к and л.

Singular-plural oppositions are illustrated by nominative plural and locative singular forms, generally accompanied by possessive pronominal modifiers and identified as plural and singular by the abbreviations "м" and "е" respectively, e.g. гра́ди ва́ша (м.) / гра́дѣ мое^м (е.), и҆зы́ и҆хъ (м.) / и҆зы́ моё́и (е.).[64] The pronominal modifiers are occasionally omitted, e.g. жо^{с}твы (м.) / жо^{с}твѣ (е.), and when they are present they almost always reflect the number of the substantive they modify, и҆хъ or ва́ши occurring with the nom. plur. forms and моємъ or моєи with the loc. sing., as if the entire noun phrase mode had to be marked for singularity or plurality as a unit: главы̀ и҃х (м.) / главѣ моєи (є.), домы̀ и҃х (м.) / домѣ моємъ (є.), дру́зи ваши (м.) / дру́зѣ моєм (є.), ну́зи и҃хъ (м.) / нозѣ моєи (є.), ҁеловѣцы̀ ва́ши (м.) / ҁеловѣцѣ моєм (є.). Identificatory modifiers other than и҃хъ, ва́ши, моєи/моємъ are rare, occurring with two adjectival pairs and one substantive: и́сты̀ ѡ̀ни (м.) / и́стѣ (є.), ще́дри ѡ̀нѝ (м.) / ѡ̀ ще́дрѣ глаго́лю (є.), ю̀ро́ѫди ѡ̀нѝ (м.) / ю̀ро́дѣ прилѣпла́ю̀щѣ͡с (є.). Occasionally, the paradigm is expanded somewhat: жи́вы̀ (м.) / живѣ̀ (є.) / живѝ (м.) (the morphological difference between жи́вы̀ and живѝ is unclear; perhaps the scribe associated stress distinctions with the already archaic -и/-ы̀ marking nom. and acc. or with the masc. vs. fem. nom. plur.?), а̀рхаггели (м.) / а̀рха́г҄геле (є.) / а̀рха́г҄геломъ. After the usual оу҆мы̀ ва́ши (м.) / оу҆мѣ̀ моєм (є.) we find the homographic verb оу҆мы̀ рѫ́ки водо́ю̀, while in another case the scribe combines the full paradigm and the singular-plural type: владыки мно́зи / владыка / владыкѫ́ / владыцѣ є̀ди́номꙋ / ѡ̀ владыко, while both the first and the second velar mutations appear in ѹ҆̀ши и҃хъ (м.) / оу҆сѣ моємⷭ (є.). In an isolated case, nom. plur. and nom. sing. long adjectival forms are juxtaposed: сватѝи наши (м.) / сватьіи нашъ (є.). The first form in the pair а̀вѝ (м.) / а̀вѣ̀ (є.) would seem to be a singular aorist and the second an adverb, to judge by the appended explanation, "рѣк҄ше оу҆ка́за̀ а̀в҄ствено"

Why just the loc. sing. in ѣ was chosen as the singular member of these pairs is not clear. It was probably convenient to be able to use the same form for both *o-* and *a-* stems (градѣ моєм, нозѣ моєи). On the other hand, there are no neuter words in such pairs; the few neuter pairs in this treatise are nom.-acc. plur./gen. sing. forms distinguished only by stress (ре́бра и҃хъ [м.] / ребра̀ моєго̀ [є.], се́рдца ихъ [м.] / се́рдца моєго [є.], слова̀ ихъ [м.] / сло́ва моєг҄ [є.], а̃дра ихъ [м.] / а̃дра̀ моєго [є.]). One can suspect a phonetic motivation for the choice of the loc. sing., namely that the Ukrainian development of *ě > [i] had brought the loc. sing. phonetically closer to the nom. plur. ы, и (the phonetic values of which were presumably in the area of [yᵉ], [i]), so that such pairs as домы̀ и҃х (м.) / до́мѣ моємъ (є.) were felt to be distinguished primarily by stress, just as in such other pairs (differing from the usual pattern described above) as рѫ́цѣ и҃хъ (м.) / рѫ́цѣ моєи (є.), сы̀ну́мъ и҃хъ (м.) / сы̀ном мои́м (є.), свои (м.) / свои (є.) and твои (м.) / твои (є.); cf. also the verbal pairs discussed below.

The earnest grammarian strove to utilize the graphic distinction of ѡ and о to mark plural and singular respectively, a distinction first made by Konstantin Kostenčeski, but the artificiality of this device is apparent in the large number of "errors": во́ды̀ / водѣ̀, домы̀ / домѣ, го́ры̀ / горы̀, слова̀ /

слова, alongside the "correct" бѹзи, нѹзи, рѹсьı, стѹгны, творцы, философы, горшди, сынѹмъ, and even (in a different section of the ms.) вѹдыı In the pairs бѹзи ихъ (м.) / б҃зѣ моемъ (е.) and христи их (м.) / хс҃ѣ моемъ (е.), the scribe follows the old rule that only the individual Christian God, Christ, and Virgin Mary are to be written under the titlo, while all other gods, Marys, etc., are to be spelled out.

The opposition of singular and plural — the only grammatical distinction that appears with some regularity throughout medieval mss. — is quite lavishly illustrated with present active participles.[65] Participial pairs have a correct old short nom. plur. masc. in -ѹще opposed to what seems to be an innovative truncated nom. sing. masc. in -ѹщи, e.g. видѧще (м.) / видѧщи (е.) (n.b. stress!), водѧще (м.) / водѧщи (е.), and similarly with живѹщ-, ка́-юще, and молѧщ-. Other pairs are adduced in long form masc. nom. plur. and innovating singular in -щїи (there is no trace of the old nom. sing. masc. forms in -ѧ, -аи etc.; it is this new nom. sing. in -щїи which leads us to interpret the -щи forms as truncated masc., rather than as old nom. sing. fem. forms), e.g. варѧщеи (м.) / варѧщїи (е.), and similarly with жрущ-, кланѧющ-....-сѧ etc. Sometimes all four masc. forms are given together, as with гл҃юще (м.) / гл҃ющи (е.) / гл҃ющеи (м.) / гл҃ющїи (е.) and similarly with порющ and хранѧщ-. In one case, a short plur. contrasts with a long sing. (рекѹще [м.]/ рекѹщїи [е.]), while in another an errant dative plural wanders into the paradigm: боѧщимⸯсѧ (м.)/боѧщесѧ (е.)/ боѧщисѧ (м.)/ боѧщенсѧ (м.)/ боѧщїисѧ (е.). In a dozen cases, these plur./sing. participial pairs are combined with stress-distinguished second-person plur. imperative/indicative pairs (on which see below): носѧще (м.) / носѧщи (е.) // носите (п.= повелительное) / носитѣ (т.= творимое), дающе́и (м.)/даю́щїи (е.)//дадите (п.)/ дадитѣ (хотѧщее быти= future), держи́те(п.) / держитѣ (бы1вшаѧ = past) // дерⸯжѧще (м.) / дерⸯжѧщи (е.). In half of these sets, we have a full six-member "paradigm", e.g. шумѧще (м.) / шумѧщи (е.) / шумѧщеи (м.) / шумѧщїи (е.) // шумите (п.) / шумитѣ (т.). In two cases, and for no apparent reason, a set of objective pronouns is added: творѧщеи (м.) / творѧщїи (е.) // твори е̂, твори и̂, твори ѧ̂ (cf. below, p. 62) // творите (п.) / творитѣ (т.); зрѧще (м.) / зрѧщи (е.) / зрѧщеи (м.) / зрѧщїи (е.) // зрите (п.) / зритѣ (т.) ӧно, его̀, ѥа, ихъ / зри е̂, зри и̂, зри ю̂, зри ѧ̂ или то̀, того̀, тѹю, тѣхъ. It is surely no coincidence that the longer full forms ӧно, его̀ etc. combine with the longer plural imperative and the clitics е̂, и̂ etc. with the shorter singular verb; this is just the sort of pseudogrammatical graphic symmetry that medieval grammarians delighted in. Similarly, when our scribe proceeds through the usual set ѹтѹще (м.) / ѹтѹщи (е.) / ѹтѹщеи (м.) / ѹтѹщїи (е.) // ѹтите (п.м.) / ѹтитѣ (т.) and then goes on to add ѹти тьı (е.) / ѹтитѣ (м.) / ѹтѣте (м.) / ѹтете (м.); he is not so much trying to provide an outline of verbal grammar as merely revelling in the luxuriant variety of different forms which result from varying the vowels and stresses in and around the stem ѵт...т-.

One of the best-illustrated grammatical contrasts in the Книга глемана Бѵквы1 is that between 2nd person plural imperative and indicative forms, distinguished only by the place of the stress.[66] As indicated above, these pairs are provided with identifying labels: бранѝте (п. = повелительное)/ бранитѐ (т. = творимое, 'indicative'). Particularly salient are the Ukrainian final stresses in the indicative forms боитѐса, бѹдитѐ, бѣжитѐ, etc. (some 15 forms), alongside the more neutral (and hence "more Russian") stem-stressed во́дите, го́ните, про́сите. In one pair, the old lengthened imperative vowel is preserved: внемлѣте (п.) / вне́млете (т.). As already mentioned, these mood pairs are sometimes combined with participial pairs, e.g. носа́ще (м.) / носа́щи (е.) // носи́те (п.) / но́сите (т.). Stress is also the only marker of the sing./plur. opposition in some noun and adjective pairs, in which unstressed (в та́инѣ) and stressed (клони́телно) -и express the number distinction, e.g. свои́ дрѹ͡г/ свои́ дрѹ́зи, мо́и до́м / мо́и вра́зи, ра́таи (sic и)[67] /ратаѝ, etc. Stressed -и̂ is one of the four "declension letters" ("клони́телныхъ Бѵквъ") recognized by our scribe, who illustrates them by the four forms свои̂, свое̂, свою̀, своѧ̀ . The fact that only е̂ и̂ ю̀ ѧ̂ / ѩ̀ were recognized as " клонительные ", together with the Slavonic tradition of writing ѧ etc. for *ę in e.g. soft masc. acc. plur. substantives (конѧ̀ vs. East Slavic конѣ, helps to explain the absence of forms with jat' from the half-dozen or so pronominal object paradigms like сохрани̂ е̂ (п.) / сохрани̂ и̂ (т.) / сохрани̂ ю̀ / сохрани̂ ѧ̂ , or with varying verbs возми̂ ѧ̂ (п.) / веди̂ и̂ (п.) / води̂ ю̀ (п.), вари̂ е̂ (п.).[68] It may be the case that the grammarian had in mind only independent (and postvocalic) е̂ и̂ ю̀ ѧ̂ as " клонительные ", since other monovocalic endings are legion in the nominal paradigms like крестъ /-а̀ /-е̂ /-и /-о /-ѵ /-ы1 /-ѣ adduced above. Or, it may be simply that he didn't bother to compare the declarations of one part of his text with the evidence of another part.

Stress is also said to mark the distinction between masculine and feminine gender in such pairs as бѣ́ла (мѹж) / бѣла̀-(женск.), стра́шна /страшна̀ , преклонѐна/преклоненà etc. There is no evidence that the scribe thought the gen.-acc./nom. case distinction was of any importance. Once again, as so frequently in these texts, what matters to the scribe is only form itself; formal distinctions are illustrated, but little or no attention is paid to the functional (grammatical) distinctions which accompany them, and this is what results in such descriptive half-truths as labelling the pair бѣ́ла / бѣла̀ only as masc./fem. This preoccupation with the importance of formal differences, coupled with such striking lack of curiosity about their real functions, also helps to explain the apparently random nature of the grammatical and lexical opposi-

tions which show up as illustrative material: nom.-acc. plur./gen. sing. in
шествїа их̈ (м.) / шествїа моего̀ (е.), dat. plur./instr. sing. in
ц̑ремъ (м.) / ца́ремъ (е.),⁶⁹ gen.-acc. plur./nom. sing. in ѿцъ ва́шиẍ
(м.) / ѿцъ мои (е.), dat./gen. fem. sing. in про́литы sic (дател.) /
про́литы (родит.), various nominal and infinitival forms in мо́щи
ст̃ых̈ / мощѝ взѧти, не́мощи 'illnesses' / немощѝ носи́ти 'be
unable', with a syntactic factor added in the triad по мѡ̈щи идох̈ / по́мощи
('help', subst.) просѧ̀ / помощи̑ ('help', infin.) ино́му хощу̀. Finally, in
the following set our grammarian was clearly delighted at what he could
accomplish by adding и on one or another side of the root: ро́дъ, и̇ ро́дъ,
и́родъ цр̑ь, роди́те (п.), родитѐ (хотащее бы̀ти),... роди́
ѐ, роди и̇, роди ю̀ (настоѧщее [sic]), but what he had in mind in the
first member of the pair напо́и (м. п. [sic]) / напо́и (е. т.) escapes me,
— perhaps a plur. noun? In none of these cases do we approach anything that
could be dignified by the name of "paradigm". Only in a few lines near the
beginning of the section entitled " а҄ сѐ ѡ̇смоучастнѣ ѿ грама-
тикїа " (451) do we find genuine, if incomplete confused verbal paradigms. "To be" is given in the present (-future):

```
бу́дѧ ѡ̈нъ         бу́дива мы̀ два̀    бу́димо со мно́ю мнѡ̈зи
бу́деши ты̀        бу́дита вы̀ два̀    бу́дите (ете in one ms.)
бу́де̄ то́и                            бу́дӯ без⁵ мене мнѡ̈зи⁷⁰
```

The "passive" paradigm is illustrated by the verb бити, first in the reflexive:

```
бїӓсѧ             бїёвасѧ            бїёмосѧ
бїёшисѧ           бїётасѧ            бїётесѧ
бїётсѧ                               би ю́тсѧ
```

No distinction is made between this and another "passive", the first-person
singular forms of which are adduced to illustrate the several tenses:

преѣ̇бы̇вшее прота́жное (imperfect): биѧ́хү мѧ
непредѣлное (aorist): би́хү мѧ
настоѧ̈щее (present): би ю́т мѧ
пома́лѣ [sc.: бы̇ва́ющее, dw] (proximate future):
    би́ти мѧ хота̄
бу́дущее (simple future): би́ти мѧ и́мӯ

Needless but sad to say, there is nothing original in any of this. The
paradigms are simply lifted out of the Middle (Bulgaro-) Serbian "Eight parts of
speech", repeating mechanically and inanely such absurdities (on East Slavic
territory) as the first pers. sing. ending -ѧ going back to the Middle Bulgarian
confusion of ѫ and ѧ (бу́дѧ, бїѧ́сѧ; the scribe himself must have been
disconcerted by бу́дѧ where the paradigm shape called for a first pers. sing.

form, and "solved" this problem by turning it into a gerund with the 3d pers. pronoun ѡ́нъ [71]), the erroneous aorist бѝхѵ (for *бѝша), the Bulg. (and now also Ukr.) 1st plur. -мо, and the -ва/-та dual. Our scribe's only contribution was to add a certain Ukrainian confusion to the stem vowels in the paradigm of быти (бу́деши but бу́днте).

The remaining brief sections of the книга глемаѧ буквы1 deal with diacritics and contain no grammatical material. Overall, we can sum up this treatise by saying that it is genuinely concerned with the importance of external form, especially monovocalic endings and stress location. The grammatical purposes served by formal distinctions are hardly of interest at all; they include above all singular/plural opposition in substantives and participles, the imperative/indicative opposition in verbs, and a variety of case forms, real and imaginary, in substantives and adjectives. Throughout, there is a clear concern with the order of elements (participial -ще/-щи pairs begin with verbs in в- and proceed through the illustrations in alphabetical order; the nominal paradigms place endings in -а before those in -є or -и, regardless of case order, etc.). This treatise is a good illustration of the modest achievements and severe limitations of medieval Russian grammatical theory. By no stretch of the imagination could it be considered a "grammar", or even a grammatical sketch, of Church Slavonic or any other language.

7. Maksim Grek

Michael Trivolis was born c. 1470 and educated in his native Greece and in Renaissance Italy. He took the name Maksim in 1506, when he entered the Vatopedi Monastery on Mt. Athos, and he acquired the sobriquet "Grek" a dozen years later, when he arrived in Moscow at the invitation of Vasilij III to help in translating religious works. Caught up in the religious and social quarrels of that turbulent century, Maksim was never allowed to return to his homeland and spent much of his later life imprisoned in various Russian monasteries.[72]

Maksim's status as an intellectual leader is secure, but his reputation as a grammarian rests on less solid ground. Enthusiasts from his own time to ours have hastened to attribute to Maksim a variety of philosophical and grammatical works, some of which were obviously not his and none of which can be proved to have come from his pen. The editors of the 1648 Moscow version of Meletij Smotryćkyj's grammar added pre- and postfaces attributed — without evidence[73] — to Maksim, and by 1794 Smotryćkyj himself had been forgotten and the entire grammar credited to Maksim.[74] A. I. Ivanov, one of the scholars most familiar with the manuscript material, states that, "До Максима Грека на Руси не было грамматики",[75] implying that Maksim was the originator of Russian grammatical tradition. Such a statement must have its origins more in the author's sympathy for Maksim's unhappy fate than in a close examination of the texts, since there is not a shred of evidence which would enable us to attribute a single original grammatical thought to Maksim. This was recognized by Jagić over eighty years ago: "Если и допустить авторство Максима Грека относительно той или другой из предыдущих статеек, все-же заслуга его заключалась лишь и том, что он перенес эту общую, по византийским учебникам широко распространенную грамматическую теорию на почву русскую. Оригинального, собственно ему принадлежащего, тут нет ничего."[76] Jagić is also much more cautious in attributing works to Maksim than is Ivanov; Jagić's argument really boils down to the absence of proof that a text was *not* written by Maksim: "Нельзя сказать, что бы она (GBL, Tr. 201, f. 525-526) не могла быть написана Максимом Греком".[77] Even Jagić occasionally seems to exaggerate Maksim's grammatical accomplishments, as when he refers to the "богатая грамматическая содержательность" of his works.[78] Final judgment of these matters must await a proper philological edition of Maksim's works.[79] In the meantime, we will risk the opinion that Maksim's grammatical works are few in number and poor in content, — perhaps even fewer and even poorer than Jagić thought.

As Jack Haney correctly notes, Maksim's "real contribution to Muscovite intellectual life... lay in the area of philology and not in grammar *per se*."[80] One might narrow this characteristic even further: Maksim's real contribution to Muscovite letters lay in his insistence on precision, and specifically on the importance of distinguishing among homophones or near homophones, many of which had arisen in his native Greek because of the simplification of the vowel system between the classical and Byzantine periods. His commentaries on earlier translations, and his defence of his own philological activities, are sprinkled with pairs or entire sets of similar-sounding words, between and among which his contemporaries failed to distinguish, such as и́ѱило́съ (ὑψηλός, DSW) 'high'/ ѱїло́съ (ψιλός) 'bare', екклиси́а (ἐκκλησία) 'church'/ еќкли́се (ἔκκλησε, aor. of ἐκκλείω) 'excommunicate',[81] or, in his treatise on the Greek alphabet, εἷς 'one'/ εἶς 'thou art'/ ἧς 'her'/ ὗς 'swine'/ οἷς 'sheep'/ οἷς 'to them'/ υἱὸς 'son'/ οἷος 'what kind of'/ οἷος 'one'/ ἡὼς 'day'/ οἵως 'what kinds of'.[82] All of this, of course, has nothing to do with Slavic grammar, but one easily understands what a delightful revelation such distinctions must have been to a Slavic scribe trying to find useful grammatical functions for the superfluous letters and graphic archaisms of his own language (inst. sing. -омь / dat. plur. -шмъ, etc.). Maksim really knew his Greek, and one can imagine the esteem in which his half-educated clerical contemporaries must have held him. Maksim made no attempt to discourage this, but on the contrary, emphasized his own accomplishments: "Оно у́бш да ве́домо е́сть ва́мъ, га́кѡ е́ллинскїй а́зы́къ, сире́чь гре́ческий, ѕѣлѡ̀ е́сть хитре́йший, не вся́къ си́це ѹдо́бь мо́жетъ достигнути си́лы егѡ̀ до конца̀, а́ще не мно́га ле́та просидѣ́лъ кто̀ бѹ́детъ ѹ нарочиты́хъ ѹчи́телей, и то́й а́ще бѹ́детъ гре́къ ро́домъ и ѹмо́мъ о́стръ, еще́ же и о́хочь, а то́й ю не тако́въ (и́же) ѹчи́тся ѹбо шѹ́части а въ совершенїе егѡ̀ не дошо́лъ, га́коже ѡбрѣта́ю слѹчьшееся и приснопа́мятны́хъ преводникѡ́въ сты́хъ писа́ней ѿ гре́ческаго а́зы́ка на ро́усскїй " (298). Elsewhere, Maksim reiterates the sacrifices necessary in order to learn Greek properly: "Грамматікїа е́с... ѹче́нїе ѕѣлѡ̀ хы́тро ѹ е́ллине́х. то бо е́с нача́ло вхо́да и́же къ філосо́фїи и се́г ра́ди не́мощно е́с ма́лы́мї реумі́ и на̀ ма́ло вре́мя разумѣ́ти си́лу ея̂, но на́добѣть седѣти ѹ ѹчи́теля до́брагѡ го́дъ ра́венъ ѹпра́нившемѹся ѿ всѣ́х житѣ́йскы́хъ пли́шь и печа́ле́х и люби́ти трезвѣ́нїе всегда̀ и въздержа́тисѣ ѿ вся́кого поко́я и ѹгоже́нїа грътанна́гѡ и сна и винопи́тїя".[83] Nor does Maksim let pass the occasion to emphasize the relative positions of Russian and Greek: "ѹче́нїе то̀ ѹ нас́, ѹ́ гре́кѡвъ, хы́тро ѕѣлѡ̀, а не́ и ѹ́ ва́с. за́не́жъ ѹ нас́ філосо́фи бы́ли и́з нача́ла вели́ки и прему́дри... ."[84] To master this ѕѣлѡ̀ хы́тро ѹче́нїе would require two years' tutoring by the master himself: "а́ще и́стинною жела́ешъ дойти конца̀ премудраго сего ѹче́нїа філосо́фъскаго, пойди сиди

у менѐ гоⷣ дрүгóй покиноүв сѧ всѧ̀ граⷣскыӕ суеты̀ й
житейска попеуéнїа й боүдеши ("even if you are", DSW) пре-
богáтый күпéць".⁸⁵

As we have seen, Maksim's opinions of these matters were shared by many of his contemporaries and later admirers. To form our own opinion, let us examine the contents of the grammatical works of which Maksim Grek, in Jagić's opinion, either was or at least might have been the author.

The 16th-century Rumjancev Museum ms. No. 264⁸⁶ contains a brief article beginning with the praise of Greek discussed above ("Граммат їкїа еⷭ...үүéнїе ѕѣлѡ̀ хытрò..."), followed by what can best be termed a brief conspectus of the "Eight parts of speech", analyzed in some detail on p. 14 ff. above. According to Jagić, Maksim knew either this redaction or some later translation of a similar Greek treatise.⁸⁷ In fact, only the latter of these two possibilities can be supported by the texts themselves. This is clear if we compare the Russian recension of the "Eight parts of speech"⁸⁸ with Rum. Mus. No. 264. The most obvious difference is in size: the older text occupies over seven pages in Jagić's edition and Maksim's less than one page (plus the half page of introductory material mentioned above). But the content, too, shows that there could not be any filiation relation between these two mss. Jagić has already called attention to a terminological difference: the terms for 'article' (ἄρθρον) and 'adverb' (ἐπίρρημα) are разлиуїе and нареуїе in the older Serbian and Russian texts, but улѣнъ and приреуїе in Rum. Mus. No. 264. Oddly enough, in view of Maksim's popularity, it is the other set of terms which appears in almost all later Russian mss.⁸⁹

But the differences are more than terminological. The "Eight parts of speech" opens with an introduction on the religious importance of grammar ("По бж҃їю ѻбразу созданному улк҃у..."), but Rum. Mus. No. 264 opens with the comments on the difficulty of learning Greek on which we have already commented. The "Eight parts" divides the noun into genders before adducing any examples, while Rum. 264 lists illustrative nouns first, then repeats some of them after the gender labels. Furthermore, the illustrative nouns themselves are quite different in the two texts:

Eight parts of speech	*Rum. Mus. No. 264*
Йма оу҆бо дѣлитсѧ нá тро е‧ в мужеско й женьско й среднее. Йма же глетсѧ, ꙗко ймать подлежащеѐ существò, ѻ нéмже есть слóво, й йма.	Йма еⷭ ꙗкоже‧ бг҃ъ аггл҃ъ улк҃ъ, пéтръ, пáвелъ, марїа, ѳеодѡра, слн҃це, нб҃о, мóре, земла, горà, й симъ подобнаа, раздѣлаеⷮ же ⷭ йма на мужеско й женьско й среднее.
ꙗвлѧетⷭ же (сѧ) сице мужьское йма бг҃ъ. ѿц҃ъ. сн҃ъ,	й мужеско еⷭ пéтръ, пáвелъ, матⷭѳéй.

а҃хъ, с҃тъ, г҃ь, а҃ггл҃ъ, ч҃лкъ,
Пе́тръ, Па́велъ, во́здухъ,
ве́тръ, ме́сѧцъ, све́тъ,
і є҆ли́ка си́мъ подо́бнаѧ.

Common to both texts are Бо́гъ, а҃ггел҃ъ, ч҃лове́къ, Пе́тръ, Па́велъ, while the "Eight parts" add ѡ҆тьць; сы́нъ, до́ухъ с҃вѧтъ, го́сподь, въ́здо́ухъ, ве́тръ, ме́сѧцъ, све́тъ, and Rum. 264 adds Матᶴѳе́и. Words in the "Eight parts" and missing in Rum. 264 prove nothing about the relation of the two texts, since Rum. 264 is so much shorter and could simply have omitted much of the older material. On the other hand, when Rum. 264 has a word missing from the "Eight parts", such as Матᶴѳе́и in this case, this would indicate a different source for the younger ms. This is even clearer in the feminine illustrations:

же́ньское же се̂· тро́ица,   женско́ж е҅· ма́рїа,
с҃таа б҃ца,⁹⁰ д҃ва, д҃ша,   стеѳані́да. ѳеодѡ́ра,
луна́, землѧ́, вода́, и́   землѧ́, гора́.
си́мъ подо́бнаѧ.

Here the only word in common on the two lists is землѧ́; the "Eight parts" adds the inconclusive тро́ица, с҃вѧтаѧ бо́городица, д҃ева, ду́ша, луна́ and вода́, but Rum. 264 adds the more indicative ма́рїа, стеѳані́да, ѳеодѡ́ра, and гора́. Exactly the same situation obtains among the neuters:

сре́днее же и́мени· ест-   сре́днее е҅ᶜ· сл҃нце, н҃бо,
ество́, су́щество, ц҃р̂тво,   мо́ре, дре́во. си́мъ по-
вла́чьство, н҃бо, ч҃л̂тво,   до́бнаѧ.
и про́чаѧ си́цеваа.

where, again, only the single word не́бо appears in both lists. Rum. 264, without including a single one of the -ство abstracts from the older list, adds words for three more natural phenomena. There is no reasonable way that these two mss. can be directly related, or even descended from a common prototype.

Similar variation occurs in illustrations of the other parts of speech. The verb is illustrated by third-person imperfects and presents in the "Eight parts of speech" but by first-person singulars from an entirely different array of verbs in the younger text:

Eight parts of speech   *Rum. Mus. No. 264*

Пе́тръ оу҆ча́ше, Па́велъ   ви́жу, слы́шу, обонѧ́ю,
посы́ла́ше, Матѳе́и бл҃го-   гл҃ю, хожу́, и и́на є҆ли́ка
ве́ствова́ше... Пе́тръ   е҅ᶜ дѣѧнїа тѣле́снаа.
оу҆чи́тъ, Па́велъ посы́-
ла́етъ, Матѳе́и бл҃гове́ствуетъ

The "Eight parts" then goes on to a fairly detailed treatment of voice and mood (see p. 16 ff. above), none of which is reflected in any way in Rum. 264. The participial illustrations which follow repeat the situation we have just seen among the nouns.

є́сть же прнча́стїе се̃·пиша́и,	причάстїе є͡с га́ко͡ж се̃·
г͡лаи̌, ві аи̌, пи́шүщи, г͡лющи,	вида́, слы́ша̀, г͡ла и хода̀,
ві ю́щи, е́же пи́шүще, е́же	твора̀ и́ си́мъ подо́бнаа.
г͡лю́ще, е́же ві ю́ще	

The older text includes fem. nom. sing. participles and the younger text none. The masc. nom. sing. participles are in the long form in the "Eight parts" but in the short form in Rum. 264. The earlier text then goes on to illustrate pres. pass. participles (пи́шемьіи, г͡лемьіи, ві є́мьіи, пи́шемаа, г͡лемаа, ві є́маа, пи́шемо, г͡лемо, ві є́мо), of which Rum. 264 shows no trace.

The two texts are closest in their treatment of the "article", which as we have seen before (p. 20 above) undergoes a Slavic metamorphosis into the anaphoric pronoun:

Eight parts of speech   *Rum. Mus. No. 264*

и́же	га́же	е́же	и́же	га́же	е́же
єго́ же	є́а̀		єго́ж	є га́же	
ємо́у̀ же	є́и̌		єму́ж	є́и́же	
	га́же			ю́же	

и́же	е́же	га́же	- - -		
и́хже	и́хже	= masc.	и́хже		
и́мже	и́мже	and fem.	и́мже		
га́же	е́же				

The differences, interesting as some of them are (acc. sing. fem. га́же / ю́же), are inconclusive as far as the relations between the two texts are concerned. The same must be said of the remaining four parts of speech, which are not treated at all in the "Eight parts" but are briefly illustrated in the later text.[91] We shall adduce this material briefly here, not because it can tell us anything about the provenance of Maksim's text, but as the first illustrations we have encountered of the second four parts of speech, the pronoun (вмѣсто и́мень), preposition (прє́ло͡г), adverb (приρѣ́чїе) and conjunction (съоу́з).

The pronoun is illustrated by the nom., gen. and dat. singular and plural of the demonstrative pronouns сєи (note the secondary form) and тъ:

сє́и	сі́и	тъ	ті́и
сєго̀	си́хъ	того̀	тѣ́х
сємо́у̀	си́мъ	томо́у̀	тѣ́мъ

Only six prepositions are listed (по̀ [note the stress], къ, съ, въ, про, низ), one of which reappears in the subsequent list of adverbs (до́брѣ, премудрѣ, си́льнѣ, прекра́снѣ, вку́пѣ, ве́рхъ, низ, вну́трь, внѣ, во́нъ, и си́мъ подо́бнаа). The conjunctions are illustrated with an equally brief list: бо̀, у́бо, но̀, понѣ̀, понежѐ, и занеже, но̀ у́бо и си́мъ подо́бнаа .

We can conclude from this comparison that Maksim's text is on the one hand not descended from the older "Eight parts of speech", but on the other had nothing original or important to offer the medieval student of Slavonic grammar. The "Eight parts of speech", awkward and incomplete as they were, at least made a serious attempt to list, describe, and illustrate grammatical categories. Rum. 264, if it indeed belongs to Maksim — and I see no reason to deny this — is nothing for him or the Russian grammatical tradition to be proud of.

A second and equally condensed version of the "Eight parts of speech" occurs in the Čudov Monastery ms. No. 34-236, which Jagić also attributes to Maksim.[92] Other aspects of this text will be discussed below (p. 72 ff.), but first let us compare these two short versions of the "Eight parts", in order to determine their relation to each other, and in order to see whether it is likely that Maksim have done essentially the same job twice.

Rum. 264, as we have seen, begins with an introduction on the complexities of Greek (" Грамматїкїа ес̃... у҆че́нїе ѕѣлѡ̀ хы̀тро̀...), which has no connection with the following "Eight parts". The latter, however, begins with its own mini-introduction, which defines grammar: " Грама-тїкїа ес̃ сказа́нїе и ꙗ҆вле́нїе преи҆спещре́ныхъ посло́вицъ фїлосо́фъскаг̃ вѣща́нїа и бесѣды мно́го разли́чныа. и сказуе́ у́ункꙋ у́инъ и о҆бра́з о́смыхъ частеи сло́ва, си́ рѣу́ ка́кѡ повѣть разумѣти и разсужа́ти и пра́вити вса́кого сло́-ва. Сло́вож е҆с нꙗ́кож се҆· б̃гъ по бл̃гти свое́и сотвори нб̃о и зе́млю и всꙗ̂ ви́дима и неви́дима. сего сло́ва ча́сти сꙋ҆, .и̃. разѣлꙗ́еса на ·и̃· ча́стеи".[93] Čud. 34, on the other hand, dispenses with introductory matter and plunges right in: " Сего̀ о҆у́бо сло́ва ча́сти (one ms.: частеи) е҆с о́смь.

The terminology of Čud. 34 is the same as that of Rum. 264 ('article' = улѣ́нъ, 'adverb' = прирѣ́чїе), and, in view of the fact that the original terms (разли́чїе, нарѣ́чїе) are much more common, this speaks in favor of a close relationship between the two treatises. However, this is almost the only evidence of a common origin.

Čud. 34 is more interested in classification than Rum. 264. The latter simply lists the eight parts of speech, but the former divides them into inflected and non-inflected: " ѿ снҲ оу҆бо пать клонатса, сй рѣуь· и҆ма, рѣуь, приуастие, улѣнъ, в҅мѣстоима. три же не клонатса прелогъ, приреу́їе, съоу҅зъ". Similarly, Čud. divides nouns into 'isosyllabic' (клонатса равноскладнъ ἰσοσυλλάδως) and 'heterosyllabic' (к. лйшескладнѣ, περιττοσυλλάβως, i.e. with more syllables in the gen. than in the nom.[94]), a distinction of no relevance to Slavic grammar.

Čud. 34, like Rum. 264, gives a list of nouns before specifying the division into genders, but restricts itself to the four masculines бг҃ъ, а҆гг҃лъ, у҃лкъ, and (uniquely) конь, whereas Rum. 264 has nouns of all three genders, as we have seen above. Čud. 34's specifically masc. nouns include only the standard бг҃ъ, агг҃лъ, у҃лкъ, петръ and павелъ, but it adds the personal names е҆катерина and і҆оу҆лїанї҆и to the feminines and omits neuter illustrations altogether. Similarly, the verbal illustrations coincide only partly, and the order in which they occur is different:

Rum. 264

вижу, слы́шу, о҆бонѩ́ю,
гла҃ю, хожу҅, и҆ и҆на елика
ес҃ дѣа́нїа тѣлесна҃а.

Čud. 34

пишѫ, гла҃ю, уѫ́, слы́шу,
вижю, и҆ елика симъ
подобна.

Čud. 34 uses the same first three verbs to illustrate pres. act. participles, which are given in the long form nom. sing. masc. (пишаи, гла҃и, проуитали). Both the long forms and the first two verbs are a direct reflection of the original "Eight parts of speech" (пишаи, гла҃и) and quite unlike Rum. 264, which as we have seen uses largely different verbs and only short forms (видѫ, слышѫ, гла҃ и ходѫ, творѫ и҆ симъ подобнаа).[95]

Čud. 34 illustrates the "article" (улѣнъ) only with the three nom. sing. forms иже, ѩже, еже, whereas Rum. 264 gave much fuller paradigms. The pronominal illustrations are completely different: Rum. 264 has nom.-gen.-dat. sing. and plur. of сеи and тъ, but Čud. 34 gives the three personal pronouns а҃зъ, ты̋, о҃нъ. Prepositions coincide only partially: Rum. 264 по, къ, съ, въ, про, низ/Čud. 34 въ, на, ѿ, съ (and note the different order).

The adverbial illustrations show an interesting combination of similarity and disparity:

Rum. 264

добрѣ, премудрѣ, сильнѣ,
прекраснѣ, вкупѣ, верхъ,
низ, внутрь, внѣ, вонъ
и҆ симъ подобнаа.

Čud. 34

добрѣ, мудрѣ, горѣ,
долу

The evidence seems clear that Rum. 264 and Čud. 34 go back to different translations of the same, or at least of very similar Greek texts: премѫ́дрѣ and мѹ́дрѣ both < σοφῶς 'wisely', вѐрхъ and горѐ < ὑπερῶς 'above', низ and до́лѹ < ὑπό 'below'.

Conjunctions are more different than similar: Rum. 264 бо̀, ѹ̈бо, но̀, понѐ, понеже, й занеже, но̀ ѹ̈бо /Čud. 34 о́ѵбо, же (< δέ), й, й оѵбо, но̀.

The differences between these two synoptic versions of the "Eight parts of speech" are so marked, and the similarities between them so few, that it seems very unlikely indeed that they or their prototypes be from the pen of a single author or translator. If one of the two is the work of Maksim Grek, the other is not.

If we leave aside the problem of the "Eight parts of speech" in Čud. 34 and turn to a more general characterization of this text, we first note that it was intended as a description not of Slavic, but of Greek. It opens with a classification of vowels (гласѡ́вна҄) and consonants (съгласна҄). The vowels are divided into inherently long (долга: ἠ, ω) or short (кратка: έ, ό), plus those which can be of either length (двоевреме́нна : ἀ ἰ ὐ). The consonants are divided into semivocalic (полѹгласо́вна) and non-vocalic (безгласна). The former group contains not only the liquids ρ and λ, which would be [+ vocalic] in a modern description, but the nasals ν, μ and, more surprisingly, σ and the affricates ζ ξ ψ. The sonorants λ ρ μ ν are termed непреложна, the affricates ζ ξ ψ are, appropriately, сѹгѹ́бна, and σ stands alone and unlabelled. The non-vocalic consonants contain three groups of three, 'medial' (средна) voiced stops β γ δ, 'thin' (тонка) voiceless stops κ π τ, and 'dense' (ѹ҄ста) fricatives θ φ χ. The author explains that ζ is composed of σ and δ, ξ of κ and σ, and ψ of π and σ. None of this would be relevant to Slavic phonology were it not for attempts to superimpose this Greek scheme onto Slavic material, for example by dividing Slavic vowels into long, short, and bitemporal.[96]

The classification of Greek vowels and consonants is transferred to Slavic in many texts, of which one published by Jagić (*Codex slovenicus...*, p. 318-319) can serve as an example. The same terminology is used as for the Greek, with the single exception of the sonorants, which are also known as 'wet' (мокрыѧ). Slavic letters not in Greek are added to the appropriate categories. In tabular form, this classification appears as follows:

Vowels гласѡ́вныѧ
    Long до́лгыѧ   и̇   ѡ̇
    Short краткыѧ   є   о
    Bitemporal двоевре́менныѧ   а   и   ѵ[97]

Consonants	согласѡвныѧ, согла́сныѧ					
Semi-vocalic	полѹгласѡ́вны ѧ					
Double	сѹгѹбы ѧ	ж	ᴣ	ᴣ	ѱ	
Unchangeable	непремѣнѧ́емы ѧ }	л	м	н	р	
(or) Wet	мокры ѧ					
[unlabelled]		с	ш	щ		
Non-vocalic	безгла́сны ѧ					
Medial	сре́днѧѧ	б	в	г	д	
Thin	то́нкы ѧ	к	ц	ч	п	т
Dense	ѧ́сты ѧ	ѳ	ф	х		

As was the case with the Greek, this is at least a first approximation of an articulatory classification, although — as was, perhaps, to have been expected — the Slavic material is less neatly grouped than was the Greek: the affricates ц and ч have been added to the 'thin' voiced stops к п т, and the palatals ш щ tacked on to the dental с. In itself there is nothing unreasonable about this; ц and ч are voiceless and do contain a stop element, while ш and щ are voiceless non-sonorants, etc.

The little attention paid to morphology in Čud. 34 is also concentrated on Greek. After the highly-condensed "Eight parts of speech" discussed above, the text goes on to illustrate one of the isosyllabic (ра́вноскла́дно кло-нѧ́емы) declensions with pure Greek endings, e.g. -ας, -ȣ͂, ά, ὰ (= -ας, -ου, -ᾳ, -α). The only interesting thing here is the remark that the nominative case (стойтелно паде́нїе) is not really a case but is termed such only from habit: " и́бо стойтелно й пра́мо не г͞летсѧ сꙋ́ще па́дение, но и҃з обы́чаѧ" (315); here we see a reflection of the Greek direct-oblique division, in which the accusative (вино́вно па́денїе) is grouped with the other oblique cases, genitive (ро́дно п.), dative (да́телно), and vocative (зва́телно).

This treatise contains a minor curiosity in its treatment of number, namely the "dual" ѹ͞ковъ in " ӵисла̀ сѹть три҆·еди́нъственно, ꙗ́коже· ѹ͞къ. дво́йно [,ꙗ́коже]· ѹ͞ковъ, мно́жественно, ꙗ́коже ѹ͞цы1" (315). The form ѹ͞ковъ clearly shows the author's ignorance of Slavic grammar, but its own provenance is not clear. It might come from analogy: the nom. masc. dual ending -а was the same as that of the gen. sing.; however, the first grammatical treatises rendered the genitive case by a poss. adjective form instead of by -а (ѹ͞къ, gen. ѹ͞ковъ),[98] and this -овъ might have been carried over to the dual. Such an error — hardly a likely one, but no better explanation comes to mind — speaks against Maksim's authorship of this text, unless it came from his first months in Moscow, before he had learned any substantial amount of Russian.[99]

After this very brief treatment of grammar, Čud. 34 turns to "prosody", i.e. to diacritics. The ten prosodic signs fall into four groups:

Forces (сѝлы):	оӟїа `	} sic
	варїа ´	
	перистомени ~	
Times (времени):	макра̀ −	
	врахїа ᴗ	
Spirits (дѵхи):	дасна̃ ᑕ	
	ѱїли ᑐ	
Passions (страсти):	ἀποστροφός ›	
	ѵ́фенъ ⌣	
	ѵ́подїастоли ;	

The confusion of the oxy- and barytone marks must be attributed to a later copyist (Čud. 34 is a late 16th c. ms.), since Maksim himself could hardly have made such an error.[100]

In the midst of a fairly complex description of diacritic distribution in Greek, the author makes a comparative comment on Russian. The vowels и ѡ ѣ ы ѵ а ѧ are long and а е і о ѵ are short. The latter are always to be written with the oxytone (here, correctly, ´), the former with a circumflex if the ultima is short but with an oxytone if the ultima is long. This passage contains the introductory phrase "оу̌ ва‵с же русѣ‵х" (316), implying that the author, if not Maksim, was some other Greek. Note, too, the gen. plur. in -ѣхъ, which as Haney points out, is typical of Maksim.[101]

Russian and Greek are compared in a number of ways in this prosodic section of the treatise. The дасїа (spiritus asper), for example, is never used in Russian, and in order to make his Russian readers understand its importance, the author compares the ⁾ / ⁽ contrast with that between ъ and ь in Slavic. His Slavic examples, гра̃дъ/гра̃дь and перстъ/пер‵сть, seem strange at first, but are probably intended as the gen. plur. and nom. sing. of these nouns, in accordance with the totally artificial 16th-century view that ь was to be used in singular endings but ъ in the plural (see the discussion of the treatise О МНОЖЕСТВѢ и о едѝнствѣ, p. 51 ff.). Russian is said not to require the long and short marks, nor does it need two of the three "passions" (ἀποστροφοсъ, ѵ́фенъ), but only the ѵ̆подїастоли . What exactly is intended by this last term is unclear. Ordinarily, it refers to the semicolon, which however functioned as a question mark. Here our author writes as if ѵ̆подїастоли alone referred to a comma: "едина оу̌ ва‵с потре́бна и ѵ̆подїастоли и собо́ю и с то́чкою си́це;...полагаетсѧ, по вопро́ сѫ (sic)[102] сло́во прочита́етсѧ, га́ково́ же ес‵ се̃... насажен оу̌хо не слы́шиши ли ; " (317).

The question of whether or not the treatise represented by Čud. 34 should be attributed to Maksim Grek must be left open. In favor of his authorship are the knowledge of Greek (assuming that the above-mentioned confusion of ˵ and ´ was the fault of a later copyist), the comparisons between Greek and the situation "оу́ вась роусѣхь", and the rare gen. plur. subst. ending -ѣхь, -ехь. Against Maksim's authorship are the many etymologically incorrect and inconsistent spellings and syntax, the ˵ / ´ error (if not a later error), and above all, the superficial character of the entire text, esp. that part derived from the "Eight parts of speech". The original "Eight parts of speech", incomplete and prescientific as it is, is incomparably more consistent and analytically deeper than either Čud. 34 or Rum. 264, which show next to no interest in grammatical matters.[103] We can leave the final decision in the form of a choice. If Maksim Grek was anything like the grammarian he was reputed to be, then he could hardly have wasted his time on such derivative banalities as these, and we can assume that he was not their author. On the other hand, if Maksim did indeed compose these treatises, then one can only wonder how he acquired such a reputation. There is nothing in any of the published writings of Maksim Grek which would earn him a significant place in the history of Slavic grammatical thought.

8. The Donatus translation

8.0.0 The lengthiest of the medieval grammatical treatises in Russia, and the only one from a tradition other than the Greek, is the 16th century translation of Donatus' introduction to Latin grammar known as the *Ars minor*.

Donatus was apparently translated in 1522 by the former diplomat Dmitrij Gerasimov (D. Tolmač); at least, this is what is claimed, in an 18th c. hand, on the binding of a latter 16th c. copy ("Дона́тѹсь си́рєѵь грама́тика и а҃збѹка переведенная Димитрїемъ толмаѵемъ съ латинскаго а҃зыка̀ 1522-го, а҃ списана 1563-го года", Jagić 528). This is the same Dmitrij who had assisted Maksim Grek in the latter's early translations (Maksim dictated his translation from Greek to Dmitrij in Latin, and Dmitrij then put the Latin into Russian). His translation is preserved in two copies from the latter 16th c., one in the (then) Imperial Library in St. Petersburg (O2), and the other, better copy in the Kazan' University Library (Kaz.).[104] The original translation, as Jagić surmised, was intended as a grammar of Latin for Russians, and for that reason it left the Latin paradigms themselves intact, providing at most marginal glosses to these Latin forms. The two copies that have come down to us, however, show almost no trace of the original Latin, giving full Russian or Russian Church Slavonic paradigms (even for such grammatical arcana as the pluperfect subjunctive); one scribe specifies that he has done this:

до з҃дѣ совершисѧ конец книги гл҃емыѧ донатѹсъ єже именѹетсѧ наѵало граматики, преведена же бысть из латиньскаго ѧзыка на рѹскиї Дїмитрїемъ Толмаѵемъ немецкаго ѧзыка ... аз же послѣди его переводѹ S.T. списах сию книжкѹ единымъ рѹскимъ ѧзы- комъ, без латиньскагѡ, да бы проѵитающимъ ю и оуѵащимсѧ въ ней болѣе раз҃ѹмно было.

(Jagić 525)

Just how раз҃ѹмно this was is open to question, since the result was a grammar of an unidentifiable language, written in Cyrillic characters and utilizing Russian and/or Slavonic morphemes, but portraying grammatical categories foreign to any Slavonic tongue. The assumption which seems to have underlain this translation, as well as many of those from Greek already discussed, is that grammar is universal ("Донатѹсъ єже именѹетсѧ наѵало грама́тики" – not, *n.b.*, "граматики латиньскиѧ", but "граматики" altogether).

8.0.1 The **Preface**, which may or may not be the work of Gerasimov himself (it is missing from O2), notes that this work is only the first of four parts of a complete grammar course: "вторую книгу ꙋчат граматикию (i.e., the full *Ars maior*), третюю книгу синтазис, четвертую прозодию " (529). This Preface mentions some of the differences between Greek and Latin ("ꙋклонении пѧть же по греческиі, а по латыньскиі шесть", etc.), and then notes the impossibiliity of translating the Latin paradigms into proper Slavic:

    Сие же да есть ведомо, иже сиі слова
    и концыі словниі преведше на словень-
    скую реч в сущем сиреч в ряду неудобь
    возможни будут в лепоту поставитисѧ.
    сего ради и непреведени суть на словен-
    скиі ꙗзыкъ в ряду, но на полех. (530)

But then he looks ahead to the possibility that

    некиі разумныи и мудрыи муж восхощет
    ѡ сих неленив быти и болиі труда при-
    ложити, і ѡнъ проучет внѧтно сию книгу
    ѿ начала і до конца, и известно ꙋразумев
    еѧ ... (sc. съможетъ, DSW) сию книгу по-
    ставити в лепоту по ѡбыічаю словеньскаго
    ꙗзыка. (*ib.*)

Dmitrij is quite specific about the non-correspondence of gender between Latin and Russian, a situation he illustrates by "Latin" сей и сиѧ сасердосъ vs. Russian сей свѧщенникъ (531). The same problem obtains in the case of Latin participles, which not even the brightest teacher ("никиі оучитель, аще и вельми хитръ будет") will be able to translate word-by-word into Russian. Finally, the Preface closes with an autobiographical note:

    азъ же сие писахъ собе памѧти длѧ
    поелику ꙋразумех, пребывая и ꙋчасѧ во
    оучилище двема грамотам и двема ꙗзыіки,
    латыіньскиѧ и немецкиѧ, а по рускиі
    преже того поучихсѧ ѿ части, а не по-
    оучивсѧ по рускиі в тамошнее оучилище
    немощно пристати. а какъ уже разума
    прибыіло. ино в то времѧ в суетах мира
    сего поспеха и силы телесныѧ оубыіло. и
    того ради сиѧ книга начисто не исправлена
    и не преписана ѡстала. а зде се того и
    не пыітаютъ. (532)

In other words, what we have before us is a work of Gerasimov's student years, and this surely explains at least some of the errors and internal inconsistencies we shall find in his translation.

8.0.2 Sandwiched in between the Preface and the Donatus grammar proper is a brief statement about the alphabet entitled Сказа́нїе ѿ бу́квех, сир҃ѣчь ѿ ѡ҆бразѣ́х а҆́збуунь іх̑ сло́въ написа́ннї толкова́нїе. The alphabet is of course in the Latin order, and consists of vowels (зва́телннї) а е ї о ѵ ü (= ї), and two classes of consonants (согласу́ющїи) which are divided into semi-vocalic (полу́звателннї) л м н р and, more surprisingly, с ҙ ҕ and mute (нѣмь і е) б ц д ф г х п к т which are however not devoid of voicing ("не ꙗ҆́ко не имѣ́ют гла́са, но еже ма́лу у҆́асть гла́са имѣ́ют" 532).

8.1.0 The main bulk of the translation is introduced by a table of contents in question-answer format (like that of the Greek erotēmata), e.g. и в҃с. Уа́сти вѣща́нїа, и҆ли́ рѣ́уи коли́ць і су́ть; Ѿ. ѡ҆смь." (533).[105] The grammar consists of two principal parts, a survey of the eight parts of speech with illustrative paradigms, and a more detailed description of verb morphology. We shall survey each of these two sections in turn, concentrating our attention not on how well or how poorly the Slavic translations render the Latin original, but on the degree to which these translations permit some insight into the state of Russian morphology in the 16th century, including the largely unexplored problem of Church Slavonic-vernacular interpenetration. Conclusions from this sort of secondary evidence can be no more than suggestive, of course, and are subject to confirmation by analysis of original texts of the same period.

The first part of the Donatus grammar proper takes up each of the traditional eight parts of speech, which are:[106]

    8.1.1 noun (и҆́мѧ, *nomen*)
    8.1.2 pronoun (проимѧ́нїе, *pronomen*)
    8.1.3 verb (сло́во, *verbum*)
    8.1.4 adverb (предло́гъ, *adverbium*)
    8.1.5 participle (прича́стїе, *participium*)
    8.1.6 conjunction (соу́з, *coniunctio*)
    8.1.7 preposition (представле́нї е, *praepositio*)
    8.1.8 interjection (разли́чїе, *interiectio*)

We shall now look at each of these parts of speech in turn.

8.1.1.0 The noun is defined as a part of speech (уа́сть вѣща́нїа) with declension (с паде́нїемъ). Nouns are proper (со́бьствено) or common (ѡ҆́бще), and are inflected for (присто́ѧт or напа́даю́т, < *accidunt*) six grammatical categories, as follows:

8.1.1.1 Quality (ка́уество, *qualitas*) is the major division of nouns into proper or common, e.g. Ри́мъ and гра́д respectively. One notes that while the translator chooses гра́д over го́род, he uses a native gen. sing. adj. ending in his definition of "proper", "є҆ди́ное ве́щи и҆́мѧ е҆́сть" (534).

8.1.1.2 Comparison (прилага́нїе , *comparatio*) shows the expected three degrees (степени, *comparationis gradus*),[107] viz. positive (положи́телнаѧ), comparative (прилага́телнаѧ), and superlative (надприлага́телнаѧ or превы́шнаѧ), e.g. ꙋ́ченъ, ꙋ́ченѣе or ꙋ́ченнѣише and предꙋ́ченнѣише respectively (*n.b.* the single -н- in ꙋ́ченѣе vs. the double -нн- in both -ѣише forms). Only descriptive adjectives (имена нарица́телныіе , *n.b.* the -ыіе ending!) can be compared. The comparative governs (слꙋжит [!]) the "negative" case (ѿрица́телномꙋ паде́нию , *ablativus* here = the genitive without preposition), e.g. ꙋчи́телнѣе ѡ́наго or ꙋ. и́нѣх; the superlative governs only the genitive plural, e.g. преꙋ́ченнѣишиі мꙋдрецовъ бѣа́ше виргили́і (*n.b.* innovative -овъ next to archaic бѣа́ше), but plurality is intended in a deeper semantic sense, since it is also expressed in collectives, e.g. наро́ꙋчитеиши ѿ наро́да , *optimus plebis*.

8.1.1.3 There are four **genders**, masculine (мꙋжески́і), feminine (же́нски́і), neuter (посреднї́і), and common (ѡбщиі[ї]), e.g. сеи́ ꙋчи́тель, сиа̀ мꙋ́дрость, сиѐ сѣдалище and сеи́ и сиа̀ ꙋлове́къ respectively, to the last of which Gerasimov, or one of his copyists, adds 'а̀ по рꙋскомꙋ іа́зыкꙋ ѡбщаго ро́да и́ма есть сеи́ и сиа̀ ꙋлкъ, и подо́бныіе томꙋ́' (535), grasping at referential sex distinctions, rather than at native epicenes, in his attempt to render *hic et haec sacerdos*.

The translator then continues with a free paraphrase of the descriptions of two further genders, universal (вса́ческиі , *omne*), and epicenes (смѣше́ныіи, *epicoenum* [*id est quod promiscuum genus dicitur*]). Understandably, he has problems in finding suitable Russian illustrations, and has recourse to borrowing in the first case (се́и и сиа̀ и́ сиѐ фели́з, е́же именꙋ́етсѧ ꙋесте́н и́ли сꙋа́стен) and to violence to Russian grammar in the second (се́и врабе́и, се́и и сиа̀ ѡре́лъ, ла́сица, коршꙋ́нъ ; *n.b.* in passing the Ch. Sl. root but native ending of врабе́и).

8.1.1.4 The category of **number** includes only the singular (еди́ньственое) and plural (множ[е]ственое), e.g. се́и ꙋчи́тель and сѣ̀ ꙋчи́тели or си́і ꙋ́лцы (*n.b.* сѣ̀ ~ си́і and the combination of archaic morphophonemics and new phonetics in the nom. plur. ꙋ́лцы).[108]

8.1.1.5 The **form** (ѡбразъ, *figura*) of a noun, like the "aspects" (види́) and "schemes" (наꙋертани́ѧ) of the Greek tradition (cf. the "eight parts of speech", p. 16 above), refer to derivational complexity. There are two levels of form, simple (единоро́дныи, сирѣꙋь простыи *simplex*) and compound (сло́жныи), for the Latin illustrations of which (*decens, potens; indecens, impotens*) Gerasimov or a copyist found the translations ми́лостивъ, моще́н, but felt obliged to illustrate the compound form with the additional, true Slavic compounds многоми́лостивъ, велемоще́н, and достовѣ́рен.

Compounds can be formed in four ways, utilizing three kinds of component (ꙋи́ны or ꙁалѡ́ги , cf. слагаютсѧ, сложны ́ є): (1) from two identical components, either whole (ѿ двꙋ цѣлы́х) or truncated (ѿ двꙋ сокрꙋшены́х), e.g. мощедѣ́йственъ O2 *efficax*, градоє́мецъ *municeps*; the examples appear in this order but would be more appropriate if reversed); (2) from a whole plus a truncated component, as непотре́бенъ *ineptus*, безсо́ленъ *insulus*; (3) from a truncated plus a whole, as тщепосла́нникъ, лженосе́ц, *nugigerulus*; (4) occasionally, from several components, e.g. непобѣди́мъ , *inexpugnalis*, нестрашли́въ , *inperterritus*. Since the Latin forms were omitted from Kaz. and O2, the resulting description could only confuse anyone interested in Slavic derivation.

8.1.1.6 **Case** (паде́нїе , *casus*) is presented in the Latin manner: nominative (именова́телное [sc. паде́нїе, DW] и́лѝ пра́вое по гре́чески), genitive (ро́дственое), dative (да́телное), accusative (вино́вное), vocative (ꙁва́телное), and ablative (ѿрица́телное); "nouns, pronouns and participles of all genders are declined, i.e. composed, according to these declensions" ("по се́м бо паде́нїємъ всѣ́х родо́въ имена́ и мѣ́сто име́нъ и[ли] проймениѧ и причастиѧ ꙋклонѧ́ютсѧ, сирѣ́ч слога́ютсѧ " 536).

8.1.1.2.0 **Nominal paradigms.** The text then proceeds to exemplify five regular and two supplemental paradigms (ѡ̈бра́ꙁы́ , сирѣ́ч подо́бники). Unlike the Greek-based texts, in which the order of case-forms is determined largely by the phonological or graphic oppositions the scribe wished to illustrate (cf. for example pp. 56 ff. above), the Donatus translation begins each paradigm with a full definition of the nom. sing. base form, and then gives the other case-number forms, always in the standard order. In other words, from the point of view of the receiving Russians, the Latin source was genuinely concerned with the systematization of grammatical oppositions, whereas most of the Greek-based sources were more interested in phonetic, graphic and diacritic — not to say purely decorative — aspects of language. In our survey, we give only the paradigms themselves, rearranged into the customary columnar order, omitting the definitional material, and adducing forms from O2 only where they differ significantly from those of Kaz., and including all paradigms in Donatus, even where their Russian translations are inconsistently repetitious.

8.1.1.2.1 The **first, masculine declension** is illustrated by ꙋ̈чи́тель in Kaz. (for O2, see below):

FIRST DECLENSION (MASCULINE)

	Singular	Plural
nom.	сєн ѵ̈чи́тєль	сѐ оѵчи́тєли
gen.	сєго̀ оѵчи́тєлѧ	сѣх ѵчи́тєлєвъ
dat.	сємѵ̀ ѵчи́тєлю	сѣм ѵ̈чи́тєлємъ
acc.	сєго̀ ѵчи́тєлѧ	сѣхъ оѵчи́тєлєвъ
voc.	ѿ ѵ̈чи́тєль	ѿ оѵчи́тєли
abl.	ѿ сєгѡ оѵчи́тєлѧ	ѿ сѣх ѵчи́тєлєвъ

Here one notes the gen.-acc. in both sing. and plur., the lack of an independent vocative form, and the new gen. plur. in -евъ but older dat. plur.-емъ (we will comment on the pronominal forms separately; cf. pp. 89 ff. below).

The O2 ms., rather than translate Latin *magister*, simply borrows it:

сй магистéръ   сїѧ̀ магистры̀ı
сê магистéрово   снѧ̀ магистровы̀ı
семоу̀ магистéру   си́мъ магистры́ıм[a]
сего̀ магистéра   си́хъ магистрѡвъ
ѿ магистéре   ѿ сїй магистры̀ı
ѿ сего̀ магистéра   ѿ си́хъ магистéровъ

[a]presumably an adj.-influenced error for -омъ.

O2 preserves the possessive adjective expression of the genitive case, in both sing. and plur. which goes back to the "Eight parts of speech" (cf. pp. 14 ff. below) but, interestingly, uses the Slavic -а genitive to render the Latin ablative. It has a separate and correctly Slavic vocative in the singular. O2 also shows an odd combination of stress-shift and vowel-zero alternation: the stress, whereever it is marked, falls on the stem-final vowel (é in the sing., и́ in the plur. except for the abl.), but the є vs. zero marking of number is strange, since Russian has never utilized this opposition for this grammatical purpose. The most cogent, though certainly not entirely satisfactory explanation is that the copyist was motivated primarily by the productive right-to-left shift distinguishing plural from singular (which, however, is characteristic precisely of feminines and neuters, not masculine!), and then omitted the unstressed є in post-tonic position, a phonetically easy step, next to the liquid ρ.

8.1.1.2.2 The **second, feminine declension** is illustrated by мѵдрость in Kaz.:

SECOND DECLENSION (FEMININE)

	Singular	Plural
nom.	сиѧ мѵдрость	сиï мѵдрости
gen.	сее мѵдрости	сѣх мѵдростеи
dat.	сеи мѵдрости	сѣм мѵдростемъ
acc.	сию̀ мѵдрость	сѣх мѵдростеи
voc.	ѽ мѵдрости	ѽ мѵдростï
abl.	ѿ сеѧ мѵдрости	ѿ сѣх мѵдростеи

Kaz. has a separate voc. in the sing. (and, at least graphically, in the plur., unless -ï is an oversight).[109] Native Russian developments are seen not only in E. Sl. gen. sing. сее, but also in the Gt. Russ. tense-jer reflex of gen.-acc.-abl. plur. мѵдростеи. There is no ready explanation in either Latin or Russian for the gen.-acc. сѣх мѵдростеи[110]

O2 builds its paradigm on сопѣль, which in Kaz. was only a marginal gloss to мѵза ; the paradigm as reproduced by Jagić 537 f.n. 18 is missing the (nom. and) gen. sing.:

сiа̀	сиѧ сопѣли
снѣ	сих̀ сопелеи
сеѝ сопѣли	сим̀ сопелемъ
сі ю̀ сопѣль[a]	сих̀ сопелеи
ѽ сопѣль	ѽ сопѣли
ѿ сеѧ̀ сопѣли	ѿ сих сопелеи

[a] ms. сі ю̀ дати сопѣль; similarly in plural

Here in the second declension it is O2 which hs no separate voc. This ms. is also careless with its root vocalism (е ~ ѣ). Otherwise, it shows the same gen. sing. pronoun in -е and Gt. Russ tense-jer -ен (-еѝ) as Kaz. and repeats the latter's animate gen.-acc.

The second declension is followed by an excursus on мѵза (here identified in the Latin manner as пéрваго ѵ́клонéниѧ, 538): there are nine muses, equated with speech organs (сирѣчь дéветь ѵ́гóде[и] или сосѵдовъ или ѡ̀ргáновъ къ глаголани ю̀ " ib., which, however, only add up to seven: " двѣ гу́бьі или оу̀стнѣ̀, четы́ре зу̀бы начáльнı е, послѣднаѧ часть ѧ̀зы́ка, горло дьı халное, гортани, тщи́на, плюча, и̇ сні девѧть оу̀гóди ѧ глагол ю̀тсѧ мѵзы" ib.[111]

8.1.1.2.3 The **third, neuter declension** is exemplified in both mss. by сѣдалище:

THIRD DECLENSION (NEUTER)

	Singular	Plural
nom.	сие сѣдалище	сиꙗ сѣда́лища
gen.	сегѡ̀ сѣда́лища	сѣхa сѣда́лищъ
dat.	семѹ̀ сѣда́лищѹ	сѣмъ b сѣда́лищамъ
acc.	сие сѣда́лище	сиа сѣда́лища
voc.	ѽ сѣда́лище	ѽ сѣда́лища
abl.	ѿ сегѡ̀ сѣда́лища	ѿ сѣх сѣдалищ

a О2 сихъ b О2 симъ

The only thing of interest here is the innovative dat. plur. m. -амъ, clearly influenced by the nom.-acc. in -а (no other Donatus paradigms show *a-stem endings extended to other stem types; cf. ѹчителемъ, магистрьімъ, мѹдростемъ, сопелемъ above and свѧщенникомъ, плодомъ below).

8.1.1.2.4 The **fourth (common-gender) declension** obviously worried Gerasimov (or a copyist), who tried to explain the problem:

Подобникъ ѹетве́ртыій, та́ко ѹ́клонѧ́ется. по латыньскиі и́мѧ ѽбщее свѧщенникъ, е́же е́сть сасердо́сь, и́мѧ нарицателное, ро́да ѽбщаго. а по рѹскии же не прииде́т та́къ, но е́сть ѹ́бо по их ꙗзьі́кѹ ѹисла единьственаго, ѽбраза единорѧ́днаго, е́же е́сть простаго, падениа именователнаго и́ вино́внаго и́ ꙁва́телнаго. еже ѹ́клонѧ́ется си́це· (539)

Having thus at least come close to specifying the difference between *sacerdos* and свѧщенникъ, the translator proceeds to mix them together in the following paradigm:

FOURTH DECLENSION (COMMON GENDER)

Singular   Plural

nom. се́и и сиѧ̀ сасердосъ,   сиï и сѣ свѧщенницы
        сирѣу свѧщенникъ
gen. сего свѧщенника   сѣх и ѡнѣх свѧщенниковъ
dat. сему свѧщеннику   сѣмъ свѧщенником
acc. сего̀ и сию̀ сасердостемъ[a]   сих и сѣх свѧщенниковъ
voc. ѿ свѧщенникъ   ѿ свѧщенницы
abl. ѿ сего̀ и ѿ сеѧ   ѿ сихъ свѧщенников
      сасердостемъ или
      сасердости[b]

    [a] О2 сего̀ свѧщенника   [b] О2 ѿ сего̀ свѧщенника;
the -мъ of сасердостемъ was supplied by Jagić.

If we ignore the awkward attempt to decline *sacerdos* in Cyrillic, the noteworthy features of the paradigm are the к ~ ц alternation in the nom.-voc. plur., the innovating -овъ in the gen.-acc.-abl. plur., and the absence of a separate vocative in both numbers (on the alternative pronouns, see pp. 90 ff. below). The paradigm is followed by a recurrent explanation that Russian свѧщенникъ is really declined not like a common-gender noun, but like the second-declension ѹчи́тель.[112]

8.1.1.2.5 Gerasimov's **fifth declension** consists of "universal-gender" nouns, which, to judge by the example фели́ксъ, meant substantivized adjectives (the Latin text had *felix nomen appellativum*, Jagić 540 f.n. 1). The paradigm has nothing to do with Slavic grammar, and we adduce it partly as a mere curiosity, partly to record the accompanying pronouns:

FIFTH DECLENSION (UNIVERSAL GENDER)

Singular

nom. се́и и сиѧ̀ и сиѐ ѵестенъ, филиксъ
gen. сего̀ фелисис
dat. сему фелиси
acc. сего и сию̀ фелисе́мъ, и сие фели́ксъ
voc. ѿ фели́ксъ
abl. ѿ сего̀ и ѿ сеѧ̀ и ѿ сего̀ фели́се или фели́си

Plural

nom.	сі́и и се̑ фелисес и сна̀ фелисиа
gen.	сих и сѣх фелисиу̑мъ
dat.	сима[a] фелисибу́съ
acc.	сих и сѣх фелисесъ и сна̀ фелисиа
voc.	ѿ фелисес і ѿ фелисиа
abl.	ѿ сих фелисибу́съ

[a] *sic*; also in O2.

The O2 ms. makes more of an attempt to Slavonize the paradigm (we give only the substantive forms, as the pronouns generally repeat those of Kaz.):

	Singular	Plural
nom.	филиксъ	фели́цыı
gen.	филикса̀	фели́цыıоу̑мъ
dat.	[omitted]	фели́цыı
acc.	фили́ксъ	фели́цыıѧ
voc.	[= Kaz.]	ѿ фелице́съ
abl.	фили́кса	фили́цыıбоу́съ

In a dogged attempt to get his paradigm translated one way or another, Gerasimov then appends the full adjective paradigms of four different possible translations of *felix*, блаженъ, счастливъ, богатъ, and честенъ. Here they have been rearranged into columnar form, with блаженъ standing for all four stems (variant endings are noted below):

Singular

	masculine	feminine	neuter
nom.	се́и блаже́н	сиа̀ блаже́нна	сиѐ блажено
gen.	сего̀ блаже́наго	сее[b] блаже́ныıа	сего блаженагѡ
dat.	сему̀ блаженому	сеи блаже́нои[c]	сему̀ блаженому
acc.	сего блаже́наго[a]	сию̀ блажену́ю	сиѐ блаже́ное
voc.	ѡ̀ блажене	ѡ̀ блаженаа	ѡ̀ блаже́ное
abl.	ѿ сегѡ̀ блаженаго	ѿ сее блаже́ныıе[d]	ѡ сего блаже́наго

Plural (all genders)

nom.	сі́и̇ блаже́нни̇
gen.	сих[e] блаженьіх
dat.	сѣм блаженьім
acc.	[omitted]
voc.	ѽ блаже́ньіа[f]
abl.	ѽ сих блаженьіх

[a]суастливагѡ [b]О2 сі́а̇ [c]бога́тѣи, честнѣи
[d]суастливьіа, богатьіа, честньіа; О2 сеа̇ блаженьіа
[e]О2 сѣх [f]суа́стливні̇, бога́тні̇, честні̇і̇, О2 блаженні
masc.; *idem* with -ьіа fem., -аѧ neut.

The most notable feature of these adjectival paradigms is their mixture of older (or Ch. Sl.) and newer (or Russian) endings, e.g. gen. sing. fem. сее Kaz. but сі́а̇ О2, dat. sing. fem. блаженои, суастливои but бога́тѣи, честнѣи. We can also note in passing that the masc. sing. has a correct archaic vocative, while the feminine and neuter use a long-form adjective for the voc., contrasted with the short-form nominatives. One also notes the somewhat insouciant attitude toward external form (single vs. double -н- in the stem, final -о vs. -ѡ, -ьіа vs. -ьіѧ, etc.), an attitude which contrasts this Latin-based grammar with most Greek-based mss., which are, generally, at least concerned with and often obsessed by such externals.

8.1.1.2.6 The **sixth declension** apparently represents the Latin fourth declension in *-us, -ūs* (*fructus, fructūs*), perhaps given as a separate gender type because the fourth declension contains nouns of all three genders (*fructus* m., *domus* f., *cornū* n.). The illustrative paradigm is a straightforward masculine:

SIXTH DECLENSION

	Singular	Plural
nom.	сеи плод	сѣ плодьі̇
gen.	сего плода̇	сѣх плодо́въ
dat.	сему плоду	сѣмъ плодомъ[a]
acc.	сего плода	сѣх плодовъ
voc.	ѽ плод	ѽ плодове
abl.	ѽ сего плода	ѽ сих плодовъ
	[a]О2 сѣмо плодома	

Here one is struck by the use of -ове as a vocative marker in the plural (whereas the sing. has no separate voc.), and by the gen.-acc. of both numbers, which is unwarranted in a Slavic grammar, although partially explained as a response not to a non-existent Latin gen.-acc., but to the Latin distinction between nom. and acc., at least in the sing. of masc. and feminine nouns (*fructus - fructum, domus - domum*). The scribe, looking for an acc. different from the nom. (as *-um* to *-us*), quite naturally borrowed his own gen.-acc. from the animate nouns, doubtless also influenced by the gen. after negation in inanimates as well.

8.1.1.2.7 The **seventh declension** is an ordinary fifth-declension Latin noun simply transliterated into Cyrillic, at least right down to the abl. plur., where the translator apparently couldn't resist the urge to insert a translation:

SEVENTH DECLENSION

	Singular	Plural
nom.	сна̀ спеснесъ	сѐ спеснѐсъ
gen.	сеѧ спеснї	сѣх спеснерүм
dat.	сѐн спеснї	сѣм спесневүс
acc.	сню̀ спеснемъ	сѣх спеснѐсъ
voc.	ѿ спеснѐсъ	ѿ спеснесъ
abl.	ѿ сеѧ спеснѐ	ѿ сих́ъ лѣпотъ

The scribe of O2 tries to Slavonize this paradigm, for example by substituting a Russian nom.-acc. for the Latin acc. -емъ of Kaz., but the result is a mish-mash which could hardly have been very informative to students of either language:

	Singular	Plural
nom.	спецьіе̋съ	[спеснесъ]
gen.	сїа̀ спецьіе̋съ[a]	спецьї
dat.	спецьіе	спецьіе̋съ
acc.	спецьіѐсъ	спесьіе̋сьї
voc.	спецьіе̋съ	спецьї
abl.	спецьіѐ	сих́ъ спецне̋съ

[a] Jagić 542 f.n. 6 "ошибочно"; the scribe might
have been thinking of forms like *vīs, vīs*.

This paradigm is followed by a paragraph explaining the various translations of *species* (лѣпота, ѿбразъ, бьітнѐ, etc.), but devoid of grammatical information.

8.1.1.3 Conclusions. This concludes the survey of individual paradigms. From the point of view of Russian morphology, they are interesting in several ways.

There is usually no separate voc. form, but in three instances the old voc. is retained (магѝстере, мѹдрости, блажене), and in two further instances an innovative voc. is created, by the use of the long-form adjectives opposed to the short forms of the nom. (блаженаӕ/блаженна, блажено / блажено) in one and by opposing a new plur. -ове to the older (ex.-acc.) -ы in the nom. (плодове̇/ плоды).

In the choice of endings, the Donatus paradigms show a mixture of archaism and innovation. The *a-stem dative plur. is extended to other stem types only in the neuter сѣдалищам, cf. ѹчителемъ, erroneous магистрыи, мѹдростемъ, сопелемъ, свѧщенникомъ, плодомъ. The old *i_2 plur. is reflected only in the к ~ ц alternation of свѧщенницы and the adj. блаженнїи; elsewhere, the old acc. *y has taken over (магистры, плоды). The gen. plur. of masc. has only the new -овъ (ѹчителевъ, свѧщенниковъ, плодовъ), with the exception of O2's adjectival genitive магистровы (paralleling the gen. sing. магистерово).[113] One must also note the innovative Gt. Russ. treatment of tense jers in gen.-acc.-abl. plur. мѹдростеи, сопелеи.

As mentioned, the accompanying pronouns will be discussed separately below (cf. pp. 91 ff. below).

8.1.2 The pronoun. After a lengthy question-and-answer drill on the Latin declension endings, containing nothing of interest to Slavic grammar, the Donatus translation proceeds to an examination of the pronoun. This second part of speech shares five grammatical categories with the noun (missing only comparison, but adding person). The pronominal categories are exemplified as follows.

8.1.2.1.1. Quality in pronouns refers not to proper vs. common, as in nouns, but to "finite" (ѹконѹалные , *pronomina finita*) pronouns which express person (ты, тои, ӧнсица) vs. the "non-finite" (неѹконѹалныа , *p. infinita*), which do not (кто, кои, etc.).

8.1.2.1.2 Gender is the same as in nouns: masculine (мѹжскиӥ), e.g. которыи (Jagić's correction for Kaz. -рые; cf. O2 -рои); feminine (жѐньскиӥ), котораѧ ; neuter (посреднии), которое ; common (ӧбщее), e.g. каковъ, таковъ — it is unclear in what sense these show common gender —; trigendered (трех родовъ) or universal (всѧческиӥ родъ), e.g. азъ, ты, своегȯ.

8.1.2.1.3 There are two **numbers,** singular (единьственое), e.g. сѐи, and plural (множественое), сиӥ.

8.1.2.1.4 Form (ӧбразъ), as in the noun, refers to the simple (единородныи) vs. complex (сложныи) morphological status of the pronoun, e.g. кто, кои and ктȯ тои (= *quisquis*; O2 кто то) respectively.

8.1.2.1.5 Case is not mentioned in the introduction to pronoun paradigms, but the latter show nom., gen., dat., acc., and abl., i.e. all but the voc. (ТЫ I and ВЫ I, however, do have the vocatives ѽ ТЫ I, ѽ ВЫ I).

8.1.2.1.6 Finally, there are three **persons**, first (пе́рвое), second (второе), and third (третне), illustrated by азъ, ты, and то́н (in margin, ѽнъсица) respectively.

8.1.2.2 Pronominal paradigms fall into four groups, not very clearly distinguished by the paragraphing of the Donatus translation: (.1) personal (азъ, ты, мы, вы, plus a mixed себ-/сво- reflexive; (.2) three demonstrative series (той, ѽнъ, сен); (.3) interrogative (кто, которын, кон); (.4) possessive (мон, твон, свон, нашъ, вашъ); the labels are ours, not in Donatus. We rearrange them here into the customary tabular form.

8.1.2.2.1 Personal pronouns exist only for the first and second persons (the third-person pronouns seemingly occupy an intermediate position between the personal and demonstrative categories), but include a strange mixed reflexive paradigm.

PERSONAL PRONOUNS

Singular

	first person	second person
nom.	а́зъ, га́зъ	ты̀
gen.	моегѡ, мое	твое, твоего[a]
dat.	мнѣ	тебѣ
acc.	мене̄	тебе̄
abl.	ѽ мене̄	ѽ тебе̄
[voc.	———]	ѽ ты̀

Plural

	first person	second person
nom.	мы̀	вы̀
gen.	на́шего, наше	ва́ше, ва́шего[b]
dat.	на́мъ	ва́мъ
acc.	насъ	васъ
abl.	ѽ нас	ѽ вас
[voc.	———]	ѽ вы I

[a]*Sic* O2; Kaz. твоемү ілн твоего
[b]*Sic* O2; Kaz. ва́шего нлн ва́шемү

REFLEXIVE

	Singular	Plural
nom.	—	—
gen.	своего	своихᵃ
dat.	себѣ	своим, себѣ[b]
acc.	себе̃	себе самѣх
abl.	ѿ себе̃	ѿ себе̃ самѣх

[a] О2 своего [b] своим is mistakenly given before the gen.

One of the most striking features of these paradigms is their treatment of "genitive" as a kind of deep-structure possessive case which surfaces as a possessive adjective (cf. similar facts in the nominal paradigm, e.g. p. 81 and f.n. 113). In all four personal pronouns, possessivity is both singly and doubly marked, the latter by the genitive case of the possessive adjective. The double marking is parallel to, and may have been inspired by, the Latin *ego*, gen. *mei*, *mei* being etymologically the gen. not of *ego* but of its poss. adj. *meus*.[114] There is no trace of the gen. pronouns мене, тебе, насъ, васъ as such, although they do appear as gen.-accusatives and as ablatives. The same confusion of derivational vs. syntactic possessive-(= gen.-)marking appears in the reflexive своего (cf. abl. себе). The disparity in the reflexive plur. between Kaz. своих and О2 своего indicates a similar hesitation about the proper referent of the category being signalled (here, number): plurality of the possessor (subjective pluralization) would still be своего, but plurality of the thing possessed (etc.) (objective pluralization) would require the surface marking своих (cf. similar confusion in plural marking in the treatise "О множествѣ и о единствѣ", p. 51 above). The added самѣх of the acc. and abl. plur. is of course only an attempt to render explicit the intended subjective pluralization.

In passing, we must also note that, alone among the pronouns, ты and вы do have vocative forms ѿ ты, ѿ вы.

8.1.2.2.2 The **demonstrative pronouns** include all three sets (in *t-*, *s-*, and *on-*), but the Donatus translation makes no attempt to distinguish them functionally, nor is it clear whether they form a coherent group or are taken as third-person personal pronouns (the fact that the reflexive себ-/сво- set comes in between the азъ-мы-ты-вы set and this тóн-ѿнъ-сен set would speak against such a view, however). The paradigms are:

то́н

	masculine	feminine	neuter	plural
nom.	то́н	та	то̀	тѣ̀
gen.	того̀	тоѐ[a]	того̀	тѣ́хъ
dat.	тому̀	то́н	тому̀	тѣ́мъ
acc.	того̀	ту̀	то	тѣ́х
abl.	ѿ того̀	ѿ тоѐ	ѿ тогѡ	ѿ тѣ́х

[a]O2 тоѧ

ѽнъ

	masculine	feminine	neuter	plural
nom.	ѽнъ	ѽна́	ѽно̀	ѽни, ѽнѣ, ѽна
gen.	ѽнаго[a]	ѽно ѧ	[omitted]	ѽнѣх
dat.	ѽному	ѽнон	ѽному	ѽнѣ́мъ[b]
acc.	[omitted]	ѽну	ѽного	ѽна [m., f. omitted]
abl.	ѿ ѽнаго[a]	ѿ ѽное	ѿ ѡнаго	ѿ ѽнѣх

[a]O2 ѽного   [b]but masc. ѽнема

The main point of interest in these two paradigms is the vacillation between Ch. Sl. and Russian endings in the gen. sing. fem.: тоѐ Kaz. vs. тоѧ O2, and within Kaz., gen. ѽно ѧ (a hybrid between онь ѧ and оноѣ), abl. ѽное; cf. also the -аго vs. -ого masc. forms, and the "animate" neuter accusative ѽного.

The near-object demonstrative сен appears twice, in nearly identical forms, (a) first as a translation of *ille, ipse* and *iste* and (b) again to render *hic*. We give the paradigm according to (a), with variants from (b):

сен

	masculine	feminine	neuter	plural
nom.	се́н	сна̀	снѐ	сні́, сѣ̀, сна̀[c]
gen.	сего̀	се ѧ[a]	сего̀	сѣ́х
dat.	сему̀	се́н	сему̀	сѣ́мъ[d]
acc.		сн ю̀		
abl.	ѿ сего̀	ѿ се ѧ[b]	ѿ сего̀	ѿ сѣ́х

[a](b) сѣѐ and O2 (b) се́н   [b](b) ѿ сеѧ   [c]In O2 (a) has the masc. plur. gen. снх, dat. снмъ and сѣ́мъ, abl. ѿ снхъ; in (b) the nom. plur. masc. = fem. сѣ̀
[d]fem. сѣма in both (a) and (b).

This formal paradigm can be supplemented by material from the pronominal forms accompanying the nominal paradigms on pp. 80-87 above.[115] There, we find a nom. sing. masc. сн in the O2 магнстеръ paradigm, and two instances of abl. sing. masc. ѿ сегѡ, in which the omega represents an attempt to find a graphic equivalent to Latin gen. -*i* vs. abl. -*o*. The gen. sing. fem. shows both Ch. Sl. and native endings and vacillation between *e* and *i* in the stem (сее 2x; снѐ; сїа̀, сїѧ̀, сеѧ), whereas the ablative shows a 6:1 predominance of Ch. Sl. forms (сеѧ 6x, сее 1x); one can draw the conclusion from this that the Ch. Sl. -ѧ ending was felt as more exotic than the native -е (< *ě*) and therefore used more consistently with the abl., which was more exotic to our educated 16th c. Russians than the gen., — in other words, even in a normative type of grammar, Ch. Sl. played a secondary role. In the plural, the noun-accompanying pronouns show more е ~ н stem variation than the formal paradigm (dat. plur. neut. сѣмъ, снм, снма acc. plur. masc. сѣх, снх, etc.). It seems clear from these ancillary сен paradigms that the pronominal system was in a greater state of flux than the "official" paradigm would indicate.

The last demonstrative pronoun paradigm, which tries to render *is, ea, id* into Slavic, is an incoherent jumble of **s-*, **t-*, and **jь-* forms, which we adduce more for completeness' sake than for the insights it provides into Slavic grammar:

	masculine		feminine		neuter	
	sing.	plur.	sing.	plur.	sing.	plur.
nom.	сѐ	снѧ̀	снѩ̀	сѣ̀	то	тѣ̀
gen.	егò	нх	сеѧ̀	снх	сегò	тѣх
dat.	емꙋ̀	нмъ	—	снма	семꙋ̀	тѣм
acc.	—	нх	снѭ	—	снѐ, тогò[a]	та
abl.	ѿ его	ѿ ннх	ѿ сеа	ѿ снх	ѿ того	ѿ тѣх

[a] ms. order снѐ, семꙋ̀, тогò

O2 has a somewhat more consistent version of this same mixed paradigm.

	masculine		feminine		neuter	
	sing.	plur.	sing.	plur.	sing.	plur.
nom.	се	снѧ	сїа̀	се	тò	тѣ
gen.	егò	нх	еа̀	нхъ	ѐгò	тѣхъ
dat.	ёмоу̀	нмъ	ен̇	іма̀	ёмоу̀	тѣмъ
acc.	ѐгò	нх̇ъ	—	—	тогò	та̀
abl.	ѿ сего	ѿ ннхъ	ѿ еѧ̀	ѿ ннхъ	ѿ того	ѿ тѣхъ

(Jagić appends a series of corrections, e.g. nom. sing. masc. сє "ѵнтаӣ сєӣ", but I see no need to try to improve on the original confusion.)

Even in such a morphological thicket of variant stem shapes as this, one discerns a few features typical of the grammar of this period, for example the dat. plur. fem. in -ма (cf. сѣма in the regular сєн paradigm on p. 91) and the pseudo-gen.-acc. sing. neut. того̀ (cf. the discussion of сѣх плодовъ, p. 86 above). As a curiosity deserving further textual investigation, let us note that the prothetic н- occurs only before stressed и́ (or, in the plur.), not before unstressed є (or, in the sing.), e.g. Kaz. ѿ єго, O2 ѿ єꙗ, but both mss. ѿ ни́хъ.

8.1.2.2.3 There is a single (indefinite and) **interrogative pronoun** paradigm, corresponding to the Latin *quis, qui*:

INTERROGATIVE PRONOUN

	masc. sing.	fem. sing.	masc. + fem. plur.
nom.	кто̀, кото́рыӣ	коꙗ, кото́раꙗ	кото́рні
gen.	коєго	ко́єꙗ	ко́ихъ
dat.	коємѵ	ко́єӣ	ко́имъ, которы́мъ
acc.	кото́раго	коюᲂ	—
abl.	ѿ коєго, котораго	ѿ коєꙗ, которы́а	ѿ ко́ихъ, которы́х

	neut. sing.	neut. plur.
nom.	ѵто̀, єже, ко́є	ко́ꙗ, кото̀раѧ
gen.	коєго	кото́рых
dat.	коємѵ	ко́имъ, кото́рым
acc.	єже, ѵто̀	ко́ꙗ, кото́раꙗ
abl.	ѿ коєго, котораго	ѿ ко́ихъ, которых

Aside from the promiscuous mixing of stems, the only notable things here are the nom. plur. fem. ≡ masc., and the absence of -ма in the dat. plur.

8.1.2.2.4 The Donatus translation has possessive pronouns for the 1st and 2nd persons sing. and plur., and the reflexive. Curiously, the 1st person pronouns, sing. and plur., have vocative forms, while those of the 2nd person do not.

POSSESSIVE PRONOUNS

First Person Singular

	masculine	feminine	neuter	plural
nom.	мо́й	мо ѧ̀	мое	мо́и, мо́й, мо ѧ̀
gen.	моего̀	мое ѧ̀	моего̀	мои́х
dat.	моемѵ̀	мое́й	моемѵ̀	мои́м
acc.	—	мо ю̀	—	мои́хъ, мо ѧ̀
voc.	ѿ мои	ѿ мо ѧ̀	ѿ мое	ѿ мои
abl.	ѿ моего	ѿ моеѧ̀	ѿ моего̀	ѿ мои́хъ

Second Person Singular

	masculine	feminine	neuter	plural
nom.	тво́й	тво ѧ̀	твоѐ	тво́и, тво ѧ̀
gen.	твоего̀	твое ѧ̀	твоегѡ	твои́х
dat.	твоемѵ̀	твое́й	твоемѵ̀	твои́м
acc.	—	тво ю̀	—	твои
abl.	ѿ твоего	ѿ твое ѧ̀	ѿ твоего	ѿ твои́х

REFLEXIVE

	masculine	feminine	neuter	plural
nom.	свой	сво ѧ̀	свое	свои, сво ѧ
gen.	своего̀	свое ѧ̀	своего	свои́х
dat.	своемѵ̀	свое́й	своемѵ̀	свои́мъ
acc.	—	сво ю̀	—	
abl.	ѿ своего	ѿ свое ѧ̀	ѿ своего	ѿ свои́х

First Person Plural

	masculine	feminine	neuter	plural
nom.	нашь	на́ша	на́ше	на́ши, наша
gen.	на́шего	на́шеѧ	на́шего	на́ших
dat.	на́шемѵ	на́шеи	на́шемѵ	на́шим
acc.	—	нашѵ	—	
voc.	ѿ на́шъ	ѿ наша	ѿ наше	ѿ на́ши
abl.	ѿ нашего	ѿ нашеѧ	ѿ на́шего	ѿ на́ших

Second Person Plural

	masculine	feminine	neuter	plural
nom.	ва́шъ	ваша	ваше	ва́ши, ваша
gen.	ва́шего	вашеа	ва́шего	ва́шихъ
dat.	ва́шемү	ва́шеи	вашемү	ва́шимъ
acc.	—	вашү	O2 вашего	—, ва́ша
abl.	ѿ вашего	ѿ ваше ѩ	ѿ вашего	ѿ ва́шихъ

These paradigms are quite straightforward; aside from the already-noted fact that only the 1st person paradigms include the voc., one notes: (1) the puzzling absence of accusative forms in the masc., the neut., and in 3/5 of the plur.; (2) the fact that masc. and fem. nom. plur. are identical, with no trace of -ѧ etc., (3) the gen. and abl. sing. fem. occur only in the Ch. Sl. form in -ѧ etc.; (4) O2's neut. "gen.-acc." вашего (cf. pp. 86, 91 above).

This concludes the description of pronouns in the Donatus grammar.

8.1.3 **The verb** is treated in two different parts of the Donatus grammar, an outline of the grammatical categories expressed by the verb (Jagić 551-555), and a complete set of paradigms, appearing as a kind of review lesson after the end of the eighth and last part of speech (Jagić 565-584). For convenience, we combine them into a single, albeit very large section here.

8.1.3.1 The verb is defined as a part of speech expressing tense and person but not case ("ча́сть вѣща́нна съ временем и́ лицем, бе́з падежніа" 551), and is either active, or passive, or both ("или дѣѩти нѣчто или страда́ти . . . или ѡ҃боє знамениѩ" ibid.). The verb expresses seven grammatical categories, which are somewhat confusingly titled: ка́чество, согласніе, род, число̀, ѡ҃браз, времѧ, and лицѐ; it turns out, however, that ка́чество subsumes both mood (зало́гъ or чинъ) and ѡ҃бразъ, so the actual seven verbal categories total eight, as follows.

8.1.3.1.1 Moods (чи́нове or зало́ги) are six in the Donatus translation, including not only the traditional indicative (указа́телньіи, e.g. утѵ̀), imperative (повели́телньіи, ути́), conjunctive[116] (сло́жньіи, егда̀ утү) and infinitive (неконча́льнь і и Kaz., нескон⁵ уа́телньі и O2, чести), but also a separate optative (жела́емьіи, да [etc.] бьіх че́лъ) rendering various *ut*- phrases (e.g. present and past imperfect ѿ люблю̀, O2 ѡ҃х люблю̀, *utinam amarem*, cf. p. 104 below), and an impersonal form (безличньіи, уте́тсѩ) presented as a separate mood.

8.1.3.1.2 Form (ѡ҃бразъ) appears twice in the list of verbal categories. Here, it refers to various kinds of intraverbal aktionsart derivation (inchoatives, interatives, desideratives, etc.). Four such forms are mentioned: (.1) inceptive (?), совершеньіи (утү), (.2) meditative or intensive, любомудр-

ствьнъіи (also called поочүателны҄, прилѣ́жныӏ҄и, поглу-
мателныӏи ; да үтү); (.3) iterative, үүащае́мыӏи (поүнта́ю); (.4)
inchoative, начинателныӏи (разгрѣюсѧ, согрѣваюсѧ). These
categories play no role in the verbal paradigms themselves. For the more usual
meaning of ѻ҄бразъ see 8.1.3.1.6.

    8.1.3.1.3 Verbal **concord** refers to conjugation ending types, of which
there are three. The first contains verbs in *-a*, the second those in *-e*, and the
third those in *-i*. The illustrations are translated in Kaz. but transliterated in O2,
e.g. Kaz. люблю̀, лю́бишъ = O2 амо (ms. моа̀), ама̀а̀съ , or Kaz.
ѵ́ую̀, ѵ́ую̀сѧ = O2 доцеѿ, доцеѿръ, etc., none of which tells us
anything about Slavic grammar.

    8.1.3.1.4 Voice ("gender", родъ словныӏи) consists of (.1) active
(дѣлниӥ), (.2) passive (страдални̏и), (.3) medial (посредственнӥ), (.4)
deponent (?),= (ѿложнӥи), and (.5) "common" (ѻ҄бщӥи), apparently also
deponents (*osculor, criminor*). Only active and passive voices are illustrated in
the paradigms, and the others are of no importance for our topic.

    8.1.3.1.5 Number consists only of singular (еди́ньственое, үтү) and
plural (множественое, үтемъ); there is no attempt to introduce a Slavic
dual.

    8.1.3.1.6 Form[2] (ѻ҄бразъ) has the same meaning as in other parts of
speech, i.e. simple (еднноряднын) vs. compound (сло́жныӏи), e.g. үтү
and небрегү respectively.

    8.1.3.1.7 There are three **tenses** (or temporal categories): present
(настоѩщее, e.g. үтѹ́), past (мину́вшее, үтохъ), and future (гр҄ѧ-
дүщ[е]е, поүтү), but five separate tense forms in conjugation, since the
past is split into past imperfect (мину́вшее несовершеное, e.g.
поүтох), past perfect (м. совершеное, Kaz. поүтох, O2 үтох),[117] and
past pluperfect (м. пресовершеное, үнтах).

    8.1.3.1.8 Finally, **person** has the usual three members, first (первое, e.g.
үтү), second (второе, үтеши), and third (третие, үтѐтъ).

    The instructional program then calls for the teacher to discuss the verb
briefly before moving on to the remaining parts of speech ("здѣ ѵчитель
[O2 магистеръ] побеседовал вкра́тцѣ... ѻ҄ словѣ, и̇ а҆ще
. . . совершѝтель [i.e., God-DW] пода́стъ време, и̇ ѵчитель
предложитъ беседы҄ı вкратцѣ і ѻ҄ про́чихъ пѧти ѵа́стеи
вѣщанїѧ [O2]..."554). We too shall proceed to discuss the verb, though
hardly вкратцѣ.

    The following discussion is based on material in Jagić 556-584.

    8.1.3.2 The Russian Donatus translation follows the original in giving the
entire first conjugation paradigm (любнтн, *amare*) and then the second
(ѵунтн, *docere*), third (ѵестн, *legere*), fourth (слы́шатн, *audire*), and
irregular conjugations (хотѣтн *volere*; бы́тн, *esse*; Donatus also included
ferre, omitted from the translation). However, since we are interested not in the

Latin verb itself but in the Slavic forms by which the Latin was translated, we shall proceed not by conjugation but by the individual mood and tense paradigms, treating for example the present indicative of all (Latin) conjugation types together, and then proceeding to the other indicative paradigms, and so on.

The Donatus verb system, as it appears in the actual paradigms, has five moods (indicative, imperative, optative, conjunctive,[118] infinitive), plus a few participial and gerundive forms. There are five tenses in all, although only the indicative and conjunctive moods have all five. Each tense-mood paradigm has active (transitive) and passive voices, the latter formed with -сѧ or a passive participle construction; in addition, there is a third person singular impersonal form (also in -сѧ or a passive participle) corresponding to each active paradigm. The individual finite paradigms have two numbers, with three persons in each number, except for the imperative, which has no first person singular forms. Not surprisingly in an attempt to fit Slavic verbs to a Latin mold, the translation shows a good many hesitations and inconsistencies.

We shall examine first the **active voice (8.1.3.2.1)**, then the passive (8.1.3.2.2), and finally the impersonal forms (8.1.3.2.3).

8.1.3.2.1.1 The **indicative** mood (ѵ҆ка́зателныи ѵинъ) has a present, a future, and three past tenses (past imperfect, p. perfect, and p. pluperfect).[119]

8.1.3.2.1.1.1 The active **indicative present** (сло́во дѣлное, ѵ҆ка́зательн ым ѵиномъ глаголемо, вре́мени настоѧ́щего) is rendered by straightforward present imperfective forms:

PRESENT INDICATIVE

1st conj.		2nd conj.	
люблю̀	лю́бимъ	ѵ҆у ю̀	ѵ҆у́имъ
лю́биши	лю́би́те	ѵ҆у́иши	ѵ҆у́ите
лю́бит	лю́бѧт	ѵ҆у́ит	ѵ҆у́ѧт

3rd conj.		4th conj.	
ѵту̀	ѵтемъ	слы́шу	слы́шимъ
ѵтеши	ѵте́те	слы́шиши	слы́шите
ѵтет	ѵтѵ́т	слы́шит	слы́шат

Except for omitted weak jers (ѵтѵ̀ etc.) and inconsistencies in marking stress and smooth breathing (ѵ҆у́иши, but ѵу́ит, etc.),[120] this is a standard Old

Russian paradigm. The same is almost, but not quite true, of the "irregular" (безпра́вильные) verbs бытн and хотѣтн :

хощу́	хо́щем	е́смь	есмѐ
хо́щешн	хощете	е́сн	есте
хо́щет	хотѧт	есть	су́ть

The innovative 1st plural есмѐ competes with есма, есмн; see the discussion of бытн on pp. 147 ff. below. хотѣтн takes the classical Church Slavonic paradigm and *tj reflexes, although, as we shall see in the discussion on pp. 147 f. below, this was an artificial paradigm for the Russian translator.

8.1.3.2.1.1.2 The Latin **future** (грѧдущее or бу́дущее) is rendered by the Slavic perfective present-future:

FUTURE INDICATIVE

возлюблю	возлюбнмъ[a]	наүү ю	наүүнм
возлюбншн	возлюбнте	наүүншн	наүү́нте
возлюбнт тон	возлюбѧт тн̈	наүүнтъ	наүү́ѧтъ[b]
поүту́	поүтéмъ	ү́слы́шу	ү́слы́шнм
поүтéшн	поүтете	ү́слы́шншн̈	ү́слы́шнте
поүтет	поүтүт	ү́слы́шнт	ү́слы́шѧтъ
восхощу́	восхо́щемъ	бу́ү	бу́дeмъ
восхо́щешн	восхо́щете	бу́дeшн	бу́дeтe
восхощетъ	восхотѧт	бу́дeтъ	бу́дүтъ

[a] *Sic* O2; Kaz. возлюбнхомъ [b] O2 omits the prefix: оу́үнмъ, оу́үнте, да оу́ү́ѧтъ

The inceptive funtion of воз-, на-, and ү- is discussed on pp. 138 ff. below; otherwise, this paradigm requires no comment.

8.1.3.2.1.1.3 The active indicative has three **past tense** paradigms, which strive — with only moderate success — to represent the Latin past imperfect, past perfect, and past pluperfect.

8.1.3.2.1.1.3.1 The **past imperfect** (мнну́вшее несвершенное) is rendered by the Slavic (prefixed) perfective aorist, except in the second and third persons singular, which take l-participle forms:

PAST IMPERFECT INDICATIVE

полюбих	полюбихомъ	пооучихъ	пооучихом
полюбисте[a]	полюбисте	пооучил еси	пооучисте
тóи полюбил	полюбиша	пооучил	пооучиша
поутох	поутохомъ	у́слы́шах	у́слышахом
поуел еси	поутосте	у́слы́шал еси	у́слы́шасте
поуел ӧнъ	поутоша	у́слы́шал есть	у́слы́шахү[b]
похотѣхъ	похотѣхомъ	бѣхъ	бѣхом
похотѣлъ еси	похотѣсте	был еси	бѣсте
похотѣл ӧнъ	похотѣша	{был есть / был бѣ	бѣша

[a] O2 полюбилъ éсть, also incorrect for ... еси (=*amabas*). [b] Imperfect ending used instead of aorist -аша; see the discussion on pp. 143 ff. below.

Except for the obviously erroneous полюбисте, the second and third person singular forms are built on the l-participle, which requires the copula in the 2nd person and permits it in the third (у́слы́шал éсть and был éсть or бѣ). The increasing artificiality of the copula is clear from this paradigm's awkward attempt to mark the 3rd sing. forms by means of various pronouns (тóи полюбил, поуел ӧнъ, похотѣл ӧн) as well as by éсть. The past imperfect forms of быти show бы1- in the l-participle forms but the old imperfective aorist vocalism бѣ- in the aorist forms. In its stem vocalism, быти shows a strange inversion of forms in this and the following paradigm: here, in the past imperfect, in which all other verbs have perfective aorist forms (полюбих, etc.), быти takes the imperfective stem forms in бѣ-, whereas in the past perfect, where the other verbs (except любити) have unprefixed, imperfective aorists (у́учихъ, утох, слышах, хотѣхъ), быти has the old perfective aorist forms бых, бы́хомъ, etc. The alternative auxiliaries éсть and бѣ are strange in this past imperfect paradigm; such alternates appear regularly only in the passive past perfect indicative (возлюбим есмь or бых, в. еси or был еси, в. есть or был, etc.).[121]

8.1.3.2.1.1.3.2 The **past perfect** tense is formed by the Slavic imperfective aorist, except for любити, which shows prefixed forms. The O2 ms., however, has prefixless любихъ, любил еси, любилъ тóи, любихомъ, любисте, любиша or любити, i.e. forms which are equivalent to those of the other verbs of this set.

PAST PERFECT INDICATIVE

возлюбих	вѡзлюбихомъª	ѹѵих̾	ѹѵихомъ
возлюбил ты	возлюбисте	ѹѵил еси	ѹѵисте
возлюбил тон	возлюбиша и тиї ᵇ (или) возлюбити	ѹѵил тон	{ ѹѵахѹ ѹѵиша

ѹтох̾	ѹтохомъ	слы̀шах̾	слы̀шахом
ѹелъ еси	ѹтосте	слы̀шал еси	слы̀шасте
ѹел ѡнсица	{ ѹтоша ѹести	слы̀шалъ	{ слы̀шаша ѹ́слы̀шати

хотѣх̾	хотѣхом	бых̾	бы̀хомъ
хотѣл еси	хотѣсте	был еси	бы̀сте
хотѣлъ ѡн	{ хотѣша хотѣти	бы̀сть	бы̀ша

ª The omega of 1st plur. вѡзлюбихомъ may represent an isolated attempt to mark plurality; cf. pp. 22,52 above. ᵇ As Jagić points out, the infinitive represents an unsuccessful attempt to render *amavere* etc.

As was the case with the past imperfect, this past perfect paradigm utilizes l-participle forms in the second and third person singular. The copula еси appears in all 2nd sing. forms except возлюбил ты (but *n.b.* О2 любилъ есѝ), where it is replaced by the pronoun ты, elsewhere used to distinguish second- from third-person forms (future opt. ind. да бы ты возлюбил / да бы тон возлюбил), and in the быти paradigm, which shows the traditional aorist бы́сть, probably for no deeper reason than that the expected былъ есть had been preempted in the preceding past imperfect paradigm (where, in turn, the use of бы̀лъ е́сть was caused by the non-existence of an l-participle with the stem vocalism -ѣ-, i.e. *бѣлъ е́сть). The 3rd person of other sing. forms is so marked by the pronoun тон, ѡн, ѡнсица, as is the 3rd plur. возлюбиша и̇ тиї. The 3rd plur. has the correct -ша ending everywhere, although ѹѵити gives the imperfect ѹѵахѹ as well.

  8.1.3.2.1.1.3.3 The **past pluperfect** of Latin is rather cleverly rendered into Slavic by iterative imperfective aorists, which although not expressing the continuity (or continued relevance) of a perfect tense, do mark the fact that the action occurred in the distant past and does not continue into the present. The forms:

PAST PLUPERFECT INDICATIVE

любливах		любливахомъ	
любливаше		любливасте	
любливал тон		любливаху тиї	
ѹѹнвах		ѹѹнвахом	
{ ѹѹнваше / ты̌ ѹѹнвалъ }		ѹѹнвасте	
ѹѹнвал тон		ѹѹнваху	

унтах	унтахом	слыхах	слыхáхомъ [c]
унтáше	унтасте	слыхалъ еси̍ [b]	слыхасте [c]
унталъ [a]	{ унтахѹ / унташа }	слыхалъ тон	слыхахѹ

хаунвах	хаунвахомъ	{ бѣх / быхвах }	бывáхом
хаунвал еси	хаунвасте	бывал еси	бывáсте
хаунвал	хаунвали	бѣаше	бывáхѹ

[a] Added from O2, missing from Kaz. [b] From O2; Kaz. has erroneous plural forms. [c] O2 has non-iterative stems: слышахомъ, слышасте

This paradigm has a number of interesting features. The 2nd sing. permits the old imperfect -аше in любливаше, унтáше alongside the l-participle forms слыхалъ еси̍, хаунвал еси, бывал еси, and gives both alternatives for ѹунти. The 3rd sing. бѣаше is one of the few non-l-participle 3rd sing. forms in the entire Donatus grammar (but cf. active optative past perfect-pluperfect wх ѹунваше). The copula is used in 2nd sing. слыхалъ еси̍, хаунвал еси, and бывал еси, but is replaced by a pronoun in ты̌ ѹѹнвалъ; pronouns also mark the third person in sing. любливал тон, ѹѹнвал тон, слыхалъ тон and plur. любливаху тиї. The 3rd plur. forms are mostly those of the old imperfect -ахѹ, but унтати also has the aorist унташа; хотѣти, interestingly, uses an l-participle form for the 3rd plur., as if the obsolete simple past tense endings were even harder to combine with the clearly innovative stem хаунва- (with E. Sl. *$tj > č$) than with more traditional stems. The быти paradigm shows the same aberrant stem vocalism as we have seen above: 1st and 3rd sing. бѣх, бѣаше, but бы- everywhere else, but the doublet бѣх ~ бывах is restricted to the 1st sing., although in auxiliary usage such doublets occur elsewhere as well, e.g. passive indicative past pluperfect ѹтени бѣхомъ ~ бывáхомъ, ѹтени бѣша ~ быша, etc.

8.1.3.2.1.2 The **active imperative** mood has paradigms for both present and future tenses, with imperative forms for all persons and numbers except the first person singular. Formally, the imperative mood is expressed by an inconsistent grab-bag of imperative, indicative, and да + indicative forms.

8.1.3.2.1.2.1 The **present imperative** paradigms are as follows:

PRESENT IMPERATIVE

		да любимъ		—	(да) ѹчим
	люби	да любите		ѹчи	(да) ѹчите
{да любитъ {да любилъ[a]		да любатъ і ѿни	да ѹчитъ	(да) ѹчатъ	
	—	ѹтемъ		—	да слышим
	ѹти	ѹтите[b]		{слѹшаи, {слыши	слѹшанте
да ѹтет		да ѹтѹтъ		да слышитъ	да слѹшаѭт

	—	бѹдем	
	бѹди[c]	{бѹдете {есте	
	да бѹдетъ	да бѹдѹтъ	

[a] Jagić considers да любилъ a "лишняя прибавка, нарушающая смысл" (567 f.n. 3), but could this not be a contamination of да любитъ and vernacular ѹтоб(ы) любилъ? [b] O2 ѹтете, probably reflecting older ѹьтѣте [c] ms. erroneously бѹѵ

The 2nd sing. forms are the expected imperatives люби, ѹчи, ѹти, бѹди, with lexically-conditioned root variation in слѹшаи ~ слыши. The 2nd plur. is somewhat less regular: only ѹтите and слѹшанте (this time without the alternant *слышите) show usual imperative forms, while любити and ѹчити utilize да- compounds, and быти has both the simple future бѹдете (perhaps a degenerate descendent of бѹдѣте) and the да-less present есте. The 1st plur. has да + present compounds in three verbs and simple indicative plurals in the other two. Third person plur. forms all have да, which as noted occurs with both indicative and l-participle forms for любити . The *audire* translation has слѹшаѭт instead of the слышатъ that we might expect by analogy with да слышитъ, да слышим ; this слѹш- form is probably just induced from the immediately preceding 2nd plur. слѹшанте .

8.1.3.2.1.2.2 The **future imperative** utilizes prefixed perfective stems in the cases of возлюб-, наѹч- and ѹслыш-, and the simple perfective future бѹд-. The fact that ѹести uses the unprefixed ѹтешн, ѹтет etc., along with such other variation peculiar to this verb as 3rd plur. проүнта ют, probably shows that үести was in the process of being replaced by үнтати at this time (*n.b.* the alternant 3rd plur. forms да үтүт ~ проүнта ют). The paradigms are as follows:

FUTURE IMPERATIVE

—	возлюбимъ
да возлюбиши ты̀	возлюбите
да возлюбит и тон	⎧ да возлюбатъ
	⎩ возлюбат и тӹï
—	да наүчим
да наүчиши ты̀	да наүчите
да наүчит тон	да наүчат
	(или) иӡүчат
—	да үтемъ
да үтеши ты̀ ⎤ᵃ	да үтете
да үтет тон ⎦	⎧ да үтүт
	⎩ да проүнта ют
	ў слы̀шим
ў слы̀ши ты̀	⎧ ў слы̀шите
	⎩ послы̀шите
ў слы̀шит тон	[omitted]
	бүдемъ
да бүдеши	⎧ да бүдете
	⎨ бүдите
	⎩ бы̀ти имате
да бүдете тон	[omitted]

ᵃO2 да поүтеши ты̀, да поүтетъ тон

Most of the second-person future imperatives use да, but возлюбите omits it, as does the entire paradigm of слышати. The 2nd sing. forms all add the pronoun ты̀, although person is unambiguously marked by verbal -ши; similarly, the 3rd sing. always has (и) тон. The third plural shows the most variation, with любити marking the imperative mood both by да and, alternatively, by the emphatic-particle-plus-pronoun construction возлюбат и тӹï. Үнти shows both на- and иӡ-, the latter perhaps an attempt to render 'study' as opposed to 'learn' (cf. the слүш-/слыш- variation discussed above and the alternative 2nd plur. form in ү- and по- in the present paradigm). вы́ти omits the 3rd plur. form altogether, but compensates for this oversight by a surabundance of 2nd plurals, including the genetically spurious вудите and the compound future вы́ти и́мате.

8.1.3.2.1.3 The **active optative** mood has three paradigms, one serving both present and past imperfect, a second for both perfect and pluperfect past, and a third for the future tense. Since no optative forms have any corresponding Slavic expressions, the translator is reduced to various more or less artificial combinations of tense endings with prefixed шх, да, вы, and pronominal forms.

8.1.3.2.1.3.1 The **present and past imperfect** optative of the four "regular" conjugations is expressed by imperfective present forms, prefaced by шх in the case of ꙋчити and слы́шати, by шх да in that of ꙗ́сти, and by ѿ, да, or ѿ да with любити (in the case of любити it is possible that the translator intended the ѿ to be understood as elliptically present in the 2nd and 3rd person forms as well). In the "irregular" хотѣти and вы́ти, on the other hand the paradigms consist not of a present but of the past imperfect tense forms (похотѣх, etc.), preceded by шх (with no да). The paradigms:

PRESENT AND PAST IMPERFECT OPTATIVE

ѿ	любл҄ю[a]	ѿ да	любимъ	шх	ꙋю́	шх	ꙋчимъ
да	любиши	да	любите		ꙋ́чиши		ꙋчите
да	любитъ	да	любатъ		ꙋ́чит		ꙋчатъ

шх да	ꙋтꙋ́	шх да	ꙋтем	шх	слы́шꙋ[b]	шх	слы́шимъ
да	ꙋтеши	да	ꙋтете		слы́шиши		слы́шите
да	ꙋтетъ	да	ꙋтꙋт		слы́шитъ		слы́шат

шх	похотѣх	шх	похотѣхомъ	шх	бѣх	шх	бѣхомъ
	похотѣлъ еси		похотѣсте		былъ еси		бѣсте
	похотѣлъ		похотѣша		былъ бѣ		бѣша

[a]O2 шх любл҄ю =*utinam amarem* [b]O2 ꙋслы́шꙋ

Here as throughout, любити uses ѿ (with the barytone stress mark specific to the exclamation "oh!"; cf. pp. 32-33 above), corresponding to шх of the other conjugations. The ѿ ~ да ~ ѿ да variation with любити is best explained by the fact that the 16th century translator, working here on the first of his six Latin conjugations types, hadn't yet settled on a coherent and consistent system of Slavic-Latin correspondences; the любити paradigms, in general, tend to differ from the others taken as a group, as for example in the past perfect indicative above, in which любити alone has prefixed forms. On the other hand, there is no immediately apparent reason for the quite different verb forms in the хотѣти and вы́ти paradigms, which as mentioned above consist of ѹҳ plus the past imperfective instead of the present indicative (the past imperf. of бьітн has an alternate 3rd sing. бьіл е́сть, not repeated here in the optative).

8.1.3.2.1.3.2 The **past perfect and pluperfective** optative is rendered by the same iterative paradigms as served for the past pluperfect indicative, preceded by ѿ̀ or ѹҳ:

PAST PERFECT AND PLUPERFECT OPTATIVE

ѿ̀ лю́блнвахъ	люблнва́хомъ
люблнвалъ есн	люблнва́сте
люблнвалъ и̂ то́н	люблнва́хѵ[a]

ѹҳ ѵ́ѵнвахъ	ѹҳ ѵ́ѵнва́хом
ѹҳ ѵ́ѵнвалъ есн	ѹҳ ѵ́ѵнва́сте
ѹҳ ѵ́ѵнва́ше	ѹҳ ѵ́ѵнва́хѵ

ѹҳ ѵнта́хъ	ѹҳ ѵнта́хомъ
ѵнталъ есн	ѵнта́сте
ѵнталъ	ѵнта́хѵ́

ѹҳ слыша́хъ[b]	ѹҳ слы́ха́хомъ
слы́шалъ есн	слы́ха́сте
слы́халъ то́н	слы́ха́хѵ

ѹҳ ха́ѵнвахъ	ѹҳ ха́ѵнва́хом
ха́ѵнвалъ есн	ха́ѵнва́сте
ха́ѵнвалъ то́н	ха́ѵнва́хѵ

ѹҳ бывахъ	ѹҳ быва́хом
бывалъ есн	быва́сте
бывалъ	{ быва́ша быва́лн

[a] O2 2nd plur. люблнва́ста, 3rd любнлн [b] O2 слы́хахъ

The translator's uncertain command of the obsolete simple past tenses is evident in the way he wavers between imperfect and l-participle forms in the 2nd sing. and 3rd sing. and plur. forms: whereas the past pluperfect indicative used both ѵ́ѵнва́ше and тьі ѵ́ѵнвалъ (without copula) for the 2nd person but only ѵ́ѵнвалъ то́н for the third, this optative paradigm has only ѹҳ ѵ́ѵнвалъ есн for the former but ѹҳ ѵ́ѵнва́ше for the latter. Similarly, indicative ѵнта́ше corresponds to optative ѹҳ ѵнталъ есн, ind. ха́ѵнвалн to opt. ха́ѵнва хѵ, ind. 3rd sing. бѣаше to opt. бывалъ, etc. Our scribe shows no greater consistency in his treatment of alternant stem forms: whereas in the ind. we find only the iterative stem слыҳ-, the opt. shows the слыш- forms in the 1st and 2nd sing. and слыҳ- elsewhere; on the other hand, the opt. has only бы в-, while the ind. alternates between бы в- and бѣ-. This sort of hesitation will be analyzed more thoroughly on pp. 141 ff. below; we adduce it here only to emphasize the obstacles faced by a translator who was not only striving to render alien grammatical categories into Slavic, but was trying to do so by means of Slavic verb forms of which he himself had only a shaky command.

8.1.3.2.1.3.3 The active optative **future** presents an inconsistent assortment of perfective present-future and l-participle verb forms, accompanied by a variety of particles and pronouns, as the translator struggled to combine futurity and volition in a single Slavic paradigm:

FUTURE OPTATIVE

да бы[a]	возлюбил		да быхом	возлюбили
да бы ты	возлюбил		да бысте	возлюбили
да бы тон	возлюбил		и тѣ	возлюбили[a]
що да бы	уунл		да быхомъ	уунли
да бы ты	уунл		да бысте	уунли
да бы тон	уунл		що да уунтъ тѣ	
{ що да утү			{ що да утемъ	
{ да быҳ уелъ			{ да быхомъ ули	
да бы ты	уелъ		що да утете	
да бы тон	уелъ		що да утутъ[b]	
що да услышү			що да услышимъ	
да услышиши			да услышите	
да услышит[c]			да услышатъ	
що восхощү			що восхотим	
восхощеши			{ восхощете	
			{ восхотите	
восхощетъ			восхотат	
що будү			що будемъ	
будеши			будете	
будет			будутъ	

ᵃAdded from O2 ᵇJagić 575 f.n. 9 remarks that the 1st person forms "are superfluous, although appropriate for Latin *utinam legam*.. . ."; comparison with the other conjugation types shows that the translator wavered among the ѫх , да , and ѫх да types. ᶜO2 да оуслы́шитъ, да слы́шу, да слы́шиши.

This optative paradigm differs in several ways from the indicative future. The indicative used the (prefixed) perfective present-future for all six Latin conjugation types (возлюблю, научу, etc.), but the optative repeats these forms (preceded by ѫх or ѫх да) only for слышати and the two "irregular" verbs. Любити and уунти have да бы plus l-participle forms (i.e., an equivalent to a CSR чтобы clause) everywhere but in the 3rd plur., where O2 provides a form in which neither volition nor futurity is apparent (и тѣ возлюбили), while уунти switches to a present (ѫх да ууатъ тѣ). Ѵести alternates between the ѫх-да-plus-present and да-бы1-plus-l-participle types. In the хотѣти paradigms one notes the intrusion of analogical -тим, -тите forms into the 1st and 2nd person plural, alongside the traditional Slavonic 2nd plur. -щете.

8.1.3.2.1.4 The active **conjunctive** mood has the same five tenses as the indicative, and is, by and large, rendered into Slavic by the corresponding indicative forms preceded by ѐгда̀.

8.1.3.2.1.4.1 The **present conjunctive** paradigm is as follows:

PRESENT CONJUNCTIVE

```
ка́ко
 или ⎫ люблю      да любимъ      ка́ко у́ю      ка́ко у́имъ
 егда ⎭ любишь    да любите           у́иши          у́ите
        любитъ    да любатъ           у́ит           у́ат

      да уту      да утемъ     егда̀ услы́шу    егда̀ услы́шимъ
      да утеши    да утете          услы́шиши        услы́шите
      да утет     да утутъ          услы́шит         услы́шат

егда ⎧ волю   егда ⎧ волимъ    егда̀ е́смь     егда е́сме
     ⎩ хощу́        ⎩ хотим          е́сѝ           е́сте
       во́лиши       во́лите          е́сть          су́тъ
       во́литъ     ⎧ во́латъ
                  ⎩ хотатъ
```

The verbs appear in unprefixed present-tense forms, except for слышати, which for no evident reason takes its usual prefix ү-. The translator seems suddenly to have discovered the existence of Slavic волити, which he uses as an alternative to or substitute for хотѣти in the conjunctive paradigm (except the future) – doubtless pleased by its similarity to *volēre*. He appears to have had some difficulty in choosing the appropriate conjunction for these conjunctive forms: for любити, here and throughout, he hesitates between ӂако and егда; for ү̑чити he uses only ӂако, for чести only да (with the result that the conjunctive often coincides with the optative, e.g. in the present 1st plur. да үтемъ); слышати, хотѣти/волити and быти take only егда̀. Among individual forms, one notes: innovative хотим corresponding to хо́щем of the present indicative; the same есме that appeared in the indicative paradigm.

8.1.3.2.1.4.2 The **future conjunctive** is a faithful reproduction of the future indicative, with the expected addition of егда̀ and (with ү̑чити only) ӂако :

FUTURE CONJUNCTIVE

егда̀	возлюблю		возлюбимъ
	возлюбиши		возлюбите
	возлюбитъ		возлюбѧт
ӂако	научу	ӂако	научим
	научиши		научите
	научитъ		научатъ
егда̀	почту	егда	почтем
	почтеши		почтете
	почтет		почтут
егда	үслышу	егда̀	үслышим
	үслы́шиши		үслышите
	үслышитъ		үслы́шат
егда̀	восхощў	егда̀	восхо́щемъ
	восхо́щеши		восхо́щете
	восхощетъ		восхотѧтъ
егда̀	буду	егда	будем
	будеши		будете
	будетъ		будут

The only difference between these conjunctive forms and those of the indicative (aside from graphic details like оу-/ѵ-) is that the latter adds a pronoun to the 3rd person любити forms (возлюбит той, -бѧт тѝі). There are no irregularities and no innovative forms.

8.1.3.2.1.4.3 The **conjunctive past** has the same three subdivisions as the indicative past: imperfect, perfect, and pluperfect. By and large, the latter two repeat the corresponding indicative forms, adding only егда̀ or ꙗко, but the imperfect conjunctive differs considerably from its indicative counterpart.

8.1.3.2.1.4.3.1 The **past imperfect conjunctive** paradigm is as follows:

PAST IMPERFECT CONJUNCTIVE

егда полюбих		егда̀ полюбихом
полюбилъ еси		полюбисте
полюбил и той		полюбиша
ꙗко пооучих		ꙗко пооучихомъ
тьі поучил		пооучисте
той пооучил		поучиша
да утѵ		да утемъ
утеши̇		утете
утет		утѵтъ[a]
егда̀ слы́шѵ		егда̀ послы́шахомъ
слы́шиши		послы́шасте
слы́шитъ		послы́шаша
егда̀ ⎰волих		егда̀ во́лихомъ
⎱хотѣх		
во́лилъ еси		во́листе
во́литъ		во́лиша
егда̀ е́смь		егда̀ ⎰есмы̀
		⎱бѣхомъ
е́си		⎰бы́сте
		⎱е́сте
е́сть		бѣша

[a] An obviously erroneous paradigm, or perhaps an editorial oversight, repeating the present conjunctive. Comparison with the other conjugation types would lead us to expect егда̀ (or ꙗко) поуто́хъ, etc.

Similarity to the indicative paradigms is restricted to the first two verbs, which there as here have the prefix по- and aorist endings, except for the 2nd and 3rd sing. in an l-participle (there are minor differences: the conjunctive omits the copula and marks person pronominally in ӻко ты̏ поѹчил, ӻко тон поѹчил, while the indicative includes еси but has no pronouns in поѹчил еси, поѹчил; cf. however ind. то́н полюбил, conj. полюбил и то́н). As noted, the да ѹтѹ paradigm is an obvious error for the expected егда̀ поѹтох, after ind. поѹтох. Whereas the ind. of слы̏шати had only past-tense (aorist/imperfect/l-participle) forms and the stem form ѹслы̏ш- everywhere, the conjunctive has unprefixed present-tense forms in the singular but aorists with the prefix по- in the plural, a grammatical inconsistency the cause of which is best sought in the differing sequence-of-tense rules in Latin and Slavic. The ind. had похотѣ- and the usual aorist and l-participle endings, but the conjunctive substitutes волити for хотѣти everywhere but in the alternative 1st sing. волих ~ хотѣх, and shows an inconsistent mixture of unprefixed forms, e.g. 1st sing. aorist волих, 2nd sing. participial волил еси, 3rd sing. present волит. Nor does the conjunctive past imperfect of бы̏ти have much in common with its indicative relative: the ind. had only past-tense forms (imperfective aorists in бѣ, except compound participial бы̏л еси, бы̏л е́сть or бѣ in the 2nd and 3rd sing), but the conjunctive shows present-tense forms in the singular (егда̀ е́смь, е́си, е́сть) and an incoherent assortment of present and both perfective and imperfective aorists in the plural; one notes, incidentally, that the 1st plur. ends in -мы̏, not the -ме of the paradigms adduced above.

8.1.3.2.1.4.3.2 The **past perfect conjunctive**, unlike the past imperfect just discussed, is much the same as its indicative counterpart:

PAST PERFECT CONJUNCTIVE

ӻко / егда̀	возлюбих	егда̀	возлюбихомъ
	возлюбил и ты̏		возлюбисте
	возлюбил он		возлюби́ли и ти̏ⁿ[a]

ӻко	ѹчих̀ъ	ӻко	ѹчихомъ
	ты̏ ѹчил		ѹчисте
	тон ѹчил̀		ѹчиша

егда̀	ѹтох	егда̀	ѹтохомъ
	ѹел еси		ѹто́сте
	то́н ѹел		ѹто́ша

егда̀	слы́шах	е́гда̀	слы́шахомъ
	слышал еси		слышасте
	слышал есть		слышахү

е́гда̀	и́звѡ́лих	е́гда̀	и́звѡ́лихомъ
	и́зво́лил еси		и́звѡ́liste
	и́зволилъ		и́зволиша

егда̀	бѣх	егда	бы́хом
	бѣаше ты̀		бы́сте
	был ѡн		бы́ша

[a] егда added here from O2, which however has a quite different paradigm:

е́гда̀	любих	е́гда̀	люблѧ́хом
	любл҄ѧ́ше ты̀		любл҄ѧ́сте
	любл҄ѧ́ше ѡн		любл҄ѧ́хоү

Here we find the usual minor differences between indicative and conjunctive in copulas and pronouns (ind. возлюбил то́н /conj. возлюбил ѡн, ind. ү́чил еси/conj. ты̀ ү́чил, ind. чел ѡнсица/conj. то́н чел, etc.), and a noticeable amount of grammatical variation as well. The ind. 3rd plur. had aorists возлюбиша, слы́шаша, to which the conj. responds with participial возлюби́ли in the first case but imperfect слы́шахү in the second; on the other hand, while the indicative permitted ү́чахү alongside ү́чи́ша, the conj. gives only the latter. The conj. substitutes волити for the ind. хотѣти throughout, but the grammatical forms themselves are the same. Only in the singular of бы́ти do the ind. and conj. shows substantial differences: ind. бы́х/conj. бѣх, ind. был еси/conj. бѣаше ты̀, ind. бы́сть/conj. был ѡн, in all of which we can see the translator's evident inability to move comfortably among the old past tense forms.

8.1.3.2.1.4.3.3 The **conjunctive past pluperfect**, like its indicative model, makes use of iterative stem forms:

PAST PLUPERFECT CONJUNCTIVE

егда[a]	любливахъ	егда̀	любливахомъ
	любливаше и ты̀		любливасте
	любливал и то́н		любливахү

ӓко	ү́чивах	ӓко	ү́чивахом
	ты̀ ү́чивал		ү́чивасте
	тон ү́чивал		ү́чиваша

єгда̀ ѹ҆ита́х	єгда̀ ѹ҆ита́хомъ
ѹ҆ита́лъ є҆си	ѹ҆итасте
тои ѹ҆елᵇ	ѹ҆ита́ѹ
єгда̀ слыіха́х	єгда слыіхахом
слыіхал еси	слыіхасте
слы́ішал є҆стьᶜ	слыіха́ѹ
єгда ѹ҆а́ѹивах	єгда ╭ и҆звѡ́ливахом
	╰ ѹ҆аѹивахом
╭ ѹ҆а́ѹивалъ еси	и҆зво́ливасте
╰ и҆зво́ливал є҆си	
╭ и҆звѡ́лилъ	и҆звѡ́ливахѹ
╰ ѹ҆а́ѹивал ѡ҆н	
є҆гда̀ быіва́х	єгда быіва́хом
быівал є҆си	быівасте
быіва́шеᵈ	быіва́хѹ
вѣа́ше	

ᵃAdded from O2. ᵇO2 ѹ҆ита́лъ, which as Jagić notes fits in better with the rest of the paradigm. ᶜO2 слыіхалъ, but elsewhere слыіш– ᵈUnclear whether быіваше is intended as a 2nd- or a 3rd-person form.

In this past pluperfect paradigm the differences between indicative and conjunctive are of the same order as in the past perfect just above, that is, substantially fewer than in the past imperfect. The лю́бити paradigms differ only in their use of pronouns: ind. лю́бливаше /conj. єгда̀ лю́бливаше и҆ ты̀, ind. лю́бливахѹ ти /conj. лю́бливахѹ) and similarly for other verbs. Some vacillation is evident between aorist and imperfect endings in 3rd person forms (ind. ѹ҆ѹи́вахѹ /conj. ꙗ҆ко ѹ҆ѹиваша, ind. ѹ҆ита́хѹ or ѹ҆иташа / conj. only ѹ҆ита́хѹ), as well as between finite and participial forms (ind. both ѹ҆ѹиваше and ты̀ ѹ҆ѹивалъ / conj. only ты̀ ѹ҆ѹивал, ind. ѹ҆ита́ше / conj. ѹ҆ита́лъ є҆си, but on the other hand ind. ѹ҆а́ѹивали /conj. и҆звѡ́ливахѹ). The быіти paradigms are identical in the plural, but show some variation in the singular (ind. бѣ́х or быіва́х /conj. only быіва́х; conj. has быіваше missing from ind.).

8.1.3.2.1.5 The **active infinitive** mood has three tense forms, only the first of which corresponds to the Slavic infinitive. The present (and past imperfect: *amāre*, etc.) caused the translator no trouble, but he was hard-pressed to render the past (perfect and pluperfect: *amavisse*, etc.) and double future (*amatum ire*, *amaturum esse*) forms. What he came up with is as follows:

PRESENT AND PAST IMPERFECT

любити	ѵчити
ѵести	слышати
хотѣти, вѡлити	быти

PAST PERFECT AND PLUPERFECT

любити было[a]	ѵчивати, ѵчивано
ѵитьівано[b]	слыхано
[любливати][c]	быти

FUTURE

любимо быти	ѵчимо быти
возлюблено быти[d]	изѵчено быти
ѵтомо быти	слышанѵ быти
поѵтено быти	оуслышанѵ быти

---

[a] O2 любливати   [b] O2 ѵчитати   [c] sic   [d] O2 dativus cum infinitivo: любимѵ быти, возлюблено быти

The only feature of any interest to Russian linguistics in these forms is the translator's attempt to render the -*um ire/-urum esse* distinction by present (imperfective) passive/past (perfective) passive participles, e.g. ѵтомо быти = *lectum ire*/поѵтено быти = *lecturum esse*. *N.b.* that these are all active participles; for the corresponding passives, see p. 132 below.

8.1.3.2.1.6 Gerunds and participles (всеѵчиновные или причастные словеса, *gerundia vel participialia verba*) are rendered by Slavic verbal substantives, present gerunds (old short-form nom. sing. masc. or fem. pres. act. participles), and present passive participles, corresponding to *amandi-amando-amandum, docendi-docendo-docendum*, etc.:

любленна	ѵченига	ѵтенига[b]	слышанна	хотѣнia	бываниа
любаѵи	ѵѵа	ѵтѵѵи	слыши[c]	хотаѵи	бываа
любимо[a]	ѵѵимо	ѵтомо	слышимо	хотимо	бываемо

[a] O2 любленига, любимо   [b] O2 ѵтени   [c] sic, for expected слыша(ѵи)

The most interesting feature of this form is the colloquial **tj > č* in любаѵи, ѵтѵѵи, хотаѵи; here, as in the past pluperfect paradigms (любливах, etc.), the translator has recourse to native Russian forms when no appropriate

Slavonic item suggests itself. Cf. the present active participles in -щ- (любащъ , etc.) below.
   There are two supine forms (исходнӥ, *supina*), which appear in Slavic
as the neut. nom. and dat. sing. of the pres. pass. participle:

любимо	оучимо	ѹтомо	оуслышано
любиму	оучиму	ѹтому	оуслыш[ан]у[a]

[a]Ms. оуслышу . It is not clear why слышати alone uses a past pass. participle.

The translator makes no effort to utilize the old Slavic supine (любитъ , etc.).
   The two active participles (причастиа) of Latin, the present (настоѩщее) and future (градущее) appear in Slavic as a present active participle and a compound infintive respectively:

любащъ	оучан[a]	оутущии
будетъ любити	будет оучити	оучести будетъ
слышащъ	хотащ	его[b]
оуслышати будет[c]	— —	—

[a]О2 оуча [b]Jagić points out that the translator evidently misread *eus* as *eius*,
   whence the possessive [c]Misprint in Jagić: баует

The present participles show how little our translator understood of the old
participle system: оучан is an old long form nom. sing. masc., любащъ ,
слышашъ, and хотащ are old acc. sing. masc. short forms, which were
now evidently felt as nom., the long variant of which was in -ии, as in оутущии
(a form with no identifiable ancestor). Nor does he attempt to capitalize on
auxiliary participial forms to render the Latin future participle (*amaturus*, etc.),
although Church Slavic could have provided him with models that might have
served to provoke more imaginative translations such as *хотащее любити, *имающии оучити, * будущии слышати, etc. Once again
we see that our translator was hampered not only by the non-correspondence of
Latin and Slavic grammatical categories, but also by his own ignorance of the
resources available to him in Slavic.
   8.1.3.2.2 The **passive voice** (слова страдалны[е] или терпѣл-
ны[е]) has the same indicative, imperative, optative, conjunctive, and non-
finite paradigms as the active. Formally, the passive voice is rendered by a
mixture of -са and passive participle constructions with auxiliaries built on
various items of быти or, more rarely, имати (оучими есте ~ оучитеса).
Alternative forms are more frequent than in the active voice, and occur especially often in the auxiliary verb.
   8.1.3.2.2.1 The **passive indicative** has a present, a future, and three past
tenses, all of which show a substantial amount of variation in tense and aspect
form (stem shape, prefixation, present vs. past passive participle, etc.), both

within individual paradigms and from one verb to another. All in all, one has even more strongly the impression already created by the active voice, namely that the translator was really faced with the doubly difficult task of rendering alien grammatical categories into a target language which was itself an incoherent jumble of obsolete and innovating forms.

8.1.3.2.2.1.1 The **present indicative** passive paradigms are as follows (хотѣти and бꙑти have no passive voice):

PRESENT INDICATIVE PASSIVE

любимъ єсмь[a]	⎧любими єсма[c] ⎩любимса	ѹчюса[d]	ѹчимсѧ
⎧любиши сѧ[b] ⎩любити сѧ	любитесѧ	⎧ѹчимъ єси ⎩ѹчитисѧ	⎧ѹчими єсте ⎩ѹчитесѧ
любитсѧ	любатсѧ	ѹчитсѧ	ѹчатсѧ

поучаюсѧ	⎧ѹтемсѧ ⎩поучаемсѧ	слышусѧ	слышимсѧ
⎧поучаешисѧ ⎩ѹести	ѹтетесѧ	⎧слышишисѧ ⎩слышатисѧ	слышитесѧ
ѹтетсѧ	ѹтѹтсѧ	слышитсѧ	слышатсѧ

[a] O2 любляса, with unexpected Bulgarian-type ending (-ꙗ < -ꙗ < -ѫ); = amor. [b] O2 любимъ еси [c] O2 єсмы [d] O2 also has a 1st pers. participial form оѹчим есмь

We shall ignore the 2nd person singular "infinitive" forms (любитисѧ, ѹчитисѧ, ...) here and throughout, as uninteresting for Slavic grammar. Otherwise, we note that ѹести and слышати use only -сѧ for the passive, whereas любити and ѹчити also have participial forms, любити in the 1st pers. sing. and plur. (and in O2 also in the 2nd sing.), ѹчити in the 1st plur. (also sing. in O2) and 2nd sing. and plur. The 3rd plur. seems to be immune against participles, and in fact third person (non-addressor) forms tend rather to gravitate toward -сѧ rather than toward participial passives. Within the individual verb paradigms above, we see the alternate stem forms of ѹести (ѹт-/поѹчай), and note the єсма ~ єсмы variation in the 1st plur. of любити (the present indicative of бꙑти had only єсме, cf. p. 98 above).

8.1.3.2.2.1.2 The **future passive** indicative is formed by adding -сѧ to the form of the future active:

FUTURE INDICATIVE PASSIVE

{возлюбл҇юса / возлюблен буду	возлюбимса
{возлюбишиса / возлюбитиса	возлюбитеса
возлюбитса і ѡнъ	возлюбатса
научюса	научимса
{научишиса / научитиса	научитеса
научитса	научатса
поутуса	поутемса
{поутешиса / уестиса	поутетеса
поутетса	поутутса
у҆слы́шуса	услы́шимса
{услы́шишиса / услы́шатиса	услы́штеса
услы́шитса[a]	у҆слы́шатса

[a]Ms. erroneously у҆слы́шатса

Only the 1st sing. alternate возлюблен буду shows a participial passive; as we saw above (p. 104), the "first conjugation" любити paradigm tends to be somewhat more experimental, less systematic, than the subsequent three.

8.1.3.2.2.1.3 The **past passive** indicative paradigms fall into two distinct groups: the imperfect, which like the future utilizes only -са forms, and the perfect and pluperfect, which use passive participles (present passive in the case of любити, past passive with the other three verbs).

8.1.3.2.2.1.3.1 The **past imperfect** paradigms are as follows:

PAST IMPERFECT INDICATIVE PASSIVE

полюбихса	полюбихомса
полюбилса ты̀	полюбистеса
полюбилса и то́и	полюби́шаса
поуча҇юса	поучахомса
{поучаешиса / поучатиса	поучастеса
поучаетса	поучахуса

поутохса	поутохомс ҩ
⎰поуелс ҩ еси	поутостес ҩ
⎱уестиса	
поутес ҩ	поутошаса
у̇слы́шахса	у̇слы́шахомса
⎰у̇слышалса еси	у̇слы́шастеса
⎱у̇слы́шатиса	
у̇слы́шаетса	у̇слы́шашаса

In general, these passive paradigms follow their active prototypes (pp. 98-99), but there are a number of differences, especially in the paradigm of учити: there where the active used perfective aorists throughout, except for the l-participial 2nd and 3rd persons singular, the passive forms also contain an odd combination of imperfectives (in the singular) and imperfects in the plural (учити). On the other hand, слышати, which otherwise repeats its active model (except for the obviously erroneous present-future у̇слы́шаетса), uses a 3rd plur. aorist instead of the imperfect у̇слы́шахѵ.

A note on the emphatic particle. Commenting on the 3rd sing. полюбилса и то́и, Jagić 569 f.n. 7 considers и а "лишняя вставка", but it is clearly an emphatic device used quite intentionally, e.g. возлюбиша и ти́ї, да любат і ѡ̇ни, да возлюбит и тои, возлюбат и ти́ї, люблива́л· и то́и, и тѣ возлюбили, etc. Some of the Donatus paradigms are translated not as bare charts but as sentences, e.g. in the passive optative present, "ѽ любим е́смь, а ты́і любим же, и тои любимъ есть". The differences among the three persons are brought into relief by this emphatic и which is used primarily in participial constructions which could otherwise express person only by means of the obsolescent copula.

Both the perfect and the pluperfect past are expressed by passive participles, and both have dual sets of быти auxiliaries, present or бы- pasts in the perfect, and вѣ- or быва- pasts in the pluperfect. This distinction parallels that between the perfect and pluperfect past active, the latter of which uses iteratives (любливах, слыхах, хачивах,...) to render the fact that the action occurred in the distant past and is not still relevant in the present; here, the imperfective and iterative aorist (etc.) auxiliaries accomplish the same purpose, and incidentally provide us with one of the unfortunately few instances where the Russian translator made rather clever use of the Slavic verbal material at his disposal.

8.1.3.2.2.1.3.2 The **past perfect** paradigms are:

PAST PERFECT INDICATIVE PASSIVE

возлюбимъ[a]	⎰ есмь ⎱ быхъ	любими	⎰ есме ⎱ быхомъ
["]	⎰ еси ⎱ былъ еси	["]	⎰ е́сте ⎱ бы́сте
["]	⎰ есть ⎱ былъ	["]	суть быша быти
у́ченъ[b]	⎰ есмь ⎱ быхъ	у́чени	⎰ есмѧ ⎱ быхомъ
["]	⎰ еси ⎱ былъ еси	у́ченї	⎰ е́сте ⎱ бы́сте
["]	⎰ е́сть ⎱ былъ	["]	суть быша быти
утен	⎰ есмь ⎱ былъ есмь	утени	⎰ есми ⎱ быхомъ
["]	[былъ еси][c]	["]	⎰ е́сте ⎱ бысте
["]	⎰ былъ е́сть ⎱ бысть[d]	["]	суть быша быти[e]
слы́шанъ	⎰ есмь ⎱ быхъ	слы́шани	⎰ есмѧ ⎱ быхом
["]	⎰ еси ⎱ былъ еси	["]	⎰ есте ⎱ бысте
["]	⎰ е́сть ⎱ бы́сть	["]	суть быша быти

[a] O2 has unprefixed любимъ е́смь, etc., which corresponds better to the other paradigms [b] O2 has оучнм, оучнми throughout [c] Added "по смыслу" by Jagić; O2 has бывалъ есѝ; comparison with the other paradigms would suggest both еси and былъ еси [d] O2, more consistently, былъ [e] O2 бывши

The choice of present vs. past passive participles appears to be a matter of chance. Incidentally, one notes the consistent use of the old nom. plur. masc. ending -и, which must have been an archaism at this time. The auxiliaries are used fairly consistently throughout the paradigms, although слышати uses an aorist бы́сть instead of the expected былъ; only the singular of ѵести is aberrant, with otherwise unknown compound auxiliaries былъ есмь and былъ éсть. The 1st plur. of быти appears with all three vowels: есме, есмѧ, есми.

8.1.3.2.2.1.3.3 The **past pluperfect** paradigms are as follows:

PAST PLUPERFECT INDICATIVE PASSIVE

люби́мъ	{ бѣх { бы́вах	люби́ми	{ бѧхом { бывáхом
["]	{ бѣ ѧ́ше { бы́ ваше	["]	{ бѣѧсте { бывáсте
["]	{ бѣ { бы́ вáше	["]	бѣша тни́ (или) о́ни бы́ша[a]
ѵ́ѵен[b]	{ бѣх { бы́вах	ѵ́ѵéни	{ бѣхомъ { бывáхомъ
["]	{ бѣаше { бѣѧше	["]	{ бѣсте { бывасте
["]	{ бѣ { бѣаше	["]	{ бѣѧхѵ { бывáхѵ
ѵтен	{ бѣх { бы́вах	ѵтени	{ бѣхомъ { бывáхомъ
["]	{ бѣаше { былъ еси	["]	{ бы́сте { бывасте
["]	{ бѣ { былъ бѣ̆	["]	{ бѣша { бы́ша[c]
слы́хан	{ бѣхъ { бѣах	слы́ханн	{ бѣхом { бѣáхом
["]	{ бѣаше { былъ еси	["]	{ бѣсте { бѣăсте
["]	{ бѣ { былъ бѣ	["]	{ бѣша { бѣáхѵ

[a]Here, as in the passive conjunctive past pluperfect, the different auxiliaries are co-ordinated with different pronouns; there is no apparent motivation for this. [b]O2 has present passive participles throughout. [c]O2, more consistently, бываш[а].

Here our translator comes close to floundering in a sea of past auxiliaries. He chooses from among six different tense-aspect sets: imperfective aorist (вѣх, вѣ; вѣхомъ, вѣсте, вѣша), imperfective imperfect (вѣах, вѣаше; вѣахом, вѣасте, вѣаху), perfective aorist (вы́ша), iterative imperfect (вы́вах, вы́ваше; вы́вахом, вы́васте, вы́ваху), perfective perfect (вы́лъ еси), and perfective pluperfect (вы́лъ вѣ), – plus the ahistorical 1st plur. вѣахом in the любити paradigm.[122] In addition, the translator uses the iterative stem form слы́ха- throughout this paradigm.

8.1.3.2.2.2 The **passive imperative**, like the active, (pp. 102-104 above), uses Slavic imperative, indicative, and да-plus-indicative forms; unlike the indicative, however, it uses no participial forms.

8.1.3.2.2.2.1 The **present passive** imperative forms are given below:

PRESENT IMPERATIVE PASSIVE

	да лю́бимса
люби́ти его[a]	да лю́битеса
да лю́битса о́нъ	да лю́батса
	поо́учимса
учи́ти	учи́теса
да учи́тса	да у́ятса
	почтемса
чести	почтетеса
да чтетса	почту́тса
	(да) слы́шимса
слы́шати	слы́штеса
слы́шатса[b]	слы́шатса

[a] erroneous for *amāre* (Jagić) [b] As Jagić points out, an error for да слы́шитса

Leaving aside the awkward transitive infinitive translations of the Latin 2nd person singular imperative forms, we shall note only that люби́ти uses да throughout its paradigm, just as in the active imperative. The other three verbs mix imperative and да-plus-indicative forms, but with a different distribution than in the active. There, учи́ти took да in all three plural forms, along with the third singular,[123] but here we find three different imperative devices: an extra prefix with the indicative (or old imperative, although there is no evidence our translator distinguished the two moods formally – e.g. несемъ-несѣмъ in the 1st plur.); the regular 2nd person plur. imperative, and the да-plus-indicative form in the third person. Incidentally, the translator shows no sign of having been aware that adding -сѧ to ѹчити gives a quite different (and hardly "passive") result than appending the same particle to любити or ѣсти.

Similar non-correspondences are found in the other verbs. In the active imperative, ѣсти used да only in the third-person forms and had ѹтемъ, ѹтите in the 1st and 2nd plur., whereas the passive uses the added prefix по- for all three plural imperatives. In слышати, the passive shows no trace of the слуш- form of the root. It is possible that 1st plur. (да) in this paradigm was intended to apply to the 2nd and 3rd person forms as well.

8.1.3.2.2.2.2 The **future imperative** passive, like its active counterpart, uses mostly prefixed verb stems, but the prefixes are different, as is the distribution of prefixed and non-prefixed forms. The paradigms:

FUTURE IMPERATIVE PASSIVE

———	да полюбимсѧ
да любишисѧ ты̀	да полюбитесѧ
да любитсѧ тои	да полюбѧтсѧ[a]
———	поѹчаемсѧ
да поѹчишисѧ ты̀[b]	поѹчантесѧ
да поѹчитсѧ тои	да поѹчаютсѧ
———	да поѹтемсѧ
да поѹтѣшисѧ ты̀	да поѹтетесѧ
да поѹтетсѧ тои	да поѹтѹтсѧ
———	да ѹслышимсѧ
да ѹслышишисѧ ты̀	да ѹслышитесѧ
да ѹслы́шитсѧ то́и	да ѹслышатсѧ

[a] O2 retains prefixless forms in the plural: да любимсѧ etc.
[b] O2 наоѹчишисѧ, with на- as in the active.

Here the use of да is nearly ubiquitous, missing only from the 1st and 2nd plur. of ѹтити. Note, incidentally, the apparently unmotivated switch to an -aj-stem in the plural of this paradigm. Why the prefix по- has been used for любити, ѹчити and ѣсти is a similar mystery; one would have expected the same prefixes воз-, люби-, наѹч- as in the active (where ѣсти was not prefixed at all, except for the unexpected да проѹчитаютъ). The use of pronouns here duplicates that of the passive, with ты̀ in every 2nd- and то́и in every 3rd-person singular form, although the 3rd plur. of любити does not attempt to replicate the active возлюбѧтъ и ти́и.

8.1.3.2.2.3 The **passive optative** shows a variegated set of plain and prefixed, ѡҳ, да бы and ѡҳ да particles combined with -сѧ indicatives, passive participles, etc. etc. There is little consistency in this part of the grammar, either among the four verbs within any one tense paradigm, or among the three paradigms themselves, or between active and passive forms.

8.1.3.2.2.3.1 The paradigms of the passive optative **present and past imperfect** reflect more the present than the past imperfect meanings of their Latin sources.

PRESENT AND PAST IMPERFECT OPTATIVE PASSIVE

ѽ любим есмь   ѽ любими есме
а ты̀ любим же   любими есте
и той любимъ есть

ѡҳ ѹчюсѧ   ѡҳ ѹчимсѧ
  { ѹчишисѧ   ѹчитесѧ
    ѹчит(и)сѧ
    ѹчитсѧ   ѹчатсѧ

ѡҳ поучаюсѧ   ѡҳ поучаемсѧ
  { поучаешисѧ   поучаетесѧ
    поучатисѧ
    поучаетсѧ   поучаютсѧ

ѡҳ ѹже слышусѧ   ѡҳ ѹже слышимсѧ
  { слышишисѧ   слышитесѧ
    слышатисѧ
    слышитсѧ   слышатсѧ

Only любити uses participial constructions for this tense, just as it was the only verb to include a participle in its future passive indicative. In the singular, this verb shows less a textbook paradigm than a narrative sentence. Ѹчити has no surprises, as it simply affixes -сѧ (or -сѧ; here and throughout these spellings seem to occur in free variation) to the corresponding active voice forms. Ѹести, on the other hand, builds its passive in a way completely different from that of the active, which has unprefixed ѡҳ да ѹтѹ̀, да ѹтеши, etc., whereas the passive uses only -сѧ forms from the secondary по-...ай- verb stem; this vacillation (between ѹтѹ and поучаю forms) merely reflects the gradual disappearance of the simplex verb. Finally, слышати is unique in including the particle ѹже (stress *sic*) into its paradigm here, but in other respects it is simply the passive mirror of active ѡҳ слы́шу, etc.

DONATUS

8.1.3.2.2.3.2 The **past perfect and pluperfect** optative passive consists of a passive participle and the same dual бъіти auxiliaries that we saw in the passive indicative above (pp. 119-120):

PAST PERFECT AND PLUPERFECT OPTATIVE PASSIVE

ѿ люби́мъ	{ бы́хъ бываҳъ	ѿ люби́ми	{ бѣҳомъ бываҳомъ
["]	{ былъ еси бывалъ еси	["]	{ бысте бываете
["]	{ то́и { былъ { бѣ ꙗ́ше	["]	{ бѣа́ху бывахꙋ
ѿ ꙋчи́мъ	{ бѣҳъ быва́ҳъ	ѿ ꙋчи́ми	{ бѣҳомъ бываҳомъ
["]	{ былъ еси бывалъ еси	["]	{ бѣсте бываете
["]	{ бѣаше [a] бѣаше	["]	{ бѣша бываша
ѿ ꙋчен	{ бѣҳъ быва́ҳъ	ѿ ꙋченни	{ бѣҳомъ бываҳомъ
["]	{ былъ еси бывалъ еси	["]	{ бѣсте бываете
["]	{ бѣаше бывалъ	["]	бѣша бѣа́ху быва́хꙋ
ѿ ꙋслы́шанъ	{ бѣҳъ бываҳъ	ѿ ꙋслы́шанни	{ бѣҳомъ бываҳомъ
["]	{ бѣа́ше былъ еси	["]	{ бѣсте бѣа́сте
["]	{ бѣ былъ есть	["]	{ бѣша бываете [b]

[a] O2 бѧ́ше и҆ли бѣаше, Jagić "должно быть бываше" (574 f.n. 4) [b] *Sic*; error for бываша or быва́хꙋ

Again, there seems to be no motivation for the choice of present participles for любити, учити but past participles for үести and слышати (*n.b.* in passing that the plural үтенни has acquired a double -нн-), nor is it apparent why слышати takes the prefix у- whereas the other three verbs are unprefixed. The ѡ of любити vs. ѡх of the other verbs is standard in Donatus. On the complexities of the быти auxiliaries, see pp. 147 ff. below.

8.1.3.2.2.3.3 The **future optative** passive utilizes да бы and ѡх да particles, and shows both -са and participial passives, but unlike its active counterpart, it never has recourse to l-participles; that is, l-participles cannot be combined with -са in the passive optative (cf. in the past imperfect passive indicative полюбился ты, поүелся еси, etc.). The paradigms:

FUTURE OPTATIVE PASSIVE

да быхъ любимъ былъ	да бымы любимы были
да бы ты любимъ былъ (или) любитися	да бысте любимы были
да бы тóй любимъ былъ	да бы тѣ возлюбилися
ѡх да уүюса	ѡх да уүимся
да уүишися	да уүитеся
(или) уүитися	
да уүитсяᵃ	да уүатся
ѡх да үтуся	ѡх да үтемся
{да үтешися	да үтетеся
үестися	
да үтется	да үтутся
ѡх да услышуся	ѡх да услышимся
{услышишися	да услышитеся
услышатися	
услышится	да услышатся

ᵃ Corrected from erroneous уүатся in both mss.

Here, as in two earlier paradigms (see pp. 115 and 122 above), only любити has participial constructions, while the other three verbs use only -са forms. The слышати paradigm is identical to its active counterpart (except of course for the added -са). The passive учити paradigm has the same -са forms as слышити, whereas its active counterpart (p. 106) has ѡх да бы plus l-participles (only the 3rd plur. has the present ѡх да уүатъ тѣ). The passive үести forms, too, have only -са, while the active alternated between the ѡх да үту and the да быхъ үелъ types.

8.1.3.2.2.4 The **passive conjunctive** has the same array of tenses as the active: a present, a future, and three past tenses. The present and past imperfect (and, for любити, the future as well) are formed by adding -са to the corresponding active forms (with some variation in prefixation), while the future and the other two past tenses utilize passive participle constructions with the same dual array of auxiliaries as we have seen in the optative above.

8.1.3.2.2.4.1 The passive **conjunctive present** is formed by adding -са to the active forms:

PRESENT CONJUNCTIVE PASSIVE

егда люблюса	егда любимс ѩ
да ⸨любишиса	любитеса
⸜любимъ еси̇	
егда любитса	лю́батса
да ꙋчюса	да ꙋчимс ѩ
да ꙋчишис ѩ	да ꙋчитес ѩ
(или) ꙋчитиса	
да ꙋчитс ѩ	да ꙋчатс ѩ
да ꙋти́са	да ꙋте́мса
да ⸨ꙋте́шиса	да ꙋтетес ѩ
⸜ꙋ́естиса	
[да] ꙋтетса	да ꙋтꙋтса[a]
егда слы1шꙋса	егда̀ слы́шимс ѩ
⸨слы1шишиса	слы́штеса
⸜слы1шатиса	
слы́1шитса	слы1шатса

[a] Added from O2

The use of particles differs somewhat, but apparently not significantly, from active to passive: ꙗ̈ко ꙋ́чю̀ but да ꙋчюса, да любимъ but егда любимс ѩ, etc. Here as elsewhere, любити differs from the other three verbs in its choice of -са vs. participial forms: да любишиса, but also and unique да любимъ еси̇. Слы1шати, for no evident reason, has dropped the prefix in the passive: егда̀ ꙋслы1шꙋ, but егда слы1шꙋса.

8.1.3.2.2.4.2 The passive **future conjunctive**, unlike the present, does not merely add -са to the active form (except — again — for most of the любити paradigm), but instead uses passive participles with two sets of auxiliaries:

FUTURE CONJUNCTIVE PASSIVE

егда ⎰ возлюблюса   возлюбимса
     ⎱ возлюбленъ буду

     ⎰ возлюбишиса   возлюбитеса
     ⎱ возлюбитиса

     возлюбитса и ѡнъ   возлюбатса[a]

егда учимъ ⎰ буду   егда учими ⎰ будемъ
            ⎱ быти имамъ   ⎱ быти имамы

            ⎰ будеши   ⎰ будете
            ⎱ быти имаши   ⎱ быти имате

            ⎰ будет   ⎰ будут
            ⎱ быти имат   ⎱ быти имуть

егда учен   ⎰ буду   егда учени ⎰ будемъ
            ⎱ быти имамъ   ⎱ быти имамы

            ⎰ будеши[b]   ⎰ будете
            ⎱ быти имаши   ⎱ быти имате

            ⎰ будетъ   ⎰ будутъ
            ⎱ быти имать[c]   ⎱ быти имут

егда оуслышан ⎰ буду   егда услышани ⎰ будемъ
              ⎱ быти имам   ⎱ быти имамы

              ⎰ будеши   ⎰ будете
              ⎱ быти имаши   ⎱ быти имате

              ⎰ будет   ⎰ будут
              ⎱ быти имат   ⎱ быти имутъ

[a]Both O2 and the repeated section of Kaz. have only participial constructions: O2 любимъ боудоу или боудоу (< *ero vel fuero*), Kaz.₂ любим буду and быти имам, etc. [b]From O2; Kaz. erroneously будетъ [c]3rd sing. forms added from O2

The passives use егда̀ throughout, except for the (probably elliptic) omission in the plural of любити, whereas the active had ꙗко for the entire paradigm of учити. Любити and слышати use the same prefixes in both active and passive forms (воз-, у-), but учити, which had на- throughout the active (ꙗко научю, etc.), uses the prefixless present active participle учимъ, учими in the passive, and у̓ести, which had по- in the active

(егда̀ поүтѵ̈, etc.), also has prefixless passive participles ѵтєн, ѵтєни in its passive. Of the four verbs, only ѵѵнти uses the present, rather than the past passive participle. The dual auxiliaries (бѵ̈дѵ̈ or бы́ти и́мамъ , etc.) are presumably an attempt to render *ero* and *fuero*, rather than a distorted reflection of the older distinction between simple and proximate future (бити хощю̀, бити и́мамъ in the "Eight parts of speech; cf. pp. 18-19 above); this is the only use in the Donatus translation of the имати auxiliary.

8.1.3.2.2.4.3 The **past conjunctive** passive has two quite different types of paradigm, an imperfect built on -са forms, and perfect and pluperfects utilizing passive participles. There is no apparent grammatical basis for this distinction, in either Latin or Slavic.

8.1.3.2.2.4.3.1 The **past imperfect** is, by and large, a -са version of the corresponding active conjunctive paradigm:

PAST IMPERFECT CONJUNCTIVE PASSIVE

```
егда любихса              егда любихомса
ты {любилса              любистес[а]
     любитиса
тон любляшеса             любахѵ̈са

егда̀ поѵ̈чнхс ѧ           егда поѵ̈чихомс ѧ
     поѵ̈чашес ѧ           поѵ̈чистес ѧ
(или) поѵ̈читис ѧ[a]
     поѵ̈чилс ѧ[b]         поѵ̈чиша с ѧ

егда почита юса           егда̀ почитаемса
     {почитаеши са         почитаетес ѧ
      почитатиса
     почитаетс ѧ           почита ютса

егда̀ слы̏ шѵ̈са            егда̀ слы̏ шимса
     {слы́шиниса           слы́шитеса
      слы́шатиса
     слы́шитса             [omitted]
```
[a]O2 поѵ̈чатиса [b] Corrected by Jagić from Kaz. поѵ̈чнмса, O2 поѵ̈чаас ѧ

This imperfect paradigm differs in several ways from its active counterpart. The passive uses the particle егда̋ throughout, whereas the active had ꙗ́ко for ѹчити and да for ѹчсти. Only ѹчити repeats the по- prefixation of its active model throughout, while любити drops the по- of the active, and ѹчсти uses the prefixal secondary imperfective поѹта ющса etc. for the ѹт- forms of the active (which erroneously had present-tense forms, ѹтѹ etc., for the expected поѹтох etc.; see p. 109 above). The use of tenses also differs: in the active, любити and ѹчити had aorists everywhere but in the 2nd and 3rd sing., and l-participles in those two, but the passive paradigm shows a broader and quite unmotivated range of variation. Любити has the aorist егда любихса, любихомса, любистеса; l-participial егда ты любилса; imperfect 3rd persons егда тои любляшеса, любляхѹса. Ѹчити, on the other hand, has a different distribution: aorist егда поѹчихсꙗ, поѹчихомсꙗ, поѹчистесꙗ, поѹчишасꙗ; l-participial поѹчилсꙗ (but see note b above); imperfect 2nd person поѹчашесꙗ. This inconsistent and indiscriminate mixture of tenses in adjacent paradigms testifies not only to the fact that the translator was ill at ease with his verb forms, but also to a lack of concern with simple consistency, a lack of concern due to the fact that he was interested not so much in Slavic grammar as in providing some sort of better-or-worse Slavic key to the Latin forms which occupied most of his attention.

8.1.3.2.2.4.3.2 The **past perfect** conjunctive paradigm consists of passive participles and dual быти- auxiliaries:

PAST PERFECT CONJUNCTIVE PASSIVE

егда любимъ	{ е́смь быхъ[a]	любими	{ быхомъ бѣа́хомъ	
и ты любимъ	{ бы́лъ бѣаше	["]	{ бы́сте бѣа́сте	
тои	["]	{ бы́лъ бѣа́ше	["]	{ бы́ша бѣахѹ
егда ѹчимъ	{ бѣх бѣах	егда ѹчими	{ бѣхомъ быхом[b]	
["]	{ бѣаше былъ еси	["]	{ е́сте бы́сте	
["]	{ есть былъ	["]	{ сѹть [бѣша][c] быша	

егда̀ ѵтєн	є́смь / бых	єгда̀ ѵтєни	є́сма[e] / быхомъ[f]
["]	была єси / бѣашє ты̀	["]	є́стє / бѣстє[g]
["]	є́сть / бы́лъ[d]	["]	сѹть / быша
єгда̀ ѵслы́шанъ	є́смь / быхъ	єгда̀ ѵслы́шани	быхомъ / бѣахом
["]	єси / был єси	["]	бѣстє / бѣа̋стє
["]	є́сть / был бѣ	["]	бѣша / бѣахѹ

[a]О2 любимъ бѣхъ и́ли быстъ [b]О2 бѣхомъ и́ли
быва́хомъ [c]Jagić's printed text reads: "сѹть [бѣша]
и́ли быша". [d]О2 быстъ [e]О2 є́смє [f]О2 бѣхомъ [g]О2 быстє

Here there is no correspondence at all between active and passive paradigms, as the former are built on simple and l-participial pasts (ꙗ́ко ѵѵи́хъ, єгда̀ ѵтохъ, etc.). The choice of participles is erratic: любити and ѵѵити use the imperfective present passive, слы́шати the perfective past passive, and ѵєсти the imperfective past passive (unless, as is possible, ѵєсти was beginning to be felt as perfective, displaced as an imperfective by ѵита́ю). The auxiliaries in this passive set are a strange mixture of tense and aspect forms which vary from verb to verb, and from singular to plural and person to person within a single verb, as is evident, for example, if we rearrange the first auxiliaries into mini-paradigms such as (любимъ) єсмь-былъ-былъ/ (ѵѵимъ) бѣхъ-бѣашє-єсть/(ѵтєн) є́смь-был єси-єсть/ (ѵслы́шанъ) є́смь-єси-є́сть, only the last of which shows any consistency. Nor do we find any striving toward grammatical coherence in the corresponding second auxiliaries (любимъ) быхъ-бѣашє-бѣашє/ (ѵѵимъ) бѣахъ-был єси-был /(ѵтєн) быхъ-бѣашє ты̀-былъ/(ѵслы́шанъ) быхъ-был єси-был бѣ. Within the several tense-aspect stems (бы-, бѣ-, бѣа-, быва-) one can observe regularities of the sort discussed on p. 119 above in the case of the passive optative (бѣ- forms occurring as 1st aux. and бѣа- forms as 2nd, etc., but not the reverse); however, all auxiliaries will be discussed in more detail on pp. 147 ff. below, so we need not dwell on them here.

8.1.3.2.2.4.3.3 The **past pluperfect** conjunctive passive uses the same set of participles as the past perfect, except for слышати, which has prefixless слышан, and the plural of үчити, which shows the doubtless erroneous (active) l-participle үчили :

PAST PLUPERFECT CONJUNCTIVE PASSIVE

егда любимъ	{ бѣа́хъ бываѫъ	любими	{ бѣахом бываѫомъ
["]	{ былъ есѝ быва́лъ е́сѝ	["]	{ бѣасте быва́сте
["]	{ бы́стъ бы́ва́лъ	["]	{ бѣша тӥ ѡ̈ни бы́ша
егда үчи́мъ	{ быхъ[a] быва́ѫъ	егда̀ үчили (sic)	{ быхомъ[c] быва́ѫомъ
["]	{ былъ еси бывалъ еси	["]	{ бѣсте бываасте
["]	{ бѣаше бывал бѣаше[b]	["]	{ бѣша бѣаху̀
егда̀ үчен	{ бѣѫ быва́ѫ	егда̀ үчени́	{ бы́хомъ[d] бываѫомъ
["]	{ былъ еси бывалъ еси	["]	{ бѣсте быва́сте
["]	{ бѧаше ѡн быва́лъ	["]	{ бы́ша[e] быва́ша
егда̀ слышан	{ бѣаѫ быва́ѫ	егда̀ слы́шани	{ бѣхом бы́ва́ѫомъ
["]	{ бы́лъ е́си бывал е́си	["]	{ е́сте быва́сте
["]	{ бѣа́ше бывалъ ест	["]	{ бѣша быва́ша

[a] O2 бѣхъ perhaps by induction from the corresponding past perfect above. [b] O2 ваше [c] O2 бѣахомъ [d] O2 бѣхомъ [e] O2 бѣша

Here, as in the past perfect, there is no direct correspondence between active and passive paradigms, since the former consist mostly of imperfect tense forms built onto iterative stems (любливахъ, слыхахъ, etc.). To some extent, this imperfectness and iterativity is reflected in the auxiliaries of the passive paradigms, which utilizes бы - forms less and быва - forms more than does the past perfect (p. perfect 12 бы-, zero быва-; p. pluperfect 6 бы-, 14 быва -). See also the general analysis of auxiliaries on pp. 147 ff. below.

8.1.3.2.2.5 The **passive infinitive** mood has the same three tenses as the active, a present and past imperfect, a past perfect and pluperfect, and a future. Since Slavic has a form corresponding only to the first meaning of the first of these three, it is not surprising that the translator has to grasp at various more or less unlikely compounds, as below:

PRESENT AND PAST IMPERFECT

любитися   учитися
утохъ[a]   слышатися

PAST PERFECT AND PLUPERFECT

любима бывша[b]   учима бывша
любливана бывша   учима бывавша

утено бѣаше   слышано бѣаше
утено бываше   слышано бываше

FUTURE

любимо быти   учимо быти
утено быти   слышано быти

[a]Jagić 578 f.n. 5: "Может быть...утомо". [b]Whether the -а ending in the любити and учити forms represents an accusative is not clear from the mss.

Again, consistency is not the hallmark of these paradigms. It is unclear why, in the perfect-pluperfect paradigm, любити and учити have a present passive participle and a participial auxiliary, whereas уести and слышати have a past passive participle and a finite, imperfect auxiliary. Любити uses the iterative любливана for this tense, but слышати retains the слыша- stem, although the corresponding active paradigm has слыхано. Apparently, here just as in the passive conjunctive forms above, the translator felt that the meaning of distant past action, — that area of verbal semantics where the Latin pluperfect partially overlaps with the Russian iterative — was better rendered by the auxiliary than by the participle. Here, however, he does show some hesitation: for лювити, the perfect/pluperfect distinction is expressed by participial лювима / лювливана, with constant бывша, while the other three verbs have a constant participle but vary the auxiliary. Here, as frequently elsewhere, the лювити paradigm differs from the other three taken together.

8.1.3.2.2.6 The passive voice has no gerunds or supines, but does have two **participles**, a past and a future (whereas the active voice had present and future):

PAST PASSIVE PARTICIPLE

лювимъ бѣ   ѹчен
ѹтенъ   слышанъ

FUTURE

лювим будет   ѹчитися имать
ѹестися имат   ѹслышится

Here again лювити differs in form from the other three verbs, in having a present rather than a past passive participle in the first of these two paradigms, not to mention the isolated бѣ auxiliary. Again, лювити uses a passive participle in the second paradigm, while the other three verbs have -ся forms, differing among themselves: ѹчити and ѹести taking the auxiliary имать, while слышати appears as a prefixed perfective present-future. None of this variation has any significance for Slavic grammar.

8.1.3.2.3 Impersonal forms. In addition to the active and passive voices, the Donatus translation lists impersonal forms (слова безличныіе) corresponding to Latin forms like *amator* (fut. imp. ind.), *amatum esse* (past perfect and pluperfect infinitive), etc. etc. The Slavic translations are all 3rd person singular -ся or participial reflexes or passives. In some cases they are identical with the corresponding passives, in others, quite different. They are of little importance for Slavic grammar, but for the sake of completeness we adduce them here, grouped together by mood.

8.1.3.2.3.1 Indicative. The indicative impersonal forms are as follows:

PRESENT   лювится   ѹчится
           ѹтется я   слышится я

	FUTURE	ВОЗЛЮБИТСѦ[a]	ДА НАѰЧИТСѦ
		ПОѰТЕТСѦ	ОѰСЛЫШИТСѦ
	IMPERFECT	ЛЮБЛѦШЕСѦ	ѰЧАШЕСѦ
		ѰТАШЕСѦ	ОѰСЛЫ́ШАНО {ЕСТЬ / БЫ́СТЬ[c]
PAST	PERFECT	ЛЮБИ́МО {Е́СТЬ / БЫ́СТЬ	ѰЧИМО {ЕСТЬ / БЫ́СТЬ
		ѰТО́МО ЕСТЬ	[omitted in ms.]
		ѰТЕНО БЫ́СТЬ[b]	
	PLUPERFECT	ЛЮБИ́МО {БѢ ЯШЕ / БЫ́ ВА́ЛО	ѰЧИМО {БѢ / БЫ ВА́ЛО
		ѰТЕНО {БѢ / БѢАШЕ	СЛЫ́ХАНО {БѢ / БѢАШЕ

[a] From O2; Kaz. ВОЗЛЮБИТ ТѦ ; = *amabitur* [b] O2 БЫТИ
[c] O2 ПОСЛЫШАЛОСѦ

The present impersonal is identical with the 3rd person sing. of the corresponding passive paradigm on p. 115 above, and so, except for the inappropriately added ДА with НАѰЧИТСѦ, is the future. The three past impersonal sets, however, differ considerably from their passive counterparts. This is true especially of the past imperfect, whose nearly canonical Slavonic imperfects have no counterparts elsewhere in Donatus (the corresponding passives have a mixed set of prefixed present, imperfect, and aorist forms such as ПОЛЮБИХСѦ, ПООѰЧАЮСѦ, etc.; cf. pp. 116-117 above), nor does the aberrant participial ОѰСЛЫ́ШАНО ЕСТЬ or БЫСТЬ have any equivalent in the passive paradigm. The perfect and pluperfect, on the other hand, repeat the passive paradigms in their structural essentials, consisting as they do of a passive participle and a dual БЫТИ auxiliary, but within this framework of correspondence there are several non-corresponding details: the passive perfect has ВОЗЛЮБИМ ЕСТЬ or БЫЛ, with prefixed participle and 2nd auxiliary БЫЛ where the impersonal has the aorist БЫСТЬ; ѰЧИТИ uses the past passive ѰЧЕНЪ in the passive but ѰЧИМО in the impersonal, with the same differences in auxiliaries as with ЛЮБИТИ ; ЧЕСТИ uses ѰТЕНЪ in the passive but has both ѰТЕНО and ѰТОМО in the impersonal, with a perfect auxiliary БЫЛ Е́СТЬ in the passive (cf. p. 118). Within the pluperfect, the impersonal has the same participles as the passive for three of the four verbs, with only passive ѰЧЕН/ impersonal ѰЧИМО differing. On the other hand, the auxiliaries are partly different, and quite differently distributed: БѢ ~ БѢАШЕ occurs only with ѰЧЕН in the passive, but with ογενο and слышано (not with ογημο) in the impersonal, while the latter both have бѣ ~ былъ бѣ in the passive, and любити in both cases has an auxiliary pair found in no other verb, бѣ ~ бываше in the passive and бѣаше ~ бывало here in the impersonal.

8.1.3.2.3.2 Imperative. The impersonal imperative has both present and future tenses, like the passive. The forms are:

PRESENT	да полюбитса[a]	да ογчитса
	да ογтетсѧ	да слышитса[b]
FUTURE	возлюбитса[c]	(да) ογчитса[d]
	ογестиса[e]	да ογслышитса

[a] O2 (Jagić: "лучше") да любитса; = *ametur* [b] O2 ογ-слышитса [c] From O2; = *amator* [d] да added from O2
[e] From O2; = *legitor*

The present imperative has the same forms in this impersonal as in the passive, except for the erroneous по- of полюбитса (cf. note a) and the equally mistaken passive слышатсѧ for слышитсѧ. The future, however, differs almost altogether, using -сѧ infinitives for the passive's да-plus-finite forms (да любитса тои, да поογчитсѧ тои, да поογтетсѧ тои); only слышати comes close to repeating its passive counterpart да ογслышитса тои.

8.1.3.2.3.3 Impersonal forms exist for all three **optative** tenses:

PRESENT AND PAST IMPERFECT	ѽ да любитса	ѡх ογчитса
	ѡх ογтетсѧ	ѡх слышитсѧ
PAST PERFECT AND PLUPERFECT	ѽ любимо {баше / бывало[a]}	ѡх ογчимо {бѣ / бывало}
	ѡх ογтено {бѣ / бѣаше}	ѡх слыхано {бѣ / бѣаше}
FUTURE	да сѧ возлюбит	ѡх да ογчитса
	ѡх да ογтетсѧ	ѡх да слышитса[b]

[a] O2 ѡх любимо бѣ іли... бѣаше, ≅ *utinam amatum* [b] O2 ογслышитса

These impersonal forms use the same particles as the corresponding active paradigms (pp. 104-107 above), with minor variations in the case of любити. The verbs themsevles are -сѧ variants of the active 3rd sing. forms throughout the present-past imperfect, but the past perfect-pluperfect uses participial passives instead of -сѧ (ѹхъ ѹчимо бѣ corresponding to active ѹхъ ѹчиваше, etc.). As in the indicative, любити and ѹчити utilize a present, but честѝ and слы́шати a past passive participle. The бы́ти auxiliaries show the same variation discussed in several paradigms above.

8.1.3.2.3.4 The **conjunctive** mood impersonal forms are as follows:

PRESENT

е҆гда̀ лю́битсѧ	е҆гда̀ ѹчитсѧ
егда прочитаетсѧ	егда̀ слы́шитсѧ[a]

FUTURE

⎰ егда любимо бу́дет	егда ѹчимо ⎰ бу́дет
⎱ егда̀ возлюблено бу́детъ	⎱ быти и҆мат
егда почтено ⎰ бу́детъ	егда̀ ѹслы́шано ⎰ бу́детъ
⎱ быти и҆мат	⎱ быти и҆мат

PAST IMPERFECT

егда̀ любимо ⎰ бѣ́ꙗше	егда ѹꙗшесѧ
⎱ бывало[b]	
егда̀ ѹтꙗшесѧ	егда̀ послышалосѧ

PAST PERFECT

егда любимо бѣ[b]	егда ѹчимо ⎰ бѣ
	⎱ бѣаше
егда̀ ѹтено ⎰ е́сть	егда̀ ѹслышано[c] ⎰ е́сть
⎱ бѣаше	⎱ бысть

PAST PLUPERFECT

⸺[d]	егда ѹчимо ⎰ бѣаше
	⎱ бывало
егда̀ прочитае́мо ⎰ бѣ	егда слыхано ⎰ бѣаше
⎱ бывало	⎱ бѣ[e]

[a]О2 ѹ҆слы́шитсѧ [b]О2 has a past imperfect е́гда̀ любѧшесѧ і҆лѝ е҆гда̀ любимо бѣꙗше and a separate past perfect; Kaz. has no separate past perfect [c]О2 слышано [d]Same as past imperfect [e]О2 егда̀ ѹслыхано бѣ

There is no consistent relation between these impersonal forms and those of the corresponding active paradigms (pp. 107-113 above). In the present, любити and učити simply add -ся to the active verb, but ѥсти forms the impersonal on a different stem (cf. active да ѹтет), while слышати removes the prefix of ѹслышит. The conjunctive future utilizes passive participles corresponding to active егда̀ возлюбитъ, наѹчитъ, поѹтет, оѹслышитъ, in some cases preserving the prefix, in others (любимо, ѹчимо) dropping it; cf. also the optative future just above, which employs -ся rather than participial forms. The auxiliaries in the impersonal future correspond to *ero* and *fuero*, etc., and are less notable in themselves than for their complete lack of correspondence with the old double future going back to the "Eight parts of speech" (бити хощю̀ = proximate future, бити и́мамъ general future; cf. pp. 18-19 above); if Gerasimov or his copyists knew this older tradition, they show no sign of it. The past impersonal forms of любити show the same idiosyncracies we have noted in several other parts of the grammar: it alone uses participial forms in the past imperfect, and it alone has a single auxiliary in the perfect. The auxiliary hierarchy discussed elsewhere (pp. 147 ff.) is generally observed, but is inverted in the бѣаше-бѣ order of the past pluperfect of слышати.

8.1.3.2.3.5 The impersonal **infinitive** tenses correspond to those of the regular paradigms:

PRESENT AND PAST IMPERFECT	любити пригоже[a]		ѹчитися	
	ѥстися		слышатися	
PAST PERFECT AND PLUPERFECT	любимо	⎰ бывшее ⎱ бывало[b]	ѹчимо	⎰ бывшее снѐ ⎱ бывалое
	ѹтено	⎰ бывшее ⎱ бывалое	слыхано бывше слышано бывшее	
FUTURE	любиму бы́ти		ѹчиму бы́ти	
	ѹтомо бы́ти		ѹслы́шано бы́ти	

[a]O2 omits пригоже ; ≅ *amari* [b]O2 бывалое; ≅ *amatum esse vel fuit*

These impersonal forms are drawn from both the corresponding active and passive paradigms. ѹчитися and слышатися are identical to the passive infinitives on p. 131, while любити пригоже is more innovative, though hardly a better translation of *amari*. The impersonal past perfect-pluperfect repeats the general structure of the corresponding passives (*ibid.*), but with a different pair of auxiliaries (cf. ѹчи́ма бывша ~ бывавша, слы́шано бѣаше ~ бываше, etc., *ibid.*), and слышати draws its impersonal participle from both the active (слы́хано, p. 113) and passive

(слы́шано, p. 131) counterparts. The impersonal future infinitive also draws its participles from both sources, утомо and prefixed услы́шано corresponding only to active infinitives (p. 113), while the other two participles occur in both active and passive paradigms, as well as here. The overall impression left by these impersonal infinitives is even more artificial than elsewhere in the Donatus grammar, since Slavic has no impersonal forms for verbs like любити, учити, no similar passive infinitives, and most assuredly no three different tenses within the infinitive mood. Considering these handicaps, it is hardly surprising that the resulting translations are less than entirely consistent and cast but a dim light on the state of Slavic grammar at that time.

8.1.3.3 Interpretation. In what follows, we shall try to identify whatever systematic features of Slavic verbal morphology can be gleaned from the mass of partially self-contradictory data in the Donatus paradigms.

8.1.3.3.1 Paradigm incoherence. One of the more salient features of the Donatus paradigms is their relatively low degree of internal coherence. One and the same six-member paradigm may show more than one stem shape, some of its forms may be prefixed and others not, half the paradigm may be present and the other half past, l-participle past-tense forms are intermingled with old aorists and imperfects, preposed particles and postposed pronouns and copulas are appended to some forms and not to others, archaic Slavonisms rub elbows with vernacular innovations (восхощем / хаунвал, et al.), etc. Such inconsistencies are multiplied when one compares the paradigms of different verbs in one and the same tense, or some one tense paradigm in the indicative, optative, and conjunctive, or in the active and passive voices, etc. This internal incoherence is due to two factors: first, the nearly impossible nature of the task at hand, namely that of rendering alien grammatical categories like the pluperfect subjunctive or the future infinitive into Slavic; second, the deep changes which had occurred (and to some extent were still occurring) in Slavic verb morphology (confusion of aorist and imperfect endings, substitution of l-participle forms for both simple tenses, esp. in the 2nd and 3rd person singular, growth of prefixed secondary (suffixal) imperfectives for old simple stems (уести → поучтати, etc.), and so on. And, as we have already seen, the preceding centuries had not produced any grammatical tradition or significant linguistic sophistication which could have helped Gerasimov and his copyists in their struggles. When one considers the handicaps under which these men worked, one is surprised less by the inconsistency and naiveté of their results than by the fact that they managed even this well.

We are concerned here not with how well or poorly the Donatus translators managed to translate their Latin paradigms (an interesting problem, but one of no direct relevance to the history of Slavic grammar), but only with the extent to which their results can cast light on the state of Russian verb morphology at that time. Detailed examination of these Donatus paradigms brings certain regularities to light, regularities which must of course be viewed with appropriate scepticism, but which are nonetheless by no means entirely irrelevant to the history of Russian grammar. In what follows, we shall describe some of these regularities, without pretending to be exhaustive; indeed, this material is too problematical to justify an exhaustively detailed description.

8.1.3.3.2 Prefixation. The use of prefixes in the Donatus paradigms has both systematic and whimsical aspects: prefixation is correlated partly with tenses, partly with the root lexemes of individual verbs, and occasionally with nothing at all.

воз- occurs with любити and хотѣти, and serves primarily as a marker of future tense. With любити, воз- occurs in all five future active forms (indicative возлюблю, imperative да возлюбиши тьı̀, optative да бьı возлюбил, conjunctive егда̀ возлюблю, infinitive возлюблено бьıти = *amaturum esse*), and to the extent хотѣти has these forms, воз- appears in them all (ind. восхощу, opt. ѡх восхощу, conj. егда̀ восхощу). In the future passive, on the other hand, воз- appears only in the ind. возлюблюса or возлюбленъ буду and conj. егда возлюблюса or возлюбленъ буду, whereas the imperative has φ- in the sing. (да любишиса тьı̀) and по- in the plur. (да полюбимса), and the opt. and inf. only φ (да быхъ любимъ был ; любимо быти);[124] хотѣти of course has no passive voice. However, воз- also appears in most of the past perfect paradigms of любити: act. ind. возлюбих, act. conj. егда возлюбих, pass. ind. возлюбим есть or быхъ (but only in the sing.; cf. plur. любими есме or быıхомъ etc.); this seems to be an unmotivated anomaly, since no other verbs have a prefix in any past perf. form (act. ind. ꙋчихъ, ꙋтох, сльıшах, хотѣхъ), nor does even любити show one in the pass. past perf. conj. егда любимъ есмь or быıхъ.

The prefix на- serves the same inceptive function for ꙋчити as did воз- for любити and хотѣти, but somewhat less consistently. It marks the future act. ind., imp. and conj. (наꙋчю, да наꙋчиши тьı̀, ꙗко наꙋчю), but is missing from the opt. ѡх да бы ꙋчил (cf. да бы возлюбил) and the fut. pass. conj. егда̀ ꙋчимъ буду or быти имамъ (cf. егда̀ возлюблюса or возлюбленъ буду); it is replaced by an unexpected из- in the fut. act. inf. изꙋчено быти. Unlike воз-, на- appears in no forms other than the future.

По- seems to have two different functions. On the one hand, it plays the same inceptive role for чести as воз- and на- for любити, хотѣти and ꙋчити: act. fut. ind. почтꙋ̀, conj. егда̀ почтꙋ, inf. почтено быти (*lecturum esse*), and passive fut. ind. почтꙋса, imp. да почтешиса тьı̀, but does not appear in the fut. imp. да ꙋтеши тьı̀ (cf. да возлюбиши тьı̀, да наꙋчиши тьı̀). On the other hand, по- appears, with varying degrees of consistency, as a past imperfect tense marker in all five verbs: active indicative полюбихъ, пооучихъ, поутохъ, похотѣхъ (but ѹслы́-шахъ); active optative (where there is a single form for both present and past imperfect) only шх похотѣх (the other verbs use non-past forms: ѿ лю-блю̀, шх ѹчю̀, etc.); active conjunctive егда̀ полюбих, ꙗко поѹчих, егда̀ послышахомъ;[125] passive indicative полюбихсѧ, поѹчаюсѧ, поутохсѧ; passive optative шх поѹитаюсѧ (the other verbs are without prefix: ѿ любим єсмь, шх ѹчюсѧ, шх ꙋже слы́шѹсѧ); passive conjunctive егда̀ поѹчихсѧ, егда̀ поѹита-юсѧ (but єгда любихсѧ, єгда̀ слы́шѹсѧ without prefix).[126]

Finally ѹ- appears to be more lexicalized than the other prefixes. It corresponds to inceptive воз- and на- in all future forms (active ind. ѹслы́-шѹ, imp. ѹслыши ты, opt. шх да ѹслы́шѹ, etc.; pass ind. ѹслы́-шѹсѧ, etc.) and to the past imperfect marker по- in active indicative ѹслы́-шах, passive ind. ѹслы́шахсѧ, but it also occurs in three passive paradigms which are unprefixed in other verbs: passive optative past perfect-pluperfect шх ѹслы́шанъ бѣх or бывах (cf. ѿ любимъ бы́х or бывах, шх ѹчимъ бѣхъ or бывах, шх ѹтєн бѣх or бывах), passive conjunctive past perfect егда̀ ѹслы́шанъ е́смь or бы́х (cf. егда̀ любимъ е́смь or бы́хъ, etc.), and active conjunctive present егда̀ ѹслы́шѹ (cf. єгда люблю̀, etc.).

The following table shows the distribution of these prefixes throughout the verb paradigms (forms which never take prefixes are omitted):

VERB PREFIXATION

	TENSE ETC.	любити	ѹчити	ѹчести	слышати	хотѣти
ACTIVE	future ind.	воз-	на-	по-	ѹ-	вос-
	imp.	воз-	на-[a]	φ-[b]	ѹ-[c]	[no imperatives]
	opt.	воз-	φ-	φ-	ѹ-	вос-
	conj.	воз-	на-	по-	ѹ-	вос-
	inf.	воз-[d]	из-[d]	по-[d]	ѹ-[d]	[none]
PASSIVE	future ind.	воз-[e]	на-	по-	ѹ-	
	imp.	φ-, по-[f]	по-	по-	ѹ-	
	opt.	φ-[g]	φ-	φ-	ѹ-	[no passive forms]
	conj.	воз-	φ-	φ-	ѹ-	
	inf.	φ-	φ-	φ-	φ-	

		TENSE ETC.	любити	учити	уести	слышати	хотѣти
ACTIVE	indic.	past imp. past perf. past plu.	по− воз− φ−	по− φ− φ−	по− φ− φ−	у− φ−[h] φ−	по− φ− φ−
	opt.	present + past imp.	φ−	φ−	φ−	φ−	по−
	conj.	past imp. past perf. past plu.	по− воз− φ−	по− φ− φ−	φ− φ− φ−	φ−, по−[i] φ− φ−	φ− φ−[j] φ−[j]
PASSIVE	indic.	past imp. past perf. past plu.	по− воз−[k] φ− φ−	по− φ− φ−	по− φ− φ−	у− φ− φ−	no passive forms
	opt.	present + past imp. past perf. + plu.	φ− φ−	φ− φ−	по− φ−	φ− у−	
	conj.	past imp. past perf. past plu.	φ− φ− φ−	по− φ− φ−	по− φ− φ−	φ− у− φ−	
present conj. active			φ−	φ−	φ−	у−	
present pass. indicative					1		

[a]Future imperative also has из- (да науүат, or и́зүүат) [b]Except 3rd plural да утут or да проүнтают [c]And also послы́ште in 2nd plural (alongside ү-) [d]Also ф-: любимо быти, уунмо быти, үтомо быти, слышану быти [e]But Kaz. ф- in plural forms (любими есме, etc.) and O2 ф- throughout [f]ф- in sing., по- in plural cf. [i] [g]All forms but third plural are built on prefixless present passive participles (да бых любимъ бы́л, ...да бы́сте любими бы́ли), but the third plural has да бы тѣ возлюбилиса , with воз-. [h]Except the alternate (= infinitive) form of the 3rd plural, here услышати (cf. үести, хотѣти) [i]ф- in singular, по- in plural cf. [f] [j]хотѣ- and хаунва- forms have no prefixes, but past perfect is given only with вол- forms, all of which take из-; егда́ извшлих, etc.; past plup. has both хаунва - and изволива- forms. [k]воз- in singular, ф- in plural [l]ф-, but also secondary по-аи forms, поүнтаюса, ... үтемса/ поүнтаемса.

8.1.3.3.3 Stem structure.

The verb paradigms show a substantial but not absolutely consistent correlation of stem types with tense categories. In the five moods (indicative, optative, conjunctive, imperative, infinitive) of the active voice, the present tense is generally expressed by the unprefixed present stem, the future by the present stem with a prefix other than по-, the past imperfect by a по-prefixed past stem, the past perfect by an unprefixed past stem, and the past pluperfect by the past stem of an iterative verb. There are, however, a number of exceptions to these generalizations, which can best be seen in the form of a table:

ACTIVE VERB STEMS

PRESENT	FUTURE	PAST		
		IMPERFECT	PERFECT	PLUPERFECT
люби-	возлюби-	полюби-	возлюби-[m]	любливa-[q]
үүн-	наүүн-[e]	пооүүн-	үүн-[n]	үүнва-
үте-[a]	(по)үте-[f]	поүто-[i]	үто-	үнта-[r]
слыши-[b]	услыши-[g]	ү- (по)слыша-[j]	слыша-	слыха-[s]
хоще-[c]	восхоще-[h]	(по)хотѣ-[k]	хотѣ-[o]	хаунва-
е-, бѣ-...[d]	буде-	бѣ-[l]	бы-[p]	быва-[t]

[a]Imper. үти, infin. үес- [b]Conj. үслыши-, imper. слушаи- and слыши, infin. слыша- [c]Opt. похотѣ- conj. 1st pl. хотимъ [d]Indic. and conj. є-, opt. бѣ-, imper. буди, infin. бы1- [e]Opt. үүн-, imper. 3rd pl. изүү- and наүү-, infin. изүү- [f]Indic. and conj. поүте-, opt. and imper. үте- [g]2 pl. imper. also послыши- [h]Opt. pl. восхоти- throughout [i]Conj. үте-, but this is an erroneously present-tense paradigm [j]Indic. aberrant үслыша, conj. sing. has erroneous present-tense forms in слыши - [k]Conj. хотѣ- [l]Conj. є-, бѣ-, and бы1- [m]O2 has an otherwise unattested любля- everywhere but in 1st sing. [n]Indic. 3rd pl. үүаху and үүиша [o]Conj. изволи - [p]Conj. also бѣ- [q]Infin. also люби - [r]Infin. үитыва - [s]Opt. 1st and 2nd sing. and conj. 3rd pl. слыша - [t]Infin. бы1-

Among these five stem types, the simplest correlation is between the present and the past perfect, which generally use the present and the past variant of otherwise identical stems (любити is exceptional in using the prefix воз- in the past perfect, but as we have seen above, this verb frequently differs from all the others). If we assume that the original Russian distinctions of imperfect/aorist/perfect/pluperfect had largely if not completely disappeared by the 16th c.,[127] this correspondence of stem structure between present and past perfect allows us to conclude that for the Donatus translators the Latin past perfect was interpreted as a simple past. The past imperfect and past pluperfect, with their special stems (по -prefixed and iterative respectively) can then be interpreted as further temporal or durational specifications (restrictions) within the past, just as the future is a temporal specification within the non-past.[128] The fact that the past imperfect is expressed by the prefix по- suggests that the translators equated this Latin tense with a completed and temporally restricted past action, much as in the modern Russian по- perfectives from non-determined verb-of-motion stems (e.g. полетать = провести некоторое время, летая, etc.). The iterative stems utilized to render the past pluperfect strongly suggest that the Russian translators responded to this Latin form not as a relative tense, but merely as a distant past action, temporally diffuse as compared to the temporally compact past imperfect. We may then risk the generalization that our 16th century Russian grammarians were not merely struggling awkwardly through clumsy translations of Latin arcanities (although this is not in itself an entirely unfair accusation), but additionally and quite unintentionally transposed the Latin paradigms into an internally coherent and formally rather elegant Russian tense ~ aspect system, one which can be symbolized by the following diagram, in which the Slavic tense forms are exemplified by the first person singular forms of үүити, with the Latin tense labels below:

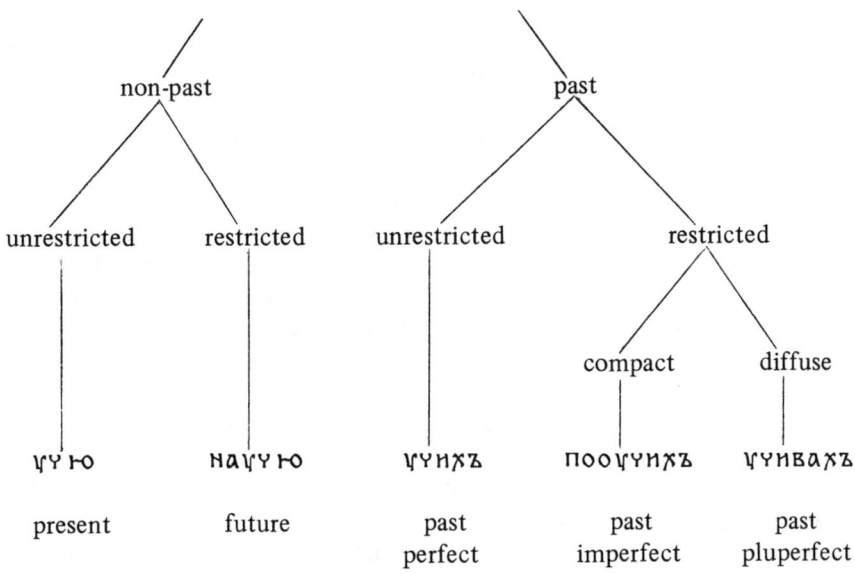

One could easily add markedness labels to the nodes in this diagram, but these would only replicate the prefixes (non-, un-) of the present labels, and would do nothing to explain the unexpected fact that within the past, it is not the unrestricted but the restricted category that is further divided.[129] One could hardly expect an entirely coherent system to emerge from our analysis, since the Slavic paradigms are after all not independently motivated by only a response to the alien and unrelated forms of the Latin prototype.

8.1.3.3.4 Verbal endings are straightforward everywhere in the non-past, but rather complex in the past.

8.1.3.3.4.1 The **present tense** has the same endings as in modern Russian, except for the still-uncontracted second person singular in –шн : –ѵ –ешн –етъ –емъ –ете –ѵт –ѵ –ншн –нт –нм –нте –ат (and their graphic variants).

8.1.3.3.4.2 The **past-tense** paradigms, on the other hand, show a good deal of variation and testify eloquently to the transitional state of verb morphology in the 16th century. This transitional state was the result of two overlapping developments. On the one hand, the old aorist and (contracted) imperfect paradigms, which coincided in many of their forms (aorist знахъ, contracted imperfect знахъ < знаахъ, etc.), were no longer distinguished with any consistency, so that we find aorist endings on clearly imperfect stems (бывашa for бывахѵ, etc.), and doublets within a single paradigm (plural ѵнтахом, ѵнтасте, ѵнтахѵ and ѵнташa in the act. indic. past pluperfect, etc.). On the other hand, and more importantly, both old simple past tenses were only bookish relics by the 16th c., having been driven out of the spoken language by the new past tense in -л. The innovative -л forms were in the process of penetrating the written language as well, and it is this process which is captured by the Donatus translation.

Innovative -л past tense forms first established themselves in the second and third persons singular, presumably because these were among the most frequent of spoken forms. Eighty percent of the Donatus past-tense paradigms have -л forms in both the 2nd and the 3rd person singular, and all without exception have -л in at least one of the two. The remainder of the paradigm consists of old simple past forms in -х, -хом, -сте, and -ша or -ху. The "standard" paradigms can be illustrated by the active indicative past imperfect of ѹчити and the active optative past perfect-pluperfect of ѥсти-ѹтати:

STANDARDIZED PAST TENSE PARADIGMS

поѹчихъ	поѹчихом (шх)	ѹтах	(шх) ѹтахом
поѹчил еси	поѹчисте	ѹтал еси	ѹтасте
поѹчил	поѹчиша	ѹталъ	ѹтаху

The Donatus grammar has seventeen paradigms of the поѹчихъ type and ten like ѹтах. Other types of paradigm are much fewer in number and are best seen as departures from the standard just illustrated.

In two cases, the paradigm includes both aorist and imperfect third plural endings, thus combining the поѹчихъ and the ѹтах types. There are the act. indic. past perfect of ѹчити and the similar pluperfect of ѹтати:

MIXED PARADIGMS

ѹчихъ	ѹчихомъ	ѹтах	ѹтахом
ѹчил еси	ѹчисте	ѹташе	ѹтасте
ѹчил тои	{ ѹчаху / ѹчиша	ѹталъ	{ ѹтаху / ѹташа

Departures from the standard 2nd and 3rd persons in -л are rather rare (in seven of the forty-two active past tense paradigms), and they are restricted to the imperfect ѹтах type:[130] we find two paradigms like act. indic. past pluperfect

любливах	любливахомъ
любливаше	любливасте
любливал тои	любливаху ти

and three like the act. opt. past perfect-pluperfect

(ѡх) ѹчнвал   ѹчнвахом
   ѹчнвал єсн   ѹчнвасте
   ѹчнваше   ѹчнвахѹ

plus the ѹнташе form, just adduced. In addition, we find one paradigm with mixed 2nd sing. forms, namely act. ind. past pluperfect

   ѹчнвах   ѹчнвахом
   { ѹчнваше
    тъı ѹчнвалъ   ѹчнвасте

   ѹчнвал тон   ѹчнвахѹ

One can assume that the reason for permitting 2nd and 3rd person singular imperfects, but not aorists, has to do with the phonological shape of these four endings: whereas the imperfects had "positive" endings in -ше ({uč-a+še}, {čit-a-+še}, etc.), the aorists had zero endings in precisely these two forms, at least in all non-consonantal stems ({u-sliš-a+ϕ}, {po-xot-ě+ϕ}, {po-uč-i+ϕ}etc.); there must have been a tendency to avoid zero endings in the Russian indicative paradigms, a tendency which is, conceivably, connected with the developing zero ending of the imperative in forms like (тронн >) тронь. It is also quite likely that this phonological factor was partly responsible for the development of -л past-tense forms first in just these two forms.

In three paradigms, the l-participle ending has been extended to the third person plural, as in the following act. ind. past pluperfect of хотѣтн:

   хаѹчнвах   хаѹчнвахом
   хаѹчнвал єсн   хаѹчнвасте
   хаѹчнвал   хаѹчнвалн

It is significant that two of the three similar paradigms occur in translations of Latin pluperfects, for which the Donatus translators utilized their native Russian iterative forms. These latter were, of course, actively spoken forms, in which the innovative l-participle past could most easily spread to forms other than the 2nd and 3rd sing.[131]

8.1.3.3.5 The **copula** appears consistently with the 2nd person sing. -л forms (почєл єсн etc.) but only sporadically in the 3rd sing. (ѹсльıшал єсть), and, as expected, not at all in the three attested 3rd plur. -л forms. The actual figures are $31/37 = 83\%$ for the 2nd sing. and $4/36 = 11\%$ for the 3rd sing. The copula is in complementary distribution with the personal article; cf. below.

8.1.3.3.6 A peculiar feature of the Donatus paradigms is the extensive use made of **person-marking pronouns** (ТЬІ, ТОН, ШН; ТНІ) in the 3rd person (singular, and occasionally plural) and, less often, in the 2nd person singular; cf. for example the act. indic. past perfect paradigm of ЛЮБИТИ:

    ВОЗЛЮБИХ   ВОЗЛЮБИХОМЪ
    ВОЗЛЮБИЛ ТЬІ   ВОЗЛЮБИСТЕ
    ВОЗЛЮБИЛ ТОН   ВОЗЛЮБИША И ТНІ

The pronoun occurs in those, and only in those forms which prefer or permit the l-participle forms (2nd s., 3rd sing., rarely 3rd pl.), although it itself is not restricted to l-participle environments, e.g. act. indic. past perfect ВОЗ-ЛЮБИША И ТНІ and act. conj. past perfect БѢАШЕ ТЬІ. The pronoun can be pre- or postposed, and in the latter case it may be preceded by the particle И, e.g., in the act. conj. past perfect, ТЬІ ҮҮНЛ, ТОН ҮҮНЛЪ, БѢАШЕ ТЬІ, ВОЗЛЮБИЛ И ТНІ, ВОЗЛЮБИЛ ШН; ШН, ШНСИЦА occurs only postposed. The distribution of pronouns by person is just the opposite of that of the copulas ЕСИ, ЕСТЬ as can be seen from the following table:

2nd sing.	{ ТЬІ	6 }	8	
	И ТЬІ	2		
3rd sing.	ТОН	13	16	24
	И ТОН	3		
	ШН	7	8	
	ШНСИЦА	1		
3rd plur.	{ ТНІ	2 }	3	
	И ТНІ	1		

Since the person-marking pronouns are in completely complementary distribution with the copulas, we can conclude that the one and the other served to mark person, above all in the new -л forms (which, like their aorist and imperfect forebears, failed to distinguish 2nd person sing. from 3rd), with the copula ЕСИ dominating in the 2nd sing. and the pronoun ТОН in the 3rd.

8.1.3.3.7 Taking into account the distribution of copula and pronominal forms, we can adduce the following as typical of the two "standard" past paradigms in Donatus:

TYPICAL STANDARD PARADIGMS

(егда) полюбихъ   полюбихомъ
полюбилъ еси   полюбисте
полюбилъ и той   полюбиша

(act. conj. past imperfect)

слыхахъ   слыхахомъ
слыхалъ еси   слыхасте
слыхалъ той   слыхаху

(act. conj. past pluperfect)

8.1.3.3.8 Irregular verbs. The "irregular" verbs хотѣти and быти (especially the latter) have a number of peculiarities setting them apart from the four "regular" conjugations and from each other. Many of these peculiarities have already been commented on in discussing the individual paradigms above; here, we shall only summarize these comments and attempt to draw a few generalizations from them.

8.1.3.3.8.1 Хотѣти is interesting only insofar as it displays a combination of Church Slavonic and Russian stem forms and endings. The present and future have Ch. Sl. т ~ щ in the singular ([вос]хощу, -хощеши, -хощетъ), and usually in the plural ([вос]хощемъ, -хощете, -хотатъ). However, the conjunctive present has Russian хотим (alongside волимъ), while the optative future mixes Ch. Sl. and Russian forms in the plural: щх восхотим, восхощете or восхотите, восхотат. In cases where no Ch. Sl. equivalent suggested itself, the translator had recourse to purely native forms and made no attempt to adhere to Ch. Sl. morphophonemic patterns: the Latin pluperfects appear as the Russian iteratives хаунвахъ etc. (not, e.g. *хащивахъ), and the equally alien gerunds as хотаун (not *хотащи or *хота, etc.). In the indicative pluperfect, the native Russian stem vocalism even induces an l-participle form in the 3rd person plural хаунвали, although the equivalent optative and conjunctive forms have the expected imperfect -ваху. Otherise, хотѣти shows the same mixture of aorist, imperfect, and l-participle forms as the "regular" verbs; cf. pp. 143 ff. above.

8.1.3.3.8.2 Быти, as is to be expected, has a much more complicated set of stem shapes and endings than хотѣти, especially in its function as an auxiliary verb with passive participles of the "regular" conjugations (pass. ind. past pluperfect ѹченъ бѣхъ and бывахъ, etc.). We shall discuss first the non-past, and then the past-tense uses of быти, subdividing the latter into the active and passive voices, in the latter of which быти functions as an auxiliary.

8.1.3.3.8.2.1 Within the non-past, the **present-tense** forms of быти show no variation except in the first person plural (the others being есмь, еси, есть, есте, суть), but this form appears with four distinct endings. In the active voice one finds only есме (active indic. present and active conjunct. present [егда есме]) and есмы (active conjunc. past imperfect егда есмы ~ егда бѣхомъ), but in the passive — that is, in its auxiliary function — all four endings occur: есме in the passive indic. past perfect любими есме (but also учени есмя, слышани есмя and утени есми), the passive optative present-past imperfect ш любими есме, and the passive conjunctive past perfect утени есме O2 (but also есмя Kaz.); есмы in the passive indic. present любими есмы O2 (but also есмя Kaz.), есмя (есмя) in the passive indic. present любими есмя Kaz. (but есмы O2), the passive indic. past perfects учени есмя and слышани есмя (but любими есме), and the passive conjunct. past perfect утени есмя Kaz. (but есме O2); есми only in the passive indic. past perfect утени есми (but учени есмя and слышани есмя). This greater variation in the passive voice is doubtless to be attributed to the un- or semi-stressed nature of the auxiliary (cf. the ending-stressed active indic. present есмѐ).

8.1.3.3.8.2.2 The **future tense** forms of быти are regular throughout, but when the same stem appears in the **imperative**, there is variation in the 2nd plur. endings: present imper. будете (sing. буди), but future imper. будите or да будете (sing. only да будеши). In the passive conjunctive future, three of the four conjugations have both simple (буду, будеши, ...) and periphrastic (быти имамь, быти имаши, ...) future forms, corresponding to *ero* and *fuero*, the only notable feature of which is the regular 1st person plural имамы.

8.1.3.3.8.2.3 It is in the **past tense** forms that быти shows the greatest complications. To facilitate our discussion, let us again adduce the paradigms (all active mood and past tense):

IMPERFECT

indicative

бѣх		бѣхом
был еси		бѣсте
{ был есть		бѣша
был бѣ		

optative

ѽх	бѣх	ѽх	бѣхомъ
	былъ еси		бѣсте
	былъ бѣ		бѣша

conjunctive

егда	есмь	егда	{ есмы / бѣхомъ
	еси		{ есте / бысте
	есть		бѣша

PERFECT

indicative

быхъ	быхомъ
былъ еси	бысте
быстъ	быша

optative
[= pluperfect; cf. below]

conjunctive

егда	бѣх	быхом
	бѣаше ты	бысте
	былъ ѡн	быша

PLUPERFECT

indicative

{ бѣх / быках	быва́хом
бывалъ еси	бывасте
бѣаше	бывахѵ

optative

шх бы1 вахъ	бы1 вахом
бы1 валъ еси	бы1 васте
бы1 вал	{ бы1 ваше
	бы1 вали

conjunctive

егда бы1 вах	бы1 вахом
бы1 вал еси	бы1 васте
{ бы1 ваше	бы1 вахѵ
бѣаше	

Many of the idiosyncracies of these paradigms have been commented on during the discussion of the "regular" conjugations above. Here, we shall be concerned primarily with the correlation of stems and endings with each other, their relation to the forms of the other Donatus verbs, and with those between these active voice (*esse*) forms and those of the passive (auxiliary) paradigms.

The most usual simple past forms to appear in these eight paradigms are the aorists of both the бѣ- and the бы1- stems, and the imperfect of the бы1ва- stem; the бѣа- imperfects occur only as scattered exceptions in the opt. and conj. sing. As in the case of all other verbs, the 2nd and 3rd person singular generally have l-participle forms, in which бы1л corresponds to both the бѣ- and the бы1- aorists, and бы1вал to the бы1ва- imperfects. Exceptions and inconsistencies do occur, but they do not detract from the overall validity of the statement just made: conj. past imperf. substitutes бы1сте for expected бѣсте, indic. past perf. 3rd sing. бы1сть for expected бы1л (есть); conj. past perf. бѣх, бѣаше for expected бы1х, бы1л еси; indic. past pluperf. 1st sing. бѣх alongside expected бы1вах ; opt. past perf./pluperf. aorist бы1ваша and l-participial бы1вали in the 3rd plur. — the former perhaps influenced by бы1ша of the corresponding indic. and conj. paradigms, and the latter a natural intrusion from the spoken language (of all the forms in all these paradigms, only бы1л(и) and бы1вал(и) were natural); the conj. past pluperf. has a бѣа- instead of a бы1ва- imperf. in the 3rd sing.

From the correspondences between the бы1ти forms and those of the four "regular" conjugations analyzed above (pp. 144 ff. above), we can assume that the бы1- aorists were the most natural (or, perhaps, the least unnatural) of these several past-tense forms, corresponding as they do to the unprefixed aorists of the "regular" verbs; that is, бы1х et al. are the least restricted (= least marked)

DONATUS 151

of all these artificial past-tense forms. The вѣ- aorists of the imperfect paradigms correspond, by and large, to the по-prefixed aorists of the regular past imperfect, which allows us to extend the meaning "temporally restricted, non-diffuse" to the вѣ-aorists of this БЫТИ paradigm. Finally, the correspondence of the БЫВА- imperfects to the regular iterative stems ЛЮБЛИВА-, ҮҮНВА- etc. is too obvious to require comment.

If we leave aside for a moment the вѣа-imperfects (on which see pp. 153 ff. below), we can outline the tense-aspects system of БЫТИ in the active voice in the same descriptive framework used for the other verbs above:

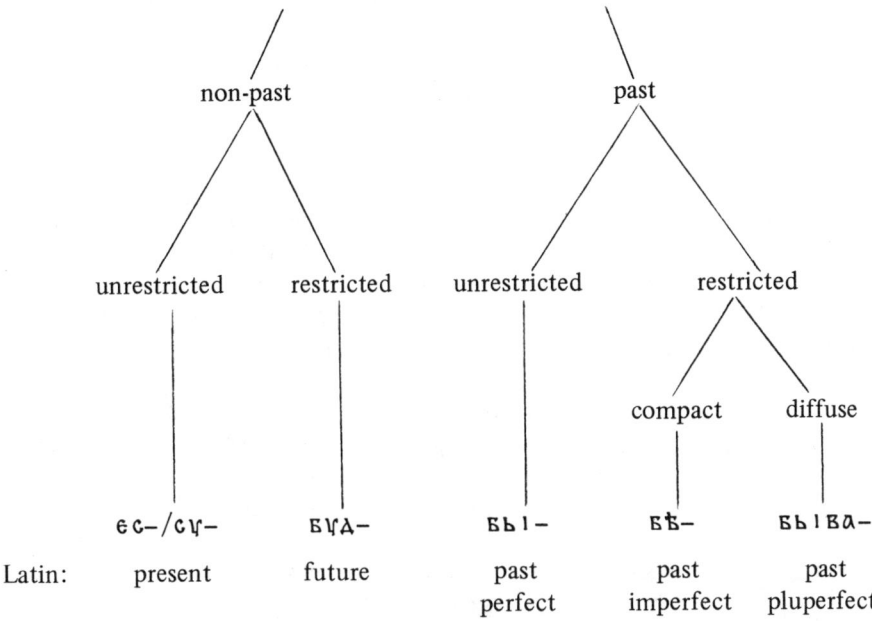

8.1.3.3.8.3 As a **passive-voice auxiliary**, БЫТИ is more complicated than in the active voice, both because of the problem in rendering the alternate Latin auxiliaries *sum/fui, eram/fueram, sim/fuerim*, etc., and doubtless because something like a pluperfect subjunctive seemed even stranger to the translators in the passive voice than in the active. We shall approach the topic first by recapitulating the auxiliary paradigms (omitting the passive participles ЛЮБИМЪ, ҮҮЕНЪ etc. and the particles ѹ, ЕГДА etc.; all are passive and past; the imperfect is omitted because it is formed with -СѦ instead of БЫТИ):

PERFECT INDICATIVE

(a) = *sum* et al.		(b) = *fui* et al.	
есмь	есме, -га, -и	бых[c]	быхомъ
еси[a]	есте	былъ еси	бысте
есть[b]	суть	{ былъ / бысть[d]	быша

[a] in one case O2 has бывалъ еси [b] with ѹченъ, былъ есть
[c] with ѹченъ, былъ есмь [d] thus with -лювимъ, ѹченъ; with
ѹченъ, слышанъ, бысть (but O2 ѹченъ былъ)

[PERFECT OPTATIVE = PLUPERFECT;
CF. BELOW]

PERFECT CONJUNCTIVE

As was noted in the discussion of complete paradigms on pp. 143 ff., the perfect conjunctives are an incoherent jumble of fractional paradigms; the correspondence between indicative and conjunctive is even lower than in the active paradigms (p. 111 above). We give the individual first (= *sim*) auxiliary paradigms in the left column, and those trying to render *fuerim* etc. on the right:

	(a) = *sim* etc.		(b) = *fuerim* etc.	
лювимъ	есмь	быхомъ	быхъ[a]	бѣахомъ
	былъ	бысте	бѣаше	бѣасте
	былъ	быша	бѣаше	бѣахѹ
ѹчимъ	бѣхъ	бѣхомъ	бѣахъ	быхом[b]
	бѣаше	есте	былъ еси	бысте
	есть	суть	былъ	быша[c]
ѹчен	есмь	есма, -е	быхъ	быхомъ[e]
	былъ еси	есте	бѣаше ты	бѣсте[f]
	есть	суть	былъ[d]	быша
ѹслышанъ	есмь	быхомъ	быхъ	бѣахом
	еси	бѣсте	былъ еси	бѣасте
	есть	бѣша	былъ бѣ	бѣахѹ

[a] O2 бѣхъ или быстъ [b] O2 бѣхомъ или бывахомъ [c] Jagić's printed text for types (a) and (b) reads "суть [бѣша] или быша" [d] O2 быстъ [e] O2 бѣхомъ [f] O2 бысте

There is not too much one can do to introduce order into such an exuberant jungle of forms, but a statistical summary can at least bring out a few tendencies:

stem and tense	(a)	(b)
ec-/cү- presents	12	0
бьı- aorists	4	8
бѣ- aorists	4	1
бѣa- imperfects	1	10
[бьıл (ecм) perfects	3	5]
	= 24	= 24

The l-participle forms are in brackets, since they are unreliable as diagnostic criteria, substituting as they do in the 2nd-3rd sing. for all three simple past tense forms. Our table shows only that the Donatus translators tended to use ec-/cү- presents for the *sim* type (a) perfect, as they did for the *sum* indicatives, but whereas the *fui* indicative was translated consistently by бьı- aorists, these aorists are outnumbered in the *fuerim* perfect conjunctive by бѣa- imperfects. All the present-tense auxiliaries occur in type (a), all but one of the бѣa - imperfects are in type (b), and the aorists are almost identically frequent in both types, the only difference being that type (b) shows a strong preference for the perfective бьı- aorist, while type (a) appears to be quite indifferent to aspect. Without wanting to establish a markedness framework which could hardly be justified by our contradictory and derivative data, we might nonetheless risk the generalization that the type (a) paradigms show a preference for auxiliaries which are temporally/aspectually relatively simple or unmarked, while type (b) auxiliaries tend to be chosen from the more complex or highly marked forms.

Another way of looking at the distinction between types (a) and (b) is in terms of individual temporal and aspectual categories:

       (a)   (b)
(1) non-past – past: 12 (ec-бьı 7, ec-бьıл 4, ec-бѣ 1)
(2) aorist – imperfect: 7 (бьı-бѣa 4, бѣ-бѣa 3)
(3) l-participle – imperfect: 3 (бьıл-бѣa)
(4) other: 2 (бѣ-бьı 1, бѣa-бьıл 1)

If we combine (2) and (3) into a single opposition of (unmarked) non-imperfect–(marked) imperfect, we can thus arrive at the generalization that in 22/24 of the paradigm forms type (a) has a relatively unmarked and type (b) a relatively marked auxiliary, or, to put it differently, the auxiliaries of type (a) are less arcane than those of type (b), which, after all, is equally true of

154   ORIGINS OF RUSSIAN GRAMMAR

sim-fuerim etc., (for a more general discussion of the hierarchal relation between (a) and type (b) auxiliaries, see pp. 156-158 below).

PLUPERFECT INDICATIVE

The pluperfect indicative paradigm, while not as incoherent as the perfect conjunctive, shows enough internal disparity to warrant listing the four verbs individually:

	(a) = *eram*		(b) = *fueram*	
ЛЮБИМЪ	БѣХ	Бѧхомъ	БЫВАХ	БЫВАХОМ
	Бѣѩше	Бѣѩсте	БЫВАШЕ	БЫВАСТЕ
	Бѣ	Бѣша ти	БЫВАШЕ	ѡни быша
ѸЧЕНЪ	Бѣх	Бѣхом	БЫВАХ	БЫВАХОМЪ
	Бѣѩше	Бѣсте	Бѣѩше	БЫВАСТЕ
	Бѣ	Бѣѩхѹ	Бѣѩше	БЫВАХѸ
ѸТЕН	Бѣх	Бѣхомъ	БЫВАХ	БЫВАХОМЪ
	Бѣѩше	БЫСТЕ	БЫЛЪ ЕСИ	БЫВАСТЕ
	Бѣ	Бѣше	БЫЛ Бѣ	БЫша[a]
СЛЫХАН	Бѣхъ	Бѣхом	Бѣах	Бѣахом
	Бѣѩше	Бѣсте	БЫЛ ЕСИ	Бѣасте
	Бѣ	Бѣше	БЫЛЪ Бѣ	Бѣахѹ

[a]O2, more consistently, БЫваш[a].

At the risk of oversimplifying somewhat, we can abstract out of the above partly contradictory data an idealized pluperfect indicative paradigm, as follows:

	(a)			(b)	
	Бѣх	Бѣхомъ[a]		БЫВАХ[d]	БЫВАХОМЪ[g]
	Бѣѩше	Бѣсте[b]	{	БЫВАШЕ[e]	БЫВАСТЕ[h]
				БЫЛ ЕСИ	
	Бѣ	Бѣша[c]		БЫЛ Бѣ[f]	БЫша[i]

[a] or Бѧхом [b] or Бѣѩсте, БЫСТЕ [c] or Бѣѩхѹ
[d] or Бѣах [e] or Бѣѩше [f] or БЫВАШЕ, Бѣѩше
[g] or Бѣахом [h] or Бѣасте [i] or БЫВАХѸ, Бѣахѹ, БЫВАШ[а]

Here the distribution of stem types is nearly as clear as in the perfect indicative, but the types used are completely different: in the perfect, the (a)–(b) distinction was rendered by єс - — вы 1 - forms, while here in the pluperfect the same distinction is expressed by вѣ - — вы ва - stem types.

PLUPERFECT CONJUNCTIVE

In the pluperfect conjunctive, the type (a) paradigms show quite a variety of вы-, вѣ-, and вѣа- forms, while those of type (b) are almost uniform. Let us examine the first of these in detail:

любимъ (a)		учим (a)	
вѣахъ	вѣахом	бы 1 х^a	бы 1 хомъ^b
бы 1 л еси	вѣасте	бы 1 л еси	вѣсте
бы 1 стъ	вѣша ты 1	вѣаше	вѣша

учєн (a)		слы 1 шан (a)	
вѣх	бы 1 хомъ^c	вѣах	вѣхом
бы 1 л еси	вѣсте	бы 1 л еси	єсте
в наше шн	бы 1 ша^d	вѣаше	вѣша

^{a} O2 вѣхъ ^{b} O2 вѣахомъ ^{c} O2 вѣхомъ ^{d} O2 вѣша

If we assume that O2 has the "correct" (i.e., more regular) readings with вѣ(а) in the four cases of ms. variation, we can without doing too much violence to the data arrive at the following somewhat idealized paradigms for the pluperfect conjunctive:

(a) - essem		(b) - fuissem	
{ вѣхъ { вѣахъ	{ вѣхомъ { вѣахомъ	бы 1 вахъ	бы 1 вахомъ
бы 1 л еси	вѣсте	бы 1 вал еси	бы 1 васте
вѣаше	вѣша	бы 1 валъ^a	бы 1 ваша^b

^{a} and бы 1 вал вѣаше, бы 1 валъ єст
^{b} and шни бы 1 ша, вѣаху

Except for the intrusion of вѣа- forms into the type (a) paradigm, the pluperfect conjunctive shows the same basic opposition of (a) вѣ- — (b) бы 1 ва- forms as we saw in the pluperfect indicative.

PERFECT-PLUPERFECT OPTATIVE

The optative mood has only a single paradigm, corresponding to both the perfect and the pluperfect of the indicative and conjunctive moods. As might be expected in such a situation, the auxiliaries are a complex assortment of all stem types:

	(a)		(b)	
ѡ любимъ	быхъ	бѣхом	бывахъ	бѣахомъ
	былъ еси	бысте	бывал еси	бывасте
	тои былъ	бѣаху	тои бѣяше	бывахѵ
ѡх уѵим	бѣхъ	бѣхомъ	бывахъ	бывахомъ
	бил еси	бѣсте	бывал еси	бывасте
	бѣаше	бѣша	бѣяше[a]	быяаша
ѡх утен	бѣх	бѣхомъ	бывахъ	бывахомъ
	былъ еси	бѣсте	бывал еси.	бывасте
	бѣаше	{ бѣша / бѣа́хѵ	бывал	бывахѵ
ѡх ѵслышанъ	бѣх	бѣхомъ	бывахъ	бывахомъ
	бѣаше	бѣсте	былъ еси	бѣасте
	бѣ	бѣша	былъ есть	бывасте (sic)

[a] О2 бяше или бѣаше ; Jagić 574 f.n. 4 "должно быть бываше", but cf. тои бѣяше just above and the l-participle forms of the two following paradigms.

It is not hard to disengage a more coherent paradigm from this variation:

	(a)		(b)	
	бѣхъ	бѣхомъ	бывахъ	бывахомъ
	былъ еси	бѣсте	бывал еси	бывасте
	бѣаше	{ бѣша / бѣа́хѵ	бѣаше	бывахѵ

Again, except for the intrusion of бѣа- forms into both type (a) and type (b) paradigms (5 and 4 times respectively), we see the basic opposition of бѣ- to быва -stems, just as in the indicative and conjunctive moods.

If we restructure the branching diagram of p. 151 to accommodate the бѣа-imperfects occurring only as auxiliaries, we can then mark the stem types used in type (a) and type (b) paradigms to show the distribution of stem types among the five past-tense passive paradigms. For reasons given on p. 153 above, we omit the l-participle forms, and for purposes of discussion we add tentative markedness values to the nodes of the branching diagram:

DONATUS

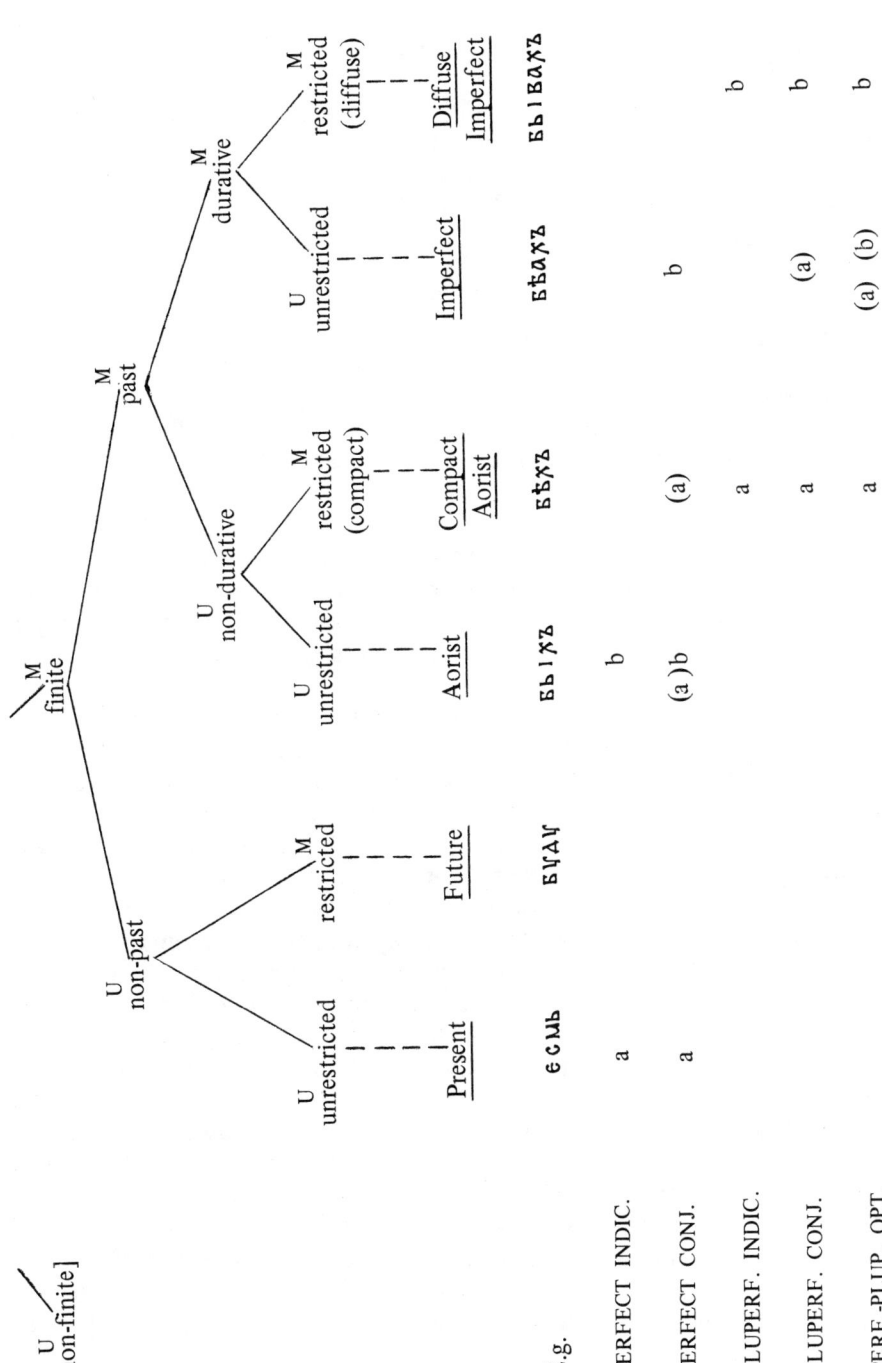

It is clear from this table that the major distinction between types (a) and (b) is between non-past and past for the perfect-tense paradigms (with some exceptions for the conjunctive), and between the non-durative and durative past for the pluperfect paradigms (again, with some exceptions for the non-indicative moods). Overall, the same generalization holds as for the perfect conjunctive (p. 153 above): type (a) auxiliaries are chosen from the less restricted (less marked) tense-aspect forms of бы́ти, and type (b) auxiliaries from those that are more restricted (more marked), and this corresponds to the more vs. less regular Latin auxiliaries (*eram–fueram*, etc.) to which the Slavic forms correspond.

This concludes our discussion of verbal paradigms in the Russian Donatus. As we hope to have shown in our perhaps overly lengthy description, this treatise contains not only abundant evidence of confusion and grammatical naiveté among its translators and/or copyists, but also a not insubstantial body of evidence (albeit partly inferential) about the state of Russian verbal morphology itself in the 16th century.

8.1.4 **Adverbs** (предлогъ словный, also предисловіе) complete the meanings of verbs ("приложена слову знаменованние его исполняетъ" 555). Adverbs have three "grammatical" features: (.1) significance (знаменование), (.2) comparison (прилаганіе), and (.3) forms (ѡбразьı).

8.1.4.1 The **significance** (знаменование) of an adverb consists in its membership in one of twenty-four semantic-syntactic classes, which are: (.1) place (мѣста, e.g. здѣ, тамо, онамо),[132] (.2) time (времени: днес, вчера, ныне, некогда, древле), (.3) number (числа: единою, двищі, трищи, четы́режды), (.4) negation (ѡрицанна: нѣсть, нѣт, ни; cf. [.18] below), (.5) emphasis (укрепленна: та́ко, мо́жет бы́ти, изве́стно), (.6) demonstrative (указанна: во́но), (.7) optative (желанна или хотенна: дабы́, ащебы́), (.8) hortative (подстрѣцанна или понуждания [*n.b.* *dj > ž]: ню, ну, also O2 помучи, поведи, подкрѣпи), (.9) modals (чина, cf. чинъ = verbal mood, p. 95 f. above: ꙗко, па́ки, посемъ), (.10) interrogative (вопрошанна: ѡ чом, почто, за кою вѣщ, чего дла), (.11) comparison (уподобленна: а́ки или ꙗко, какъ, какъ бы́), (.12) qualitative (ка́чества: у́еннѣ, краснѣ, крѣпцѣ, добрѣ), (.13) quantitative (количества: много, мало, менше́е, ме́ншні, велми; cf. [.24] below), (.14) doubt (сумнѣнıа: та́к ли, са́к ли, любо такъ а любо са́къ), (.15) personal (именны́е, O2 лиуны́а: со мною, с тобою, с собою, с нами, с вами), (.16) exclamatory (званна: ѡй, O2 ши ѡгон), (.17) response (ѡвѣщанна : а), (.18) separative (разделенна: ѡсов), (.19) oath (клатвы или работы [!]: е́й, та́ко, ни, нѣсть, не та́ко; cf. [.4] above), (.20) selection (и҆збра́нна: пригожее, па́че), (.21) inclusion (собра́нна: вкꙋпѣ, въ є҆днна́чествѣ [O2 во є҆динонача́лство], вмѣ́сте), (.22) prohibition (запреще́нна: не [O2 не трони, не ходи]), (.23) occasional (?: прилꙋча́ꙗ: се та́къ ты, се такъ), (.24) comparison (прилага́нна: па́че, болѣ, менше, превелие, малѣнше, ꙗнло [sic]). It is obvious from this list that "adverb" is too narrow a translation of предло́гъ словны́й, which actually means something more like 'adverbial (phrase)'.

8.1.4.2 Comparison (прилага́нїе) is not only a category of significance (.24) above, but also has its usual meaning of three degrees of comparison, positive (положи́телнаꙗ стꙋпень), comparative (прилага́телнаꙗ с.), and superlative (превы́спренеи or превы́шнеи с.), e.g. ꙋ҆ченѐ, ꙋ҆ченнѣ̀е, преꙋченнѣ́йше or преꙋченѣ́йши respectively.

8.1.4.3 Forms (ѻ҆́бразы) are the same for adverbs as for other parts of speech, namely, (.1) simple (є҆динора́дныи) and (.2) compound (сложны́й), which refer to unprefixed and negative-prefixed adverbs respectively: ꙋ҆ченнѣ, разꙋмнѣ; неꙋ҆ченѐ, неразꙋ́мнѣ.

The text then continues with a more detailed analysis of adverbs of place (cf. 8.1.4.1.1 above), but this contains nothing of interest for Slavic grammar and will be ignored here.

8.1.5 The **participle** (прича́стие) is cogently defined as a part of speech sharing nominal and verbal categories: "Прича́стие... є҆сть... ча́сть вѣща́ния, ча́сть прие́мла и҆мени и҆ ча́сть сло́ва (= verb, DSW) и҆ ча́сть ѿ ѻ҆боего" 558.

8.1.5.1 The participle expresses six grammatical categories, as follows.

8.1.5.1.1 Gender (ро́дъ) in the participle can be (.1) masculine (мꙋже́скы̀, e.g. сеи ꙋ҆те́нъ), (.2) feminine (же́ньскии̇: сиа̀ ꙋ҆те́на), (.3) neuter (посре́дний: сио ꙋ҆те́но), or (.4) universal (всачески̇: се́и и҆ сиа̀ и҆ сиѐ ꙋ҆то́мо — as Jagić 558 f.n. 5 points out, an incorrect rendering of *legens*). There is no trace here of common (ѻ҆́бщий) gender or epicenes (смѣ́шеныи р.); cf. the nominal genders, p. 79 f. above.

8.1.5.1.2 The participle has the same six **cases** (паде́нн ꙗ) including the vocative form, as the noun, viz.: (.1) nominative (и҆менова́телное, e.g. се́и ꙋ҆тꙋ́щь, сиа̀ ꙋ҆тꙋ́ща, сиѐ ꙋ҆тꙋ́ще [133]), (.2) genitive (ро́дственое: сего̀ ꙋ҆тꙋ́щаго), (.3) dative (да́телнѣ [*n.b.* here *et seq.* the adverbial terminology]: семꙋ̀ ꙋ҆тꙋ́щемꙋ), (.4) accusative (вино́внѣ : сего̀ ꙋ҆тꙋ́щаго, сию̀ ꙋ҆тꙋ́щꙋю, сиѐ ꙋ҆тꙋ́щее), (.5) vocative (зва́телнѣ: ѻ҆ ꙋ҆тꙋ́щии, ꙋ҆тꙋ́щее), and (.6) ablative (ѿрица́телное [sic]: ѿ сего̀ ꙋ҆тꙋ́щаго, ѿ сеꙗ̀ ꙋ҆тꙋ́щиа, neut. = masc.).

8.1.5.1.3 Tense (вре́мѧ) consists of the customary triad of present (настоꙗ́щее: ꙋ҆тꙋ́), past (минꙋ́вшее: ꙋ҆то́х), and future (грѧдꙋ́-

щее или будущее: чести ми или како честй, или како чести имам ; note that the illustrations had to be borrowed from the finite verb system.

8.1.5.1.4 The **significance** (знаменование) of a participle consists of its membership in one of several voice and tense classes: (.1) active verbs (дѣлное слово) have present (настоящее, e.g. учущїй) and future (грядущее, e.g. чести имамъ [134]) participles; (.2) passives (страдалное с.) have them for the past (минувшее, e.g. ученъ) and the future (ученъ будетъ). These four standard participles (present, future, perfect, gerundive) are illustrated below (8.1.5.2). Other significance classes are mentioned only here, with no paradigmatic illustrations: (.3) medials (посреднее с.) have only present and future participles, e.g. стоящь, станет (*sic*; = *staturus*), but (.4) deponents (шложное с.) have them for the present (глагола), past (глаголавый) and future (иже глаголати имат), and (.5) common-voice verbs (шбщее с. also deponents) have all four, e.g. present безчестни, perfect безчествованый , and two futures, безчествован будетъ and безчестен будет (*criminaturus, criminandus*).

8.1.5.1.5 **Number** consists of the usual singular (сен учщь) and plural (сїи учущїи); note the old acc. учщь functioning as a nominative.

8.1.5.1.6 **Form** (шбразъ) among the participles, as elsewhere, refers to derivational status, and in particular to negative prefixation: (.1) simple (единородный or простый), e.g. учщь; (.2) compound (сложный), e.g. нерадящ, небрегущъ.

8.1.5.2 Donatus then continues with translated **paradigms** of the four participles of *legere* (чести); we rearrange them here into the usual columnar form.

8.1.5.2.1 The **present active participle** appears as an inconsistent combination of Slavic and pseudo-Latin forms:

PRESENT ACTIVE PARTICIPLE

Singular

	masculine	feminine	neuter
nom.	сей учщїй	сия учщая [a]	сие учщїй
gen.	сего учщаго		
dat.	сему учщему		
acc.	сего учщаго	сию учщую	сие учщее
voc.	ш учщїй		
abl.	ш сегш учщаго	ш сея учщая	ш сего ⎰учщагш ⎱учщаго

Plural

	masculine	feminine	neuter
nom.	сні́ ꙋтꙋ́щрі	сѣ̀ ꙋтꙋ́щрї	сна̀ {ꙋтꙋ́ща ꙗ / ꙋто́ма ꙗ
gen.	сн҇х ꙋтꙋ́щрх	сѣ́х ꙋтꙋ́щрх	снх҇ъ ꙋтꙋ́щрх
dat.	сн҇ма ꙋтꙋ́щрма	—	—
acc.	снхъ ꙋтꙋ́щрхъ	сѣ́х ꙋтꙋ́щрхъ	сн҇х ꙋто́мьіх
voc.	{ѡ̈ ꙋтꙋ́щрї / ѡ̈ ꙋтомнї	—	—
abl.	ѡ̄ сн҇х ꙋтꙋ́щрхъ	—	—

[a]omitted forms are presumably like the masc. (following the Latin model)

Here the translator vacillated between a literal translation of the Latin, on the one hand, and the natural urge to express the grammatical categories of his own language, on the other; for example, the nondistinction of gender in nom. sing. *hic et haec et hoc legens* appears in the neut. ꙋтꙋ́щнї, identical to the masc., but the corresponding fem. makes a concession to Slavic grammar by appearing as a long-form nom. sing. fem. participle in -щна and the neut. itself appears in its Slavic -ее form in the acc. The dual abl. sing. neut. exploits the ѡ/о distinction to render the -*e*/-*i* of Latin *ab hoc legente vel legenti*, and the same graphic device is used to distinguish abl. сегѡ from gen. сего, as in the nominal paradigms on pp. 81, 85 above. The dat. plur. in -ма appears only in this pres. act. participle, cf. however the same ending among the pronouns, e.g. pp. 91 - 92 above.

8.1.5.2.2 The **future active participle** proved to be a bit more than the translator-copyists could handle; we adduce it here as a curiosity:

FUTURE ACTIVE PARTICIPLE

Singular

	masculine	feminine	neuter
nom.	сен ꙋестѝ бꙋ́детъ	сна̀ ꙋести бꙋ́детъ	снѐ ꙋтомо бꙋ́детъ
gen.	сего̀ емꙋже ꙋести	енже ꙋести	егоже ꙋести
dat.	семꙋ емꙋже ꙋести	ёнже ꙋести	емꙋже ꙋести
acc.	сего емꙋже ꙋести	сн ю̀ ёнже ꙋести	снѐ ёже ꙋестѝ
voc.	ѡ̄ ꙋтꙋ́щрї	ѡ̄ ꙋтꙋ́ща ꙗ	ѡ̄ ꙋтꙋ́щее
abl.	ѡ̄ сего емꙋже ꙋестѝ	ѡ̄ се ꙗ̀ ёнже ꙋестѝ	ѡ̄ сего емꙋже ꙋести[сѧ]

Plural

	masculine	feminine	neuter
nom.	сни́ и́мже [се] уести	сѣ̀ и́мже уести	сна̀ и́мже уести[ся]
gen.	сих и́мже уестѝ	сѣх и́маже уести	сих и́мже[b] уести
dat.	си́мъ и́мже уести	—	—
acc.	сих утѵ́ши х[a]	сѣх утѵ́ших	сна̀[c] утѵ́ма
voc.	ѿ иже уести бу́дете	—	ѿ иже вам[d] уести
abl.	ѿ сих и́мже уести	—	—

[a] О2 си́хъ и́хже утѵ́щихъ [b] Kaz. ихже, О2 и́маж [c] О2 си́н [d] О2 васъ

The only items of Slavic interest in this paradigm are, once again, the -ма datives (here, in the gen. plur.) and the fact that утомо is spelled with an о in the neut. sing. but with ѡ in the plur. Conceivably this might indicate that the scribe was aware of the Greek-based tradition of using the graphs о/ѡ to mark the sing./plur. distinction (e.g. вода/вѡдь1, cf. p. 22 above), but it is equally possible that this copyist reinvented the distinction for himself, since he also exploited it in earlier paradigms to distinguish abl. сеѡ from gen. сего (cf. pp. 81 and 85 above).

8.1.5.2.3 The **perfect participle** is classed as a present passive participle, and is rendered into Slavic by the present active -ся participle, in the masc. and fem. forms, and by the present passive participle in most of the neut.:

PERFECT PARTICIPLE

Singular

	masculine	feminine	neuter
nom.	сѐн утѣ́1нся	сна̀ утѵ́шаася	снѐ утѵ́шееся
gen.	сего̀ утѵ́шагося	сеѧ̀ утѵ́шнюася[b]	сего̀ уто́маго[b]
dat.	сему́ утѵ́шемуся	се́и утѵ́шенся	сему́ утомому
acc.	сего̀ утѵ́шаго[a]	сню̀ утѵ́шую[a]	снѐ уто́мое
voc.	ѿ утѵ́шиͥся	ѿ утѵ́шаася	ѿ утомое
abl.	ѿ сего̀ утѵ́шагося	ѿ сеѧ̀ утѵ́шнюася	ѿ сего̀ уто́маго

Plural

	masculine	feminine	neuter
nom.	сі́и ѹтѷ́шнї сѧ	сѣ ѹтѷшнисѧ[c]	сна̀ ѹтѹ́ма ꙗ
gen.	сих ѹтѷшнхсѧ	сѣх ѹтѷшнхсѧ	си́хъ ѹтѹ́мыıх
dat.	си́мъ ѹтѷшнмсѧ		
acc.	сих ѹтѷшнхсѧ	сѣх ѹтѷшнхсѧ[c]	сна ѹтѹ́ма ꙗ
voc.	ѿ ѹтѷ́шнї сѧ	ѿ ѹтѷша ꙗсѧ	ѿ ѹтѻ̀ма ꙗ
abl.	ѿ сих ѹтѷ́шнхсѧ		

[a] Jagić 561 f.n. 2 considers that сѧ was omitted by error from these forms [b] O2 omits the pronoun from both and the сѧ from the fem. (= *huius lecti, lectae, lecti*) [c] from O2

This paradigm seems to have been the work of a translator who tried, but not always successfully, to write correct Ch. Sl. His masc. nom. sing. ѹты́ исѧ is flawless, but right next to it is an innovative fem. ѹтѷ́шаѧсѧ instead of canonical *ѹтѷшн ꙗсѧ. In the plural. the fem. nom. has a nearly modern Russian form, while the vocative has an ending from Russian Ch. Sl. (-а ꙗ, < *ęję). The pronoun stem alternates, without apparent motivation, between си - and се-, and the spellings -ꙗ, -ѧ seem to occur in free variation, but ш is reserved as a plural marker, in all but the voc., of the neut. Overall, however, this is a rather coherent paradigm, especially if one compares it to the perfect participle above and the gerundive below.

8.1.5.2.4 The **gerundive**, or future passive participle, consists partly of periphrastic passives with бѹ́детъ etc., partly of various anaphoric phrases:

GERUNDIVE

Singular

	masculine	feminine	neuter
nom.	сеи ѹтен бѹ́дет	сна̀ ѹтена бѹ́дет	сиѐ ѹте́но бѹ́детъ
gen.	сего̀ егоже ѹести	[е] ꙗже ѹестѝ	е́же ѹести
dat.	семѹ̀ егож ѹести	е́нже ѹести	е́же ѹести
acc.	сего̀ егож ѹести	сиѭ̀ ю̀же ѹести	сиѐ е́же ѹестѝ
voc.	ѿ иже ѹтен бѹ́дешн	ѿ иже ѹтена бѹ́дешн	ѿ и́же ѹте́но бѹ́детъ
	ѿ сего̀ егож ѹести	ѿ се ꙗ е ꙗже ѹести	ѿ сего̀ егоже ѹести

Plural

	masculine	feminine	neuter
nom.	сиï иже ѹтени бѹдѹт	сѣ ѹтени[a]	сна ѹтома бѹдѹт[b]
gen.	сих иже ѹтени бѹдѹтъ	сѣх ѧже ѹтени бѹдѹт	сих еже ѹтоми бѹдѹтъ
dat.	симъ ихже ѹести	—	—
acc.	сѣх[c] ихже ѹести	сѣх ихже ѹести	сиѧ ѧже ѹести
voc.	ѡ ихже ѹести	ихже ѹести	ѧже ѹтома
abl.	ѿ сих ихже ѹести бѹдѹтъ	—	—

[a] О2 сïи ѹтени бѹдета (sic) [b] О2 сиѧ ѹтена бѹдѹтъ [c] Jagić 561 f.n. 10 considers this an error for сихъ

The only item of interest here is the preservation of the old *i_2 plur. ending of the participles (ѹтени, ѹтоми), and perhaps the fact that the translator or copyist has abandoned ѡ as a plur. marker in the neuter.

This concludes the exemplification of participles in the Donatus translation.

8.1.6 Conjunctions (соѹзьі) display three kinds of grammatical features: domain, form and rank.

8.1.6.1 There are five **domains** (ѿбласти), or functional classes, of conjunctions: (.1) copulative (совокѹпителньіе e.g. и, иже), (.2) disjunctive (несовокѹпителньіе : или, не, ниже[135]), (.3) complementary (дополнѧтелньіе, = adversative, concessive, and others: ѹбо, тѣмже, дабьі, сирѣѹ, ѿбаѹе), (.4) material (вещественьіе: аще, когда, наипаѹе, токмо), and (.5) concatenating (? = совѣщалньіе[136]: ибо, сего ради, понеж, тѣм же ѹбо).

8.1.6.2 Form (ѿбразъ) continues to refer to derivational complexity: понѐ is (.1) simple (простьіи, единорѧдньіи) and понеже is compound (сложньіи).

8.1.6.3 Rank (ѹинъ) refers to whether a conjunction is (.1) prepositive (предположньіи : и), (.2) subjunctive (подложньіи : кои, не), or (.3) common (ѿбщиï ѹбо, сего ради, тѣм же).

It is difficult to find anything of interest for Slavic grammar in all of this.

8.1.7 Prepositions (представлѐниа) are defined as a word-class in which the only relevant grammatical category is case ("Вопросъ. представлѐнию колицьі пристоиѧ или нападаю; [meaning unclear, DW] ѿвѣтъ. едино. вопросъ. ѹто ; ѿвѣтъ. падѐние то́кмо" 563). There are only two cases, accusative (вино́вное) and "negative" (ѿрицателное, = ablative). There ensues a list of prepositions which take the acc. in Latin (*ad, apud, ante, adversum*, etc.), but the Slavic translations require, in addition, the genitive, the dative, and the instrumental: пред, у, ѡколо, супротиву, по, надъ, etc. Anticipating some confusion on the part of the Russian schoolboy hearing that пред, у etc. take the acc., the Donatus translation then asks, " Како се есть;" and hastens to explain that, " глаголем бо' ко ѡцу, пред селомъ или у села.", etc. (563), i.e. giving some illustrative prepositional phrases with the correct Slavic rection. The same exercise is then repeated for the ablative prepositions and their translations. The only minor items of interest in these lists are the mixtures of older and newer endings: на супостатьı but про ближних, далѣ предѣловъ and промеж кораблéи but still пред свидѣтели 2x, etc.

8.1.8 The **interjection** is "a part of speech which signifies a mental desire by means of an (intellectually, DSW) unrecognizable word ("часть вѣщанна, знаменующа ума желанна гласом незнаемьıмъ" 565). The only feature of interjections is signification (знаменование), by which is meant the particular mental state expressed by the preposition. These states are: (.1) jollity (веселна ума [sic] ..., ꙗко смѣꙗнна), e.g. ха ха ха; (.2) pain or sadness (болѣзнование или туга), e.g. увьı ; (.3) surprise (удивление), e.g. ѡ се, папа (sic) (= на на?); (.4) horror (ужасъ), e.g. ух ух ух, -- или аще ꙗже сут подобна симъ" (565).

At this point the Donatus translation returns to a more detailed examination of verbal paradigms, which have already been discussed above (pp. 95 ff.); we therefore conclude our treatment of Donatus at this point.

9. Concluding Remarks

The preceding pages offer a selection of medieval grammatical material, which, we hope, may help to clarify the shadowy intellectual background from which the first printed grammars arose. Whether the selection and organization of this material are judicious is not for us to say. The material is presented primarily in chronological order, although the actual chronology is unclear in many cases, and is obviously contradicted by the subject matter itself in some instances, as when Maksim Grek uses passages adapted from the much older "Eight parts of speech". One might, perhaps, have organized the study not by chronology, but by subject, with chapters on "The History of Punctuation", "The History of Phonology", etc. Above all, it is obvious that such problems can be approached seriously only by someone with unlimited access to the libraries and archives of the Soviet Union, Bulgaria and Yugoslavia. The present volume, although not entirely devoid of original speculation, is in no way intended as a substitute for such primary archival research. We would be well rewarded for our small efforts, were they to serve as an incentive toward such study.

NOTES

ᵃ S. K. Bulič, *Očerk istorii jazykoznanija v Rossii, T. 1 (XIII v. – 1825 g.)* (= *Zapiski Ist.-Fil. Fak. Imper. SPb-skogo universiteta*, c. LXXV), SPb., 1904; V.I. Jagić, *Istorija slavjanskoj filologii* (= *Ènciklopedija slavjanskoj filologii*, I), SPb., 1910; E.F. Karskij, *Očerk naučnoj razrabotki russkogo jazyka v predelax SSSR* (= *Sbornik Otd. russk. jaz. i slov. AN SSSR*, CI, No. 1), Leningrad, 1926; Kraus Reprint, Nendeln, Liechtenstein, 1966); V.V. Vinogradov, "Russkaja nauka o russkom literaturnom jazyke", *Učenye zapiski* MGU, vyp. 106 (*Rol' russkoj nauki v razvitii mirovoj nauki i kul'tury*, 3, 1), Moscow, 1946, p. 22-147; V. D. Levin, A. D. Grigor'eva, "Vopros o proisxoždenii i načal'nyx ètapax russkogo literaturnogo jazyka v russkoj nauke XIX v.", *Učenye zapiski Mosk. gorodsk. ped. inst. im. V. P. Potemkina*, 51 (= *Kafedra russkogo jazyka*, vyp. 6), Moscow, 1956, p. 257-291; P. S. Kuznecov, *U istokov russkoj grammatičeskoj mysli*, Moscow, 1958.

ᵇ A.I. Klibanov, "*Napisanie o gramote* (opyt issledovanija prosvetitel'no-reformacionnogo pamjatnika konca XV – pervoj poloviny XVI veka)", *Voprosy istorii religii i ateizma. Sbornik statej*. III, Moscow, 1956, p. 325-379. This article was called to my attention by Professor Robert Mathiesen.

ᶜ V. Jagič, *Codex slovenicus rerum grammaticarum. Rassuždenija južnoslavjanskoj i russkoj stariny o cerkovno-slavjanskom jazyke*, Berlin, 1896 (reprinted Munich, 1968 = *Slavische Propyläen*, 25).

ᵈ This confirms the view of L. S. Kovtun, "Russkie knižniki XVI stoletija o literaturnom jazyke svoego vremeni", *Russkij jazyk. Istočniki dlja ego izučenija*, Moscow, 1971, p. 22.

ᵉ Professor Harvey Goldblatt's forthcoming book on Konstantin will argue a different view.

1. V. Jagić, *Codex slovenicus rerum grammaticarum. Rassuždenija južnoslavjanskoj i russkoj stariny o cerkovno-slavjanskom jazyke,* Berlin 1896; photo-mechanic reprint, Munich, 1968 (= *Slavische propyläen*, 25), p. 2.

2. *Ibid.*, p. 5.

3. *Ibid.*, p. 6.

4. J. Dobrovský still considered East and South Slavs as a single group, and even Maksimovič, as late as 1839, could hardly distinguish O.C.S. from Old Russian. Cf. V. D. Levin, A. D. Grigor'eva, "Vopros o proisxoždenii i načal'nyx ètapax russkogo literaturnogo jazyka", *Učenye zapiski Moskovskogo gorodskogo pedagogičeskogo instituta imeni V. P. Potemkina*, 51 (= Kafedra russkogo jazyka, vypusk 6), Moscow, 1956, p. 267-68.

5. Jagić, *Codex slovenicus* . . ., p. 6-7.

6. Cf. most recently the articles by Granstrem-Kovtun and by Vagner in *Izbornik Svjatoslava 1073 g. Sbornik statej*, Moscow, 1977.

7. L. S. Kovtun, *Russkaja leksikografija èpoxi srednevekov'ja*, Moscow-Leningrad, 1963, p. 13-154.

8. Ioan's unearned reputation as a grammarian was imputed to him by Kalajdovič and others, who thought he had translated the "Eight parts of speech". Ioan's text is found in Jagić, *Codex slovenicus* . . ., p. 32-36.

9. It has been suggested, but not yet convincingly demonstrated, that the so-called "mysterious Black Sea signs" were (perhaps via Georgian) a source of the Glagolitic alphabet; cf. N. A. Konstantinov, "Černomorskie zagadočnye znaki i glagolica", *Učenye zapiski LGU*, 197 (= Serija filologičeskix nauk, vyp. 23), 1957, p. 110-146; cf. also M. I. Privalova, "Ob istočnikax glagolicy (V diskussionnom porjadke)", *ibid.*, 267 (= Serija filol. nauk, vyp. 52), p. 17-33.

10. Jagić, *Codex slovenicus* . . ., p. 9. Note that the examples themselves occur in alphabetical order (first consonants, then vowels).

11. шь = щ ; cf. a 13th-14th c. Bulgaro-Serbian revision of this text, with exemplar phrases illustrating each letter: "ш. шестокрилли аггли слоужеть ми; ъ, еромь носимь невидѧмо; щ. що мы обвѣщаета до второаго пришествиѩ" (*Codex slovenicus* . . ., p. 16).

12. The two lists are a bit different in the later Russian text:
Greek: а в г д е з и θ і к м н 3 о п р с
т ѵ ф х ѱ ѡ
Slavic: б ж s ц ч ш щ ъ ы ь ѣ ю ѫ ѧ
(*Codex slovenicus* . . ., p. 18).

13. *Ibid.*, p. 11.

14. The Kievan period had been equally receptive to foreign (Byzantine-Bulgarian, Bohemian) cultural influences, but less mechanistic in adopting them. See, e.g. *Izbornik 1073. Sbornik statej*, Moscow, 1977.

15. Published by Jagić, *Codex slovenicus* . . ., p. 38-54.

16. This erroneous view goes back to I. Kalajdovič; cf. *Codex slovenicus* . . ., p. 38.

17. *Codex slovenicus* . . ., p. 40, 76-77.

18. Such graphic trivia would hardly be worth mentioning were it not for the fact that later "grammarians" tried to exploit them as grammatical markers (singular/plural, masculine/feminine), cf. p. 22 and 60, etc. below.

19. Greek equivalents are in most cases taken from Jagić's commentaries in *Codex slovenicus* . . ., *passim*.

20. In Greek the term παρασύντετον had referred to words derived from compounds, i.e. to words with two levels of embedding.

21. Published by Jagić, *Codex slovenicus* . . ., p. 95-199.

21a. "потрѣба би или огнь или ина каа казнь подбна сеи възнезаапоу наити на пишоущих и писанънаа, еже съжещи сих", ms. f. 10² (*Codex slovenicus* . . ., p. 108).

22. Jagić, *ibid.*, p. 81, refers to Konstantin as "čelovek, ne umevš[ij] vyrazit' svoi mysli prosto i otčetlivo i na ponjatnom jazyke"; furthermore, Konstantin was not always able to understand the very Greek he was trying to imitate (*ibid.*, p. 228).

23. E.g. in the late 14th c. Serbian Hamartolos translations.

24. Jagić, *Codex slovenicus* ..., p. 229 ff.

25. The point is clear in spite of Konstantin's substitution of the *pojerok* for ь. Later Russian mss. have diacritic substitutions for both jers.

26. Konstantin too used only ь in auslaut, but employed both ъ and ь in inlaut; in prepositions, he used кь but въ.

27. Jagić, *Codex slovenicus* ..., p. 266-67, 288-93.

28. Jagić's text, p. 278, has what appears to be a second superscript л above the о: мо͡лˊба.

29. Cf. the original in the "Eight parts of speech", p. 17 above.

30. It should be reiterated that only Jagić's printed texts are available, which introduces a degree of uncertainty into any discussion of diacritics.

31. Edited by Jagić, 360-385.

32. As Jagić 518 points out, this terminology owes more to Latin than to Greek; cf. vocalis/semivocalis, φωνῆντα/ἡμίφωνα.

33. затин = (1) a smooth, slow-flowing part of a river, near the shore; (2) an aperture for shooting, in a fortress wall.

34. Note that only the ъ-substitute (ёртица) is mentioned, not the ь-substitute (паёрокъ).

35. One must assume that а є о ѵ were considered basic and e.g. ѧ є ѡ ю secondary, but that front и was taken to be the basic member of its group. Note that in the treatise о̀ мнȯ́жествѣ і о̀ ѐді́нствѣ (p. 51-55), the basic vowels а о ѵ are used in singular endings and ѧ ѡ ю for the plural, whereas the front/back relation is reversed for sing. и ь/plur. ы ъ.

36. In some mss., ѵ.

37. See Jagić 512 ff.

38. "Nasal", probably, because of such spellings as ӓггелъ.

39. Ц is in fact omitted from a neighboring passage, in which these "сходи́телные" pairs are listed by name (бѵки с покоѐᴍ, вѣдьі с фѐртоᴍ да с дито ю...").

40. See D. S. Worth, "Metaphorical phonology in the 16th century", *Slavica hierosolymitana*, 5-6, 1981, p. 69-74.

41. Other ms.: ѡ̀бращѧ́юще, притѧгѧ́юще, совокоѵплѧ́юще (374 f.n. 12).

42. Other mss. continue: по шестерѵ, по́ седмерѵ, по́ ѡ̀смерѵ, по́ девѧтерѵ (374 f.n. 14).

43. The other mss. adduce the following illustrations of more complex syllables: і ѝ͞зѣра̀, ѡ̃ ѝ͞зѣра̀ і ѡ̃ ѝ͞зѣра̀, а̀ і ѡ̃ і͞зѣра, а̀ і ѡ̃ і ѝ͞зѣра (*sic*; perhaps the second і is an intercalated acc. masc. pronoun?).

44. Jagić's printed text, however, uses only є (not ε) in the exx.
45. *Sic* Jagić 374; sc. єй̆.
46. *Sic* Jagić 374; sc. ай̆.
47. Omitted, either in the text or inadvertently by Jagić (*n.b.* the initial о̲ of the following digraph о‫ү‬).
48. Cf. B. A. Uspenskij, *Arxaičeskaja sistema cerkovnoslavjanskogo proiznošenija* (*iz istorii liturgičeskogo proiznošenija v Rossii*), Moscow, 1968, p. 29 ff.
49. Another ms. continues on to по дєвати̇̆.
50. If we eliminate the repeated ѡ̇бращаю̇тсѧ and приклонѧ́ю̇тсѧ, we are left with five verbs, corresponding to the five full-vowel pairs (1.2.1.1-.5, 2.2.1-.5). However, the disparity in terminology (only приткновє́нїє ~ притоу̇їє having a verbal counterpart) and some apparent changes in order (притъ́ıю̇тсѧ is 4th of the five verbs but приткновє́нїє and притоу̇їє are 6/6 among the clusters) makes it impossible to attribute a particular verb to a particular cluster. And in any case, it should not be forgotten that our medieval scribes took as much pleasure in the variety of their terminology as in the multiplicity of their graphic signs.
51. The scribe uses three different vowels in order to maintain his standard quota of three examples; apparently, he couldn't think of three different CCC clusters. No examples are given here for CCCCV clusters, but of скврa on p. 36 above. Other mss. continue on to nine-consonant clusters, – without illustrations, of course.
52. Other mss. carry this game even further: а̇ і о̇ і ю̇аковѣ, а̇ і о̇ і і о і лѣ (apparently 'and also about Joil too' with і̇ 'too' between the preposition and the proper name). Interest in such phonological monstrosities has not died out; cf. и о Ии и о ииных родителях and предводитель монстрш взбзднул, both from the lips of eminent Slavists now departed.
53. Edited from two mss. by Jagić, *Codex slovenicus* . . ., p. 431-436.
54. In some cases the functions he assigned were artificial (sing. -скаа / plur. -скаѧ, etc.), but such artifice is after all only one more manifestation of the natural tendency for formal and semantic contrasts to seek and join each other; before we are too harsh on our medieval predecessors, we might remember that it was not so long ago that we distinguished gender in plural adjectives (masc.-ые / fem., neut.-ыя), and we still spell ци- in roots but -цы in endings.
55. The distinction between high (sacred) and low (profane) words, only the former of which may be written under the titlo, goes back to the Russian recension of the abbreviated Kostenčeskij text (p. 29 above). It would be interesting to learn when this binary opposition turned into a ternary one. The latter, of course, contains the seed of Lomonosov's famous "three styles".

56. A somewhat different treble reward is promised at the very end of the text: прёжде всѣ͇ х теб҃ѣ г҃лю, разу́мно с раз҄смотрёнїемь пиши бж҃твенаа слѡвеса̀, ꙗко́ж подо́бно ёсть, да ѿ б҃га мзду̀ за сѐ прїи҆меши, ꙗ҃ш҄ꙗ своѥ҆ ѿ си͇ в добрѡдѣтели ѻ҆бу҆ꙗ́еши, у҆ту́шь і͇ же и҆́маши мно́гѡ в ра́зумѣ по́л҄зовати" 436.

57. The full title reads Кни҃га г҃лемаꙗ бꙋкви и҆же в нача́лѣ ѿ грамматикі҆а ѿ просо́дна͇ ѻ҆ е҆́же ка́ко во ст҃ы͇ х҇ книга͇ х҇ ка́ꙗ҃о посло́вица писа́ти и̑ г҃лати. It was edited from ten similar mss. by Jagić, 442-456.

58. The annotation "м(ножественное)" and е(динственное)" are in the original; we have substituted the slash for the raised dot · of the original.

59. By "derivational paradigm" we mean a "nest" of derivationally related words, each of which has its own inflectional paradigm; cf. D. S. Worth, "The notion of 'stem' in Russian flexion and derivation", *To honor Roman Jakobson. Essays on the occasion of his seventieth birthday*, The Hague-Paris, 1967, p. 2269-2288.

60. Note the displaced order of и and ї; о is presumably omitted because only ѡ could appear in anlaut (but ѡ itself appears only in the "letter" ѿ); what became of ш, щ, and ꙗ is unclear.

61. Here and ff. we resolve forms under the titlo and bring superscript letters down onto the line. Possible vowel/zero alternations are normalized in the CSR manner.

62. There are few exceptions: пророчицы / пророчица , and the three *i*-stems милость/-и, милосердость/-и, and страсть/-и.

63. Jagić церковниі ; perhaps a typographical error, or perhaps influenced by the и usual in this fourth form.

64. Exceptions are rare. The genitive in го́рь і и҆х (м.)/го́рь моеѧ́ (е.) belongs with the stress-differentiated homographs like ре́бра и҆х (м.)/ребра̀ мое҆го́ (е.) treated below. Both types are combined in вѡ́ды (м.)/водь і (е.)/водѣ (е.), in the later sections of the treatise, derived from the "Eight parts of speech". The second member of the pair зе́мли и҆х (м.)/землѝ мое҆и҆ is probably the archaic *ja*-stem locative.

65. As was the case with the plur./sing. pairs already discussed, these are spread over several separately-subtitled sections of the mss., reflecting both the compilatory nature of the treatise and the unthinking mechanical activities of its copyists.

66. These too are in alphabetical order, but scattered among three separately-subtitled sections.

67. Here, once again, the scribe is incapable of following the very rules he was compiling or copying, since he goes on to say that no diacritic is to be

written over this "secret" и ("зри, ꙗко идѣже в тайнѣ шв ꙗвлѧетсѧ иже, тоу верхꙋ̃ его не пишетсѧ никоегоже просодіа, еже е́ть и сицевыⷯ· той, сей, мой, пой, чей, и в подобныⷯ симⸯ· пой, дой, лой (? — DSW) кꙋй, рой " (Jagić, 453; presumably what is intended is the distinction between [j] and unstressed but syllabic [i]).

68. The scribe cannot decide between Great Russian and other reflexes of tense jer in бїй е̊ (о̊но)/бей й (его̀, того), бей ю̃ (еѧ̀, тꙋю), бей ѧ̃ (ихъ, тѣхъ).

69. This pair violates the titlo convention referred to on p. 54 above.

70. The scribe explains the concept of (1st vs. third) person by adding "ꙗко вы нѣцыи ѿ насъ глютъ или мы ѿ другиⷯ" (Jagić 45).

71. The same seems to have been the case with the Букварь of Ivan Fedorov, cf. R. O. Jakobson, *Ivan Fedorov's Primer of 1574*, Cambridge, Massachusetts, 1955, p. 17-18.

72. V. S. Ikonnikov, *Maksim Grek i ego vremja*, Kiev, 1915²; A. I. Ivanov, *Literaturnoe nasledie Maksima Greka*, Leningrad, 1969; Jack V. Haney, *From Italy to Muscovy: the life and works of Maxim the Greek*, München, 1973. On Maksim's mss., see esp. Hugh M. Olmsted, *Studies in the early manuscript tradition of Maksim Grek's collected works* (Ph.D. thesis, Harvard Univ., 1977).

73. I. V. Jagić, *Codex slovenicus* . . ., p. 325-326.

74. Instructions from the Academy of Sciences to those engaged in preparing a new Russian grammar specified Maksim and Lomonosov as models (Ivanov, *Literaturnoe nasledie* . . ., p. 91).

75. *Ibid.*, p. 90.

76. Jagić, *Codex slovenicus* . . ., p. 321.

77. *Ibid.*, p. 311.

78. *Ibid.*, p. 298.

79. The only full edition of Maksim's works is philologically unsatisfactory: I. Ja. Porfir'ev, ed., *Sočinenija predpodobnogo Maksima Greka*, I-III, Kazan', 1859-1862, 1895-1897².

80. Haney, *From Italy to Muscovy* . . ., p. 109.

81. From his "О книжном исправлении", incorporated into the 1648 Smotryćkyj edition and reproduced by Jagić, *Codex slovenicus* . . ., p. 298-300.

82. *Sočinenija prepodobnogo Maksima Greka*, III, p. 80 (in a simplified orthography), reproduced by Jagić, *Codex slovenicus* . . ., p. 298.

83. From the 16th c. Rumjancev Museum ms. No. 264; Jagić, *Codex slovenicus* . . ., p. 306.

84. *Ibidem*.

85. Rum. Mus. No. 264 (Jagić, *Codex slovenicus* . . ., p. 307).

86. Published by Jagić, *Codex slovenicus* . . ., p. 306-307.

87. *Ibid.*, p. 307-308.

88. *Ibid.*, p. 47-54.

89. *Ibid.*, p. 308.
90. The original Serbian text has троица светаа, богородица.
91. Rum. 264 could obviously not have taken this material from the "Eight parts", but the two mss. may well have had a common ancestor. In such cases, unlike that discussed above, the presence in Rum. 264 of items missing in the older text is not of any importance.
92. Jagić, *Codex slovenicus* . . ., p. 312-318.
93. The repetition of the numeral makes it appear that the scribe may have been compiling his text from two sources, one of which had "сегѡ слова ѵасти сѫть ‧и̃‧" and the other, " се слово раздѣлѧ́етсѧ на ‧и̃‧ ѵастен". This introductory section is not taken directly from the older "Eight parts of speech".
94. Jagić, *Codex slovenicus* . . ., p. 322, adduces Greek materials illustrating this distinction: αἰνείας, αἰνείον / αἴας, αἴαντος
95. It is possible that -н of long forms in some previous text have been miscopied into the conjunctions of Rum. 264; an original superscript -н could also have been mistakenly copied as the кендема ᵛ .
96. Such a classification is found, for example, in the printed grammar of Lavrentij Zizanij 1596.
97. One ms. has а і̋ü̈.
98. Cf. the "Eight parts of speech", p. 15 above.
99. As is well known, Maksim's first translations were made from Greek to Latin, and his assistants then translated this Latin into Slavic.
100. The text also contains an error in discussing the distribution of diacritics (permitting an oxytone on the antepenult when the ultima is long); cf. Jagić, *Codex slovenicus* . . ., p. 323. This too must be taken as a copyist's error, if we wish to attribute this treatise to Maksim.
101. Haney, *From Italy to Muscovy* . . ., p. 108. The same phrase occurs several times in Čud. 34.
102. Čud. 34 is inconsistent in its spelling, especially in its use of ѫ, cf. сѵгѵ́бна / сѵгѫ́ба / соѵгѵ́ба 314, пишѫ̃ / г̃лю / ѵтѫ̃ / слы́шѵ/ ви̃жю314, соѵтъ / сѫ̃ / сѵтъ 315, среднѧ / среднѧ 314, съю̈съ/ съо̀ѵ̈съ 314, дѫхн / дѫхы 1 , both nom. plur., 315-316, etc. The syntax is no more consistent, e.g. " ѻ̀ва ѹ́бо н҄ соѵ́тъ моѹжеска...ѻ̓ва же ес̃ же́н҅ска " (315).
103. The same is true of the isolated comments on correct and incorrect translations in his commentaries and theological tracts, and even of the pre- and post-faces to the 1648 Smotryćkyj.
104. Donatus was edited by Jagić, 524-585, using Kaz. as his primary source. In our discussion, as in his edition, unattributed paradigms or quotations are from Kaz. while material from O2 is identified as such. Incidentally, a certain degree of scepticism about the accuracy of individual forms as cited here would not be inappropriate: Jagić did not see either ms. himself, but worked from

copies made for him by colleagues. Let us note in passing that Kaz. and O2 were not independent revisions of Dmitrij's original translation; they are so close in many (but by no means all) ways that, either one was copied from the other, or both go back to a common intermediate version.

105. The question-answer format is defined by a phrase which shows that Gerasimov (or a copyist) was acquainted with the Greek tradition: "поста́влены̀ воспро́сы̀ а́ки в лицѐ оу҆чи́телево, и ѿвѣща́нна а́ки в лицѐ оу҆ченнчѣ" (533); cf. the full title of the Написание языком словенским о грамоте: "Написа́нїе ꙗзы́ком словенским о грамотѣ і̏ о е҆ѧ̀ строе́нїи, в не́мже о҆ бѹ́квѣ и҆ о е҆ѧ̀ писмене́х, вопроша́нїа оу҆чи́тел'скаꙗ, ꙗ̀ко в лицѐ оу҆чени́ческо, и҆ ѿвѣща́нїа оу҆ченни́ческа, ꙗ̀ко в лицѐ оу҆чи́тел'ско " (cf. p. 35 above). This is one of the very few pieces of evidence showing interaction of the Greek and Latin traditions in early Russian grammar.

106. The grammatical labels differ considerably from those arising from the Greek tradition (cf. pp. 14 ff. above), in which pronoun was мѣсто и́мени, verb рѣчь, adverb на- or прирѣчие, etc. However, we are concerned here not with grammatical terminology but with grammar. Nor were these distinctions especially important to Dmitrij Gerasimov, who adduced the Greek-based labels ("И҆ в Дамаскинѣ мѣсто и́мени" etc.), but added, "сло́во и҆ рѣч за ѡ҆дно̀ стои́т і вѣща́ние ко́е хо́щешь то рцы̀" (533).

107. Jagić 534 f.n. 7 and *passim* discusses the (in)adequacy of Dmitrij's terminological translations.

108. As Jagić 535 f.n. 11 and 626 notes, the later Prostoslovija version of Donatus adds a dual to both noun and verb.

109. There is no tradition which might support the opposition of sing. -и to plur. -ї. On the contrary, sing. -ї was opposed to plur. -ы̀ in, e.g., nom. sing. fem. -скїа vs. nom. plur. -скыꙗ; cf. p. 52 above.

110. However, the tradition itself of "illicit" gen.-acc. forms is a venerable one; cf. for example acc. sing. neut. е҆сте́ства in the "Eight parts of speech", p. 15 above. Perhaps the most likely explanation of сѣх му́дростеи is that the original Latin had an animate fem. noun. Cf. f.n. 111.

111. The only linguistic interest of this passage is that it strengthens our suspicion that the Latin original declined *mūsa*.

112. This remark was probably added by a copyist, who knew the traditional Latin declension numbering, whereas Gerasimov (perhaps by a schoolboy error) gives ꙋчи́тель as an example of the first declension (p. 81 above).

113. The copyist of O2 may have known the South Slavic tradition of using a possessive adjective instead of a genitive case form, as e.g. in the "Eight parts of speech" (ꙋчлвѣкъ, gen. ꙋчлвѣковъ; жена̀, gen. женина̀; е҆сте́ство, gen. е҆сте́ствово, etc.; cf. p. 15 ff. above. The possible influence

of such -ов- adjectives on the [v] -pronunciation of gen. sing.-ого and on the expansion of the gen. plur. in -ов will be examined in a separate study.

114. I am indebted to Emily Klenin for this observation.

115. This supplemental material is probably more indicative of the actual state of (morphological, graphic, etc.) affairs than the formal pronominal paradigm, in which the scribe was likely to concentrate on being "correct".

116. Cf. f.n. 118.

117. This hesitation about form is partly reflected in paradigms.: prefixed возлюбих vs. ѹчих̾, ѹтох̾, слышах̾: cf. p. 100 below.

118. We prefer this term to "subjunctive", since it reflects the Latin (coniunctivus) and Russian (соѹзныи ѹчнъ) more closely; cf. German "Konjunktiv".

119. The present and future, rendered by Slavic imperfective present and perfective present-future respectively, will be presented first, since the Slavic forms are natural and correspond directly to the Latin; the Russian text itself follows the Latin order present-past-future.

120. No jers have been added to final-consonants lowered from ms. superscripts (любн̾ → любнт, etc.).

121. See also the discussion of быти as auxiliary, pp. 147 ff. below.

122. The forms and functions of these auxiliaries will be discussed separately on pp. 147 ff. below.

123. However, Jagić prints да in the plural in (unexplained) parentheses, which may indicate the да was supplied by him, or taken from O2.

124. But see the 3rd. plur. fut. opt. ind. да бы тѣ возлюбилисѧ.

125. The singular forms omit the prefix: егда слышѹ etc.

126. По also appears as an alternative to ѹ- in the active future imperative 2nd plur. ѹслышите ~ послышите, and, with the secondary imperfective suffix -aj-, in the passive indicative present, e.g. ѹтемсѧ ~ поѹчтаемсѧ (cf. p. 115), in which one observes the replacement of the old simplex ѹести by the innovating suffixal imperfective поѹчтати (-аѭт), a development quite unrelated to the use of по- as a tense marker in the Donatus paradigms.

127. Cf. S. D. Nikiforov, *Glagol, ego kategorii i formy v russkoj pis'mennosti 2-j poloviny XVI veka*, Moscow, 1952. Cf. also pp. 143 ff. below.

128. These further specifications are at least as much aspectual or aktionsartig as they are temporal, but such problems cannot be discussed with the limited and inconsistent material at our disposal.

129. This objection could of course be obviated by requiring markedness reversal within marked categories, in which case the (M) past would exfoliate into a (M) unrestricted and an (U) restricted subcategories, the latter of which would in turn expand into the (U) diffuse and (M) compact. It is hard to see what is to be gained from such diacritic manipulation in this case; cf., however, p. 157 below.

130. The only exception is вьість in the act. indic. past perfect; the passive has a single почтесѧ in the indic. past imperfect.

131. The second instance is вывали, which occurs alongside въ і ваша in the act. opt. past perfect-pluperfect of быти; in addition, in the same paradigm, O2 has ѡх лювили for Kaz. ѡх лювливахү. The only non-pluperfect 3rd plur. in -л is возлювили и тиї of the act. conj. past perfect, — and лювити, the first of the four conjugations (= *amāre*) is frequently idiosyncratic.

132. We do not give all exx. of every class.

133. Corrected in the ms. from the mistranslation of *legens* " сѐи и снà и снѐ ꙋтьıи" 558.

134. A mistranslation of *lecturus*, Jagić 559 f.n. 2.

135. We make no attempt to give complete lists, especially because the synsemantica are even harder to translate than the autosemantica.

136. A catchbag category containing translations of Latin coordinating causals (*enīm, etenim*) and illatives (*ergō, īgitur, idcircō*) and subordinating causals (*quoniam, propterea*), etc.

Other Books From
Slavica Publishers, Inc.
PO Box 14388
Columbus, Ohio 43214

American Contributions to the Eighth International Congress of Slavists Vol. 1: Linguistics & Poetics; Vol. 2: Literature.

P. M. Arant: *Russian for Reading.*

H. I. Aronson: *Georgian A Reading Grammar.*

Balkanistica: Occasional Papers in Southeast European Studies, Vol. III; Vol. IV; Vol. V; Vol. VI.

H. Birnbaum: *Common Slavic Progress and Problems in Its Reconstruction.*

H. Birnbaum: *Lord Novgorod the Great Essays in the History and Culture of a Medieval City-State, Part I The Historical Background.*

H. Birnbaum & T. Eekman, eds.: *Fiction and Drama in Eastern and Southeastern Europe.*

K. L. Black, ed.: *A Biobibliographical Handbook of Bulgarian Authors.*

M. Bogojavlensky: *Russian Review Grammar.*

R. C. Botoman: *Imi place limba Romana/ A Romanian Reader.*

E. B. Chances: *Conformity's Children An Approach to the Superfluous Man in Russian Literature.*

C. V. Chvany & R. D. Brecht, eds.: *Morphosyntax in Slavic.*

F. Columbus: *Introductory Workbook in Historical Phonology.*

R. G. A. de Bray: *Guide to the South Slavonic Languages.*

R. G. A. de Bray: *Guide to the West Slavonic Languages.*

R. G. A. de Bray: *Guide to the East Slavonic Languages.*

B. L. Derwing & T. M. S. Priestly: *Reading Rules for Russian.*

D. Disterheft: *The Syntactic Development of the Infinitive in Indo-European.*

J. S. Elliott: *Russian for Trade Negotiations with the USSR.*

J. M. Foley, ed.: *Oral Traditional Literature A Festschrift for Albert Bates Lord.*

Folia Slavica, a journal of Slavic, Balkan, and East European linguistics, 1977 ff.

R. Freeborn, ed.: *Russian and Slavic Literature.*

V. A. Friedman: *The Grammatical Categories of the Macedonian Indicative.*

Other Books From
Slavica Publishers, Inc.

C. E. Gribble, ed.: *Medieval Slavic Texts, Vol. I, Old and Middle Russian Texts.*

C. E. Gribble: *Reading Bulgarian Through Russian.*

C. E. Gribble: *Russian Root List with a sketch of word formation, second edition.*

C. E. Gribble: *Slovarik russkogo jazyka 18-go veka/ A Short Dictionary of 18th-Century Russian.*

C. E. Gribble, ed.: *Studies Presented to Professor Roman Jakobson by His Students.*

G. J. Gutsche & L. G. Leighton, eds., *New Perspectives on Nineteenth-Century Russian Prose* (J. T. Shaw festschrift).

W. S. Hamilton: *Introduction to Russian Phonology and Word Structure.*

P. R. Hart: *G. R. Derzhavin: A Poet's Progress.*

M. Heim: *Contemporary Czech.*

M. Hubenova and others: *A Course in Modern Bulgarian, Part 1; Part 2.*

International Journal of Slavic Linguistics and Poetics.No. 23 1981 ff.

R. Jakobson: *Brain and Language.*

R. Katzarova-Kukudova & K. Djenev: *Bulgarian Folk Dances.*

A. Kodjak ed.: *Alexander Pushkin Symposium II.*

A. Kodjak: *Pushkin's I. P. Belkin.*

A. Kodjak, ed.: *Structural Analysis of Narrative Texts.*

D. J. Koubourlis, ed.: *Topics in Slavic Phonology.*

M. Launer: *Elementary Russian Syntax.*

R. Leed & A. & A. Nakhimovsky: *Beginning Russian, Vol. 1; Vol. 2.*

R. L. Lencek: *The Structure and History of the Slovene Language.*

J. F. Levin: *Reading Modern Russian.*

M. I. Levin: *Russian Declension and Conjugation: A Structural Description with Exercises.*

A. Lipson: *A Russian Course, Part 1; Part 2; Part 3.*

H. G. Lunt: *Fundamentals of Russian.*

P. Macura: *Russian-English Botanical Dictionary.*

T. F. Magner, ed.: *Slavic Linguistics and Language Teaching.*

M. Matejic & D. Milivojevic: *An Anthology of Medieval Serbian Literature in English.*

Other Books From
Slavica Publishers, Inc.

A. Nakhimovsky & R. Leed: ***Advanced Russian.***

L. Newman, ed.: ***The Comprehensive Russian Grammar of A. A. Barsov.***

F. J. Oinas, ed.: ***Folklore, Nationalism & Politics.***

H. Oulanoff: ***The Prose Fiction of Veniamin A. Kaverin.***

J. L. Perkowski: ***Vampires of the Slavs.***

S. J. Rabinowitz: ***Sologub's Literary Children: Keys to a Symbolist's Prose.***

L. A. Rice: ***Hungarian Morphological Irregularities.***

D. F. Robinson: ***Lithuanian Reverse Dictionary.***

R. A. & H. Rothstein: ***Polish Scholarly Prose A Humanities and Social Sciences Reader.***

D. K. Rowney, ed.: ***Russian and Slavic History.***

E. Scatton: ***Bulgarian Phonology.***

W. R. Schmalstieg: ***Introduction to Old Church Slavic.***

M. Shapiro: ***Aspects of Russian Morphology, A Semiotic Investigation.***

O. E. Swan: ***First Year Polish.***

C. E. Townsend: ***Continuing With Russian, corrected reprint.***

C. E. Townsend: ***Czech Through Russian.***

C. E. Townsend: ***The Memoirs of Princess Natal'ja Borisovna Dolgorukaja.***

C. E. Townsend: ***Russian Word-Formation, corrected reprint.***

D. C. Waugh: ***The Great Turkes Defiance On the History of the Apocryphal Correspondence of the Ottoman Sultan in its Muscovite and Russian Variants.***

S. Wobst: ***Russian Readings and Grammatical Terminology.***

J. B. Woodward: ***The Symbolic Art of Gogol Essays on His Short Fiction.***

D. S. Worth: ***Bibliography of Russian Word-Formation.***

M. T. Znayenko: ***Gods of the Ancient Slavs Tatischev and the Beginnings of Slavic Mythology.***

OHIO UNIVERSITY LIBRARY

book as soon as you
order to avoid a
latest date